In the Shadow of the Rocking Chair

In the Shadow of the Rocking Chair

Shirley Owens

ISBN: 1530456320
ISBN 13: 9781530456321

With love to my family—wherever you go, my heart will follow, always.
To mend broken dreams and to complete things un-
done: encourage one another, always.
To my daughter, Dawn, without whose uplifting spir-
it my inspiration to write would have fallen by the way-
side; you helped me find my voice, always.

To ...
Robin, beautiful and bright inside and out, always
Dawn, who is inclusive, always
Tracy, my happy angel, always
Lonnie, who adds spice and keeps us on our toes, always
Earl, my best friend and helpmate, always
I love you all.

Contents

Dreams and Things

ON ANY GIVEN afternoon, you may find this sentimental old woman in her usual place of escape. Nothing else is as comforting as settling back into the trusted arms of a rocking chair.

Inside our kitchen, two rocking chairs offer a welcoming first impression. The straight-back chairs around the table are less often taken. There is a sense of family spirit, a blending of the young and the old, which the rocking chairs symbolize.

You are sure there is plenty of time. Then it passes so quickly... almost unnoticeably. You blink and it is gone. These moments will never come again. I reminisce, wistfully, of loved ones who have vanished from my life. I miss them beyond words. Yet words are the means I have left to restore my memories of them.

Even though I remembered struggling with insecurities, a stirring of nostalgia moved me to revisit my childhood. Making reckless wishes was a part of my growing up. I thought I wanted to be a copy of some other girl, someone prettier, smarter, and more confident.

For sure, I am a dreamer, open to every possibility, even looking on unique experiences—dreams and things—as miraculous signs. Sometimes, I can only wonder at the beauty of it all.

Before I was a wife, before I was a mother, first I was His child. God knows my limitations better than I ever will. On this note, my memoir begins.

Preface

GRANDMA MOLLIE'S WORDS echoed from the past. "Someday, Shirley, you'll realize how wonderful it was to be young and carefree. My childhood was the best time of my life."

I stared in awe at the work of her hands. Grandma's quilt block started the wheels of my mind to turning. Who would have guessed, after all these years, that this forgotten piece of my history would come home to me?

If I could do it all over again, I thought, I would not be in such a hurry to grow up. As I reminisced, the years fell away.

Until I spread out my life around me in pages of handwritten detail, I was blind to its significance. Sleeping memories somehow awakened, filling in the vacant lines as if by a will of their own. I desire to hold on to the loves of my childhood days and to pass forward these early experiences to my children and beyond.

I am sadly convinced that just a few simple stories, told now and then, would not be enough to outlast the present generation nor do my people justice. Without some sort of permanent reminder, the essence of who these unique personalities were would be lost. At the same time, I want to protect the privacy of some characters. Their names have been changed to protect the guilty, as well as the innocent.

I think whatever befalls us should not be tossed aside or explained away as simply a matter of fate. When obstacles are thrown in our path, none of us is truly alone.

It was while I was consumed with sorting out my own life that I observed how crucial were all the other lives that had crossed mine. We become who we are because of—and sometimes even despite—those we have loved or collided with on all those yesterdays.

Some yesterdays are better than others. Not every idea that crosses my mind is good enough to run with. There was a time to laugh, and after a few wrong turns, a time to cry. But if there is something to be learned—a truth that rises out of the ashes—it is that I am not here by chance nor am I the sole maker of my own destiny. With peace in my heart, I leave the mystery of my being to the mind of God.

A mysterious order holds all humanity together, and our world on its axis. I believe we exist in the palm of God's hand. With every dawn, He gives us a new beginning, breathing life into us—body and soul—and we have another chance to get it right. The voice that tells you, "You are as loved as any of my children" truly comes from God.

There are a few shining moments—a wealth of hopes and dreams, really—that I want to share. Just the same, my book would not be complete without including the face of troubles that graces the opposite side of the coin and which is equally a part of the story.

It is my sincerest hope that the turning of these pages will be many. Like the journey of a handed-down, treasured patchwork quilt block, my book reminds me of tradition.

Similar to the cherished piece of coverlet or other family heirlooms, with God's blessing, may these pages pass graciously, from the hands of the generation before and into the next. May the whole book, like the comfort of a quilt, warm hearts.

CHAPTER 1

Bend an Elbow, Break a Heart

FROM ACROSS THE empty center room, Grandma calls out a final goodnight. "Shirley... honey, Grandma set your shoes at the edge of the bed."

"Okay, Grandma."

At least for tomorrow, there would not be another frantic shoe hunt amid the clanging of the bell coming from the schoolhouse, directly behind our house. Grandma's vigilance would head off an eruption of tears from her young charge. I think the shoe devil hides my shoes when I'm asleep.

Grandma Mollie and Grandpa Alf retire for the night to their respective bedrooms, and the house grows silent. I lie still for a while, thankful that this is my home, as it is for any of us who needs it. But the fall of darkness can cast a surreal mask over everything it touches, and it can bring out the worst in some of us.

A masculine voice shatters my dreams. The man is weeping. I recognize the sound as coming from one of Mom's older brothers. Uncle Al is penniless, and his home is in our backyard. He lives in Grandpa's shed that he crammed with the bare necessities.

I tuck the frayed edge of the worn quilt under my chin. The sobs go on. What to do—what to do? My thoughts whirl. Wave on wave of raw emotion pours into my bedroom from somewhere in the house.

Gradually, curiosity overtakes fear. I creep from my bed, daring to investigate further these wretched cries of a woebegone someone.

1

I peek around the doorway and look into the front room.

The anguished cries and guttural sounds are coming from Grandma's room. I edge closer. Tiptoeing across the threshold, I brave the shadows to get a better view into Grandma's room and at that tormented soul.

I grope my way along the front room wall until I'm in line with Grandma's bed. Piercing the black of night, I see the crumpled form of Uncle Al. Is he drunk again?

He is hunched forward, kneeling at Grandma's bedside. Silvery rays from the light of the moon pour through slits in the drawn shades. The mounded pillow where Grandma rests her head, glows dramatically white against the darker background.

"Please, please, Mama," he pleads. "Let me have a little money. Oh, Mama. You don't *know* what it's like. It's so awful. I can't stand it! You can't know the hell I'm in. I have to have me a drink. I need it. I think I will go crazy and kill myself. Please... Mama, give it to me!"

Just a few feet away is the spectacle of a grown man kneeling at his mother's bedside, bawling like a baby and begging for drinking money.

The scene defies logic. Could this be the same fellow who will prod any unsuspecting kid to "pull my finger"? There is an unexpected rend in the fabric that I thought men were woven from. I never knew they could cry.

My face burns with scorching humiliation that rightly belongs to him. Does Uncle Al imagine that the entire household sleeps like the dead? Come morning, will he be able to face any of us? Tonight, I am learning that addiction knows no shame. Tomorrow, I will pretend that I never heard any of it.

Grandma's nightgown must be sopping wet from his tears. "No," she says. "I'll not. You go on now. Leave me be. What little dab I've got in my pocketbook, I'll need it to pay for my medicine."

"I'm so sorry, Mama," he says. "I can't help myself."

I want to help, but I don't know how. Lord only knows where Grandma last hid her pocketbook. Could she even locate it on her own? I can't help her rummage for it now. I don't know how to intervene. My young feet turn to clay.

There is another presence in the front room. The moving form flows discreetly along the wall across from me. I hold my breath as the adult shadow advances in step with an old man. Darkness does little to conceal a set of white long johns on the march. He glows like a ghost.

I can tell Grandpa Alf is straining to hear their voices. He is oblivious of me. Standing here in pitch blackness, I can almost reach out and touch him.

The old man and his shadow progress together until he has a clear line of vision to the drama going on inside Grandma's bedroom.

Grandpa does not attempt to come between Mollie and their son. This other, older, hard drinker hangs his head and backs away, retreating to his own room.

Uncle Al presses his grateful lips against Grandma's careworn hand. "Thank you, Mama. Oh God, thank you! You're so good! You're just an angel, Mama—an angel." It was incredibly moving. His words would stay locked in my consciousness forever.

Grandma Mollie is unimpressed. Sweet talk flows freely, and she has heard it all before from his father. "I'll not do this again," she vowed. "Don't you come to me another blessed time. Not a red cent more, I'll declare."

"I'll pay it all back, Mama. I will, I will. I swear, I will," he promises. Uncle Al is needing to quench his thirst. His hands shake from withdrawal, and his bended knees are ready to be welcomed by the nearest vacant barstool.

I follow my shadow as it rises and falls along the center room wall, crosses the doorway of my bedroom and swiftly climbs into bed, a step ahead of me. And we lie there awake in the dark, my shadow and I, staring into the darkness.

Early next morning, I overhear Grandpa confront Grandma. "You handed him the money, didn't you? Now that you give it over, I got me a good idea, he'll come back a whinin' and a blubberin' for some more. I'm a heap satisfied, you'll not ever be a shut of it a'tall."

I see the flash of fire in her eyes.

"Alf, don't you say another blessed word to me! Who was it what took our son to the pub, when I begged you not to do it? He was just a little tad of a fellow, too young to even sit on a barstool, when you took him with you. You set that child, our boy, on top of the bar—right up next to his ol' daddy. It was all right then! You thought he looked pretty cute then!"

I want to reach out and stop the flow of words—words that can never be taken back. But it's too late. You can't put the cork back in the bottle. One person's addiction affects many other lives.

"You wouldn't listen to a thing I had to say." Grandma's words rain down on him like powerful blows. "I asked you not to take our boy to town with you. Now look at him. If our son is a drunkard, I'll abide you made him that a way!"

Grandma's resentment had been building for years as she competed with the local pub for the family paycheck. Her torrent of words and wrath is unleashed, sending Grandpa limping for cover.

CHAPTER 2

—— ✿ ——

Mollie's Shadow

To six young castaways, she was like an angel sent from Heaven. God gave her on loan so that they might have someone to love them. This wonderful old woman became my grandmother. Her earth name was Mollie.

In memories from my childhood, Grandma Mollie remains full of life. She was of slight build, a frail woman who would not stand out in a crowd, except for her eyes. Mollie's bluest of eyes are a gift passed forward; she looks back at me from the mirror.

Mollie was an ordinary person who journeyed through an extraordinary time, and she shared her journey with me in countless hours of storytelling. She always followed her heart. And when the path grew dark as night, love shone a light to illuminate the way.

When I grew to call my grandparents' house "my home," I filled the shoes of many other children who had come before me. Sometimes, when I got older, it felt like my and Grandma's roles were reversed; I was very protective of her. How is it that one so vulnerable and frail could give strength to so many others? One of Grandma's daughters-in-law once told me, "Mollie ain't afraid of anything. She could walk into a den of snakes with nothing but a club in her hand."

As a child, I marveled at Grandma's courage, questioning from where it flowed. Once I was grown, I concluded that her source must have been the quiet faith, born of her own unique survival experiences. In troubled times, I had seen a look of bewilderment etched on her face, but I didn't see her cry. It may be that Grandma held back her emotions until there came a solitary time.

Because I grew up in her shadow, following in her footsteps, I am a better mother. I had an angel watching over me. Without Grandma's example, where could a restless child, such as I, have learned patience? Being "backward" presented another challenge. All that Grandma had to give me was her full attention and stories of hope. Because of the shy nature I was born with, those were the things I needed most.

Grandma's life story reads like an old-time stage play filled with performers from her youth. I see, with the eyes of my heart, a cast of heroes and villains. These characters are all strangers to me. I had never been anywhere except Southern Illinois, and the Kentucky she came from seemed like a foreign land.

Through Grandma's stories, I was introduced to the people with whom she had crossed paths. This was a time when ancient customs spawned a most worrisome sort of villain. Grandma was mindful of dangers lurking all around us, and she cautioned us against trusting strangers.

The villains of her childhood were comprised of strange and violent men who would mistreat women and children. "They would steal children," she told. "Their families would never see or hear from them again." Finally, she added, "They were just gone." These words struck fear in my heart.

In my childhood, though, there was another villain: mental illness. Emotional difficulties were gradually overwhelming our mom, and it left us helpless. I wished I could stretch out my arms and hold back the invisible thing that was stealing her.

Divorce was imminent. Six needy youngsters, ranging in age from 4 to 13, needed shelter. Grandma Mollie and Grandpa Alf made room for us. These easygoing folks welcomed their youngest daughter, Norma, whose mental health was plainly declining, and her youngsters into their home until "come a better day." For a while, my dad was there, too.

There were five girls and one boy in our family. Dee was the oldest, and she was our star. We all looked up to her. Sonny, the fearless one, was our only brother, a year or so younger than Dee. Next came Mary and then Nancy, born just a year apart. They were a contradiction to each other in that they couldn't be together in harmony, but neither could they bear to be separated by any distance. I was born three years before our youngest sister, Carol, who remains my lifelong friend. My name is Shirley and this is my story.

When my siblings and I think of home, what comes to mind is the place where our mother grew up and the house that we shared with our grandparents.

Mollie and Alf had already raised sixteen children of their own, and they were well into their twilight years when they began sharing their everything with us. Our grandparents made certain that not one of us ever went to bed while we were hungry, even though the wolf was pawing at their door before our arrival.

My mouth begins to water when I recall how I used to stir up a concoction of powdered sugar and milk into icing, and then smear it across a stack of graham crackers. I wish I could say to her, "Grandma, you're the best grandma in the world because you let me do it myself."

The two of them gave us anchor. Despite knees swollen from arthritis, Grandpa walked across town, almost daily. He would return home with the mail in one hand, and a burlap sack filled with necessities to sustain life thrown over the opposite shoulder.

Grandma cared for us through measles, mumps, scrapes, and bumps. With her home remedies, she could take away the sting from our hurts, including the pain of a broken heart. In times of my uncertainty, it felt like mine would shatter.

Just as a bandana conceals the face of a child playing cowboy, shyness is a mask that protects the hearts of those who wear theirs on a sleeve. Grandma talked for me. She could form just the right words, providing an answer that a little dreamer couldn't get out all by her insecure self.

Whenever I felt like a nobody, Grandma told me stories born of her childhood experiences. Those were the days that made her strong—times that filled the blood coursing through her veins with the blue/black iron of determination. Hers were stories that ended with a moral, shaped the way I saw the world and changed little nobodies into heroes. Grandma made me believe that there is triumph of good over evil.

Peace always is an impossibility. None of us is made perfect, and sometimes we dance out of turn. Without the occasional misstep in our lives, we would not recognize happiness when it came calling. Some have said that what makes us who we are is in the blood, and that history repeats. I believe that to be true.

Our grandparents were very accepting of all our shortcomings. They made us feel that no matter what we did, we could always come home. Family is everything. I want my children to have that same sense of belonging. Pass acceptance on.

For reasons known only to order, an uneventful day is changed into one that is enduringly close to my heart. I doubt that it is simply by chance that I am able to recall in vivid detail the history behind Grandma's quilt block. I estimate that the calendar may have read 1946. This would have given me eight birthdays.

I consider my unusually clear childhood memories a gift from Someone who truly loves me. He lifts me up when I'm at my lowest, gladdens my soul and makes time stand still long enough for me to remember and record it.

My imagination ran wild. Curled up inside Grandpa Alf's oversized rocking chair, I could change the world—unless, of course, Grandpa's wobbly legs approached me before a daydream could begin. On these occasions, he would gruffly invite me to move on. "Shirley," he'd say, "you go on now and get yerself outta my chair, aggravatin' young'n. I need to set down there." Grandpa needed his chair to rest his bones.

On another and more fortunate afternoon, the rocker was mine, and I began to daydream. I didn't see "hide nor hair" of the old guy, so my skinny bones draped themselves into a comfy spot. I was almost swallowed up in the great hulk of wood. Just the same, there is not a better place, anywhere, than a rocking chair to begin a good story. And so it was with Grandma's interesting tales of olden days.

Grandma was born in 1871. She had a knack for making her past experiences spring to life. I was curious about the parade of ancestors that marched through her stories of frontier living.

"We all had chores," Grandma said, "even the little ones." She went on to describe the games she and her siblings made up and played on their daily trek to fill their water pails at the spring. More serious issues to contend with included her fearsome days spent trapped in a log cabin during a winter blizzard. However, the best thing of all were her stories of Indians.

When Grandma Mollie was a child, it was a sign of the times to say that the native people of our land were Indians. We, as youngsters, never played "cowboys and Native Americans." I believe, with all my heart, that under the heavens—we are one people.

Grandma was an awesome storyteller. She could hold the attention of this impatient youngster when hardly anyone else could. I remember it like it was yesterday. The soft light of day spread from our front room window, falling across Grandma's bowed head. She appeared to have nodded off from the gentle motion of the rocking chair. Her eyes opened to let me know that she was only resting. A story hour was approaching. Grateful for a break in an otherwise tiresome afternoon, I listened closely as she unwrapped the newest sample of her early adventures. The story concerned the life and hardships of a boy called Pin 'em.

CHAPTER 3

— ✢ —

Pin Them

"He had a hard row to hoe, that boy … livin' deep in the woods and away from everybody. There wasn't a single button on anything that poor lad put on. Every stitch he wore was mismatched and ragged. My friend's shirt and trousers were nothing short of some old rags held on him and fastened together with big old safety pins."

"Because of how he dressed himself, his schoolmates took to calling the young fellow "Pin Them," Grandma said.

Nothing hurts more than ridicule. A never forgotten encounter with some girls in the next grade, invaded my thoughts.

At first, they are just three blurry objects in the distance. Then slowly, as they walk closer, I recognize them. Although I hesitate, wanting to take to the street, by now any change of course from the sidewalk would look obvious. I can only swallow hard and keep walking straight ahead.

My old faded clothes and scuffed shoes were a reminder that I wasn't their equal. Wishing with all my heart that I could glide past them, I put on a brave front, forced a shy smile, and offered a friendly, "Hi there."

Shelly, the most intimidating of the three, stepped forward. Then with palms pressed against the exaggerated swaying of her hips, she mocked my nervous movements. There was no escaping her taunting.

"Well … hi there." I heard sarcasm in her voice; I saw contempt in the broad, unnatural grin on her face, and I felt all the blood drain from mine. I didn't cry.

I heard one of the girls express regret. She said, "Oh … Shelly, you shouldn't have done that."

"Why not?" Shelly answered, "She ain't nobody." Nobody…I turned the name over in my mind as I listened to Grandma recount the hardships of Pin Them, and I noted the similarity of our backgrounds. Was he ever shunned by a classmate? I wondered.

Grandma explained their olden ways. "The kids all greeted one another and when they saw him coming, they'd call out, 'Pin Them! Here comes Pin Them.' And it wasn't very long, you know, till the name stuck. And then it was shortened to Pin 'em. His chums never meant it ugly, nor nothing that-a-way. Lots of young'ns had a second name of some sort."

I felt that I had walked in Pin 'em's shadow. When my choices were few, the lowly safety pin made my siblings clothes fit me, as well as them. Let's see… an unlucky kid is shunted aside, and nobody cared enough to help him. "What about his mother?" I asked. "Why didn't she sew buttons on his clothes?"

"He didn't have a mama. She died in childbirth," Grandma recalled. "Him and his pa lived alone in a shanty out in the woods, and they kept to themselves. The pa didn't mistreat Pin 'em, except when the old man was suckin' on the bottle. When the pa went to rantin' and ravin', Pin 'em lit out and hid till his pa laid down and commenced to snore. He was afraid of takin' a lickin' if his pa could catch him."

Dismayed at Pin 'em's misfortune, I stammered, "You mean to say—that a drunk could beat up on a little kid, and nobody would put a stop to it?"

"You know, it was all folks could do to mind after their own," Grandma confessed. "And none of us knew of Pin 'em ever takin' a beatin'. He stayed out of the way when his pap was tootin'. The drunkard couldn't stumble around quick enough to lay hands on him."

"Law … we all had us a long, cold walk to school, but we'd bundle up good. Pin 'em throwed on more ragged wraps."

I imagined the destitute shanty as Grandma described it. Living in the wild, I concluded that Pin 'em was mostly on his own there. The image of a scared little boy flashed through my mind.

"Winters," Grandma explained, "were much harsher back in those days."

I wondered how Pin 'em escaped freezing to death. With his pa standing in the open doorway and calling out his given name, Pin 'em hardly dared to breathe.

Saving him from an untimely end, in my thoughts—I pictured Pin 'em, huddled in a corner of the shack. Crouching next to the large firewood box, he could hide there until his pa's rage was spent.

I think he couldn't cry, either. It was on these terms that Pin 'em grew into manhood.

Grandma's story is not just a random recollection on her part: She has a moral example to pass on. "Pin 'em never lost heart; he kept up with his chores and stayed in school." She applauded Pin 'em's character. "By and by, he matured and left these parts. My, oh my! But what a success he became! How taken aback everybody was to learn the news that Pin 'em had begun a business and was made the head of a large corporation. He was a man of some wealth. Nobody that remembered Pin 'em begrudged him that."

With heaps of praise that she reserved for the downtrodden, Grandma exclaimed, "Law … who would have thought it? The ragged little nobody, whose chums used to call Pin 'em, has a Mr. in front of his name. He is some … body!"

Grandma used Mr. Pin 'em's dirt-poor climb to respected community leader, as an anecdote that proved success came to those who persevered.

The dividing line between fate and coincidence is often just a blur. Only a short time ago, I was listening to Grandma's recollection of Pin 'em. Then, unexpectedly, I seemed to be living it.

The place where I grew up is still a vivid memory. I know, by heart, everything just as it was when the house was alive with a mix of the young and the old.

We girls sack out in the largest bedroom. What our quarters lack in frills is made up for in comfort, and we can be ourselves in here. The old folks don't find it necessary to breathe down our necks.

The room has three windows, which are framed with straight tiers of lace, and each one has a pull down shade. A well-traveled sidewalk passes directly by this bedroom. Anytime I am undressing in here, my eyes are drawn to the window shades. Before my clothes come off, I pull the chain on the glaring overhead bulb. I lay my things out ahead of time so that I can easily dress in the dark.

The reason I am uneasy about changing my clothes at night is that an admirer confided that he (while walking past the house, in the dark) could see my shadow and even the outline of my body through the drawn shades. Nothing is sacred to an amorous young boy.

Inside the girls' room and directly across from the entrance is a dark walnut table. It stands against the east wall and next to the center window. A walkway to the table separates two full-size beds. A beige scarf, crocheted in a pineapple design, covers the square tabletop.

Since Grandma never learned to crochet, the scarf must have been a luxury that she saved her pennies to buy. This dainty extravagance extends over the table edges and on down the spindle legs another inch or so. A dull orange stain, made by a careless kid who spilled iodine, is hardly noticeable on the beige threads. The kind purchaser of the scarf would have promptly forgiven the clumsy fingered one who was responsible for the spill. Grandma never held your mistakes against you.

The entire bedroom wall to the right of the doorway is lined from floor to ceiling with the homemade shelves built by a younger Alf. Our belongings, as well as Grandma's comforters, are loosely folded and stored on the cream color boards. These shelves were the place I turned to on that morning when poverty struck home.

I was dressing for school when it happened: my threadbare dress, weakened from repeated wear and washings, snagged on something that caused a jagged rip down the side. My only alternative was dirty.

What's a poor child to do? On the verge of tears and against the odds, I went to the last resort wall of shelves. I searched there for something, anything that would get me by (please God) just for today. Grandma came in to see what was delaying me, and I showed her my ruined dress.

Her face mirrored the empathy she felt for me, but she assured me, "Honey, there's nothing on these shelves for you. I'll wash your other shirtwaist and make out an absence slip. You can go in at noon recess. It'll be dry right directly."

As I continued in my desperate rummaging for clothing, I grew so frustrated that I could have bawled. If my classmates should find out that I was absent because I hadn't anything to wear, I would be too crestfallen to show my face.

Suddenly, in my distress, my fingers closed around a brown paper bag. It was crammed full at the bottom and rolled shut at the top. Grandma stood by while I pulled my brother's outgrown western outfit from the bag. I held the pieces of it up to me. They looked to be a close fit.

The red shirt was still in good condition. It had slit pockets, trimmed with white braid to form arrows. The black pants were typical cowboy style (faded but wearable) with more white braid stitched along the length of the pant leg, from waist to ankle.

Only someone who has been poorly dressed can understand how grateful I felt for this windfall. There was Grandma and I—no one else to cry to or make the poverty go away.

"These are boy clothes," Grandma commented. Then having second thoughts and acknowledging my predicament, she kindly added, "but if you want to, by golly, you can put 'em on and see."

While I slipped into Sonny's castoffs, gathered up my books and finally located my shoes, Grandma dished out some pensive urging alongside my breakfast bowl. She always looks for the best in the midst of calamity. The optimism she had dealt out to me in the guise of the saga of Pin 'em sent me skipping off to school.

Shortly after I had worn Sonny's old clothes, Grandma shuffled out of her bedroom, holding a catalog in her hands and a tape measure draped around her neck. She handed these intriguing items to Mom.

Carol and I became instantly involved, and we stood straight and tall while Mom measured us. Excitedly, we scanned the pages of Grandma's wish book, choosing new dresses for ourselves. The same pretty dress jumped out at both of us.

At the instant I saw the narrow red and white stripes, the vision of a peppermint candy stick popped into my head. This fantasy-come-true, the candy cane dress, boasted of six full yards of whirling circular skirt.

As I stared at the page, I could almost feel the breeze I'd churn up from spinning around and around in the dress. I pictured myself, gracefully making the most of the cotton skirt floating at my waist.

There was one last hurdle standing between me and that dress— and my heart leapt when I found my size. Carol and I never ended up sharing alike dresses because that particular style dress was not offered in her size. Initially, Carol felt let down, but she soon made a second choice.

I haven't a clue where the money for the dresses came from. It pleased me to think my father bought them.

Mom filled out the order form. Carol and I anxiously waited for our dresses to arrive in the mail, not at all sure of our choices. Sometimes mail order descriptions exaggerate their wares.

It was worth the wait. The candy cane dress was wonderful beyond my expectations. I tried it on, and it fit perfectly. Yards and yards of peppermint skirt soared and twisted at my hips as I danced and twirled. Some days are really, really good.

CHAPTER 4

❦

The Quilt Block

GRANDMA'S ATTENTION EVENTUALLY turned from entertaining an antsy grand-daughter to a needed task. Beside her, resting at her feet, is an ancient woven basket that holds her sewing notions. Grandma can do amazing things using only scraps of cloth and bits of ribbon. She pokes through the odds and ends in the basket. Her gaze soon fixes on success, and her hands bring up a length of white cloth and a long strand of red embroidery floss.

Grandma used to have a sewing room. Now, because of Grandpa Alf's restless sleeping habits, that small area is a separate bedroom for her. In his advanced age, Grandpa is awake much of the night, wander-ing back and forth from bed to creaking rocking chair. He can't seem to stay put anywhere. The old gentleman roaming about and clad in his long johns and moonlight is a familiar sight.

Grandma's antique, treadle sewing machine was idle now, and most of her sewing consisted of replacing a button or closing a ripped seam. Her eyes had weakened, so I was accustomed to threading her needles for her. We help each other this way. I see close up for her and she sees distance for me. She let me sew some and instructed me on the basics. I was beginning to learn the art of embroidery. Although my first stitches looked crooked and too long, with Grandma's direction my fingers soon adapted. As for her own sewing, though, Grandma seemed to have lost interest. She would rather rock-a-bye in her favorite chair and tell us stories full of olden day wonders. I am a lucky little girl to have these experiences; I just cannot realize this yet.

So, it was unusual for Grandma to begin a new sewing project, and I took notice of her preparations. She measured and cut a square piece from the white cotton cloth. Then she stretched it out flat, holding it between her hands. Scooting to the edge of my seat on the larger rocker, I watched her fingers struggle with the obstinate piece of cloth, trying to hold it steady as she embroidered across it. I watched her follow a pencil line, using slow, deliberate stitches.

"Grandma, why don't you use my embroidery hoop?" I asked. "I'll run and get it for you. I'm sure a hoop would make that so much easier for you."

"Well, there's not but a little dab of sewing to it. A few more letters of my name is all that's here. I'll be done right directly, honey."

I asked her what she was making, and Grandma explained her project to me. "I'm making this piece, to become a part of a friendship quilt. I saw a finished one. It was put together in the church basement. It was just real nice."

I pictured the quilt as Grandma described it. Through her eyes, I saw it in full color, rolled out across the wooden quilting frames. It certainly had turned her head.

"Each one of the friendship blocks," Grandma explained, "was signed with the handwritten signature of a friend or neighbor that I knew well." That personal touch impressed her.

I realized then that Grandma expected that this single quilt block, with her name, would live on and eventually become linked to similar blocks from other friends. Once compiled, it would become a wedding gift. My Grandma was quite the optimist.

I hoped the block would measure up to her expectations. Could those old, wrinkled hands make the magic she expected of them? My doubting self moved to her side to better view her progress. I looked at Grandma's painstaking work. She had penciled in her full name to fit across the center of her block. Surprising to me, her name was legible.

I wondered, can you wish something into being? Her quilt block did last but in a strange way that neither she nor I would have anticipated.

Some time went by. The letters of her last name were yet to be completed when a perplexed expression covered an old woman's care worn face. Abruptly, Grandma dropped the piece of white cloth to her lap. Saying not a word, she slid the ancient brass thimble from her finger.

"Well, I'll declare. Gol blessed thing!" This was as firm a reprimand of her handiwork and the nearest thing to swear words that I had heard fall from her lips. Then, showing the "un-blessed" object of distress to me for acknowledgement that we had a supply-and-demand problem, her cramped fingers produced the final strand of red floss. I could see that she might not have enough thread to finish her name.

"Grandma, it's gonna be really close. What will you do if there's not enough thread left?"

Quietly, I wished we weren't so poor. I wished Grandma could buy something fancy—like silverware or maybe nice dishes—for the wedding couple. Moreover, without voicing my opinion (I would never say anything that would hurt Grandma's feelings.), I asked myself, would just one square of embroidered cloth be a good enough present for a wedding? What does a child know of such social things?

I reviewed Grandma's handiwork on the quilt block. She had divided the last strand of red embroidery floss to finish it, making the letters at the end of her last name noticeably thinner. I wondered whether the wedding couple would even know that the handmade piece was Grandma's noblest effort at giving to them a token of her best wishes. A small gift can appear better when there is nothing fancier to compare it with—silverware, dishes. Then there is the biblical lesson of a poor widow who gave the coins, all she had.

Worry, worry, and more worry. It weighs too heavily on a little one's shoulders. I could never have imagined how worthy that humble wedding gift would become to me in a future time.

CHAPTER 5

The Shadow Box

IT WAS LATE morning on one of my abundant celebration of days on earth when improbability struck. Following a fair night's sleep and a happy weigh-in, I went on with my routine. A pre-breakfast treat, first thing, buffers the aspirin that I take every morning before coffee.

The magic of caffeine and aspirin brought me fully awake, and I unwound to become more human. For the better part of the next hour, I lingered in the arms of my own kitchen rocking chair, sipping coffee and glancing through the newspaper.

The morning was nearly spent when I reached for my Bible. It tops the stack of mostly health related magazines that collect on the small table next to that comforting old rocker of mine. Reading, over coffee, is the best way to start my day. Some of the Bible verses are uplifting and reassuring. I find meaning as I read.

Since I don't take my thoughts as gospel, neither do I accept, without question, anyone else's. Gratefully, in our more fair and optimistic age, there is hope for an enduring faith for all people. My thinking is that God's love is just not meant to be so complicated.

After placing the Bible back on the table, I was armed with a wealth of good intentions, and I felt ready to face come-what-may with faith, hope, and love.

I pulled on a pair of well-worn house slipper boots, preparing for a wintertime workout throughout the house. Just as I set course for a round of stair-climbing, the phone rang. I almost didn't answer it because it was likely a sales call. But my intuition led me to pick up the receiver.

"Is this Shirley?" The voice did not sound familiar.

"Yes, I'm Shirley."

"Shirley, I'm your cousin Don. I had to call around to get your number. Do you remember me?"

Immediately, I could place him. Don was the oldest child of Aunt Lela, Mom's sister. There was quite an age difference between us, over two decades.

"Why sure I do," I said. "It's been a long time. How are you?"

"Oh, I'm getting by pretty fair," he said.

Before Don's call, I hadn't spoken with this older cousin in a very long time. So it was puzzling to hear from him now.

Don, at the request of his mother was on a mission to place a family heirloom into my care. He went on to describe the contents of a shadow box. Grandma's quilt block was at the center of it. I welcomed the gift.

Where there is always room for one more, there is also a place of honor for a family keepsake

A week after Christmas, the gift arrived. Earl lent a willing hand to its unveiling. When the packaging came off, years fell away, revealing a forgotten moment in time.

It was an unassuming square of white cloth: nothing anyone would take notice of or place value on. But despite its poor showing in the beginning, an invisible hand guarded its mysterious journey across time. Seemingly worthless, this single quilt block came to hold great significance in the restoration of my past. It never became a part of anything more. Other friendship squares did not materialize.

Passed down, unexpectedly, to this once very shy one—no dishes, silverware or fancies of any kind can compare with the work of Grandma's own gentle hands. Neither could those more costly things best my memories of her sheer determination to finish what I now consider art. The time we share with those we love is truly short.

I have tried to make an accurate account of our words and actions surrounding the 1940s. Although I may have taken some small liberties with exact conversations between Grandma and me, my memory of that day, so long ago, remains very clear.

Grandma's gift to the wedding couple was an unusual one, and later, when her quilt block and thimble came to me, these things brought home a flood of memories. It borders on miraculous—how the forgotten piece of cloth endured without stain, rip, or decay. Normally, the wear and tear of passing seasons brings a lessening of everyone and everything. How could Grandma's quilt block and thimble not be lost to me? I have to believe in a Heavenly Presence that keeps even the smallest of miracles on track.

With the passing of more than sixty years, the wedding gift that Grandma had put her heart into making faded from my memory. Her gesture of best wishes was meant for another grandchild, but somehow fate had made it mine.

Wayfaring across the years, this piece of cloth made its way back to its home in my heart, in what seems like an impossible journey from my childhood. Love survives the test of time.

23

The quilt block that I had doubted would ever matter, came to light. In my heart, I believed Grandma was the guiding force. And I thought, Grandma's things have come home.

One of Grandma's favorite expressions was the word "royal," which she would use to describe anything outstanding. And she easily broke into laughter at the absurdity of human nature.

Once again, the merry twinkle in those bluest of eyes, had taken me by surprise. As a wonderful old woman watches the journey of her quilt block and thimble, there is royal laughter from somewhere beautiful.

Earl hauled the large glass enclosed case from room to room, hoisting it up against a number of walls for me to appraise. Finally we agree that it belongs in our kitchen.

Grandma's memento hangs just above our kitchen table—the place where four generations of our family gather for holiday celebrations. When we offer our prayer of gratitude, there is one royal angel among us.

The eyes of newcomers to our home are just naturally drawn to the display case, and I am always happy to satisfy their curiosity about it. After looking over the contents, some of our guests have even remarked, "I should do this." My heart sings every time.

Grandma has been lost to us (Heaven's gain) since 1960, but her legacy lives on. Our children never had the opportunity to know her, except through these stories about her life.

Here, then, is not so much an ending to the history of the quilt block and shadow box; it is more of an introduction to other rocking chair adventures: a new beginning.

CHAPTER 6

❦

Oak Street Escapades

SETTING SAIL FOR my earliest memories, takes me on a long and adventurous voyage back in time. My five siblings and I shared passage on a failing vessel that I'll call "The Wib and Norma."

"Shirley!" Daddy called out from the back porch. As fast as my little legs could carry me, I hurried over to where he stood. "Go tell the kids Daddy wants them," he told me. I started around to the front of the house to look for them. Their shrieks and giggles guided my footsteps.

"Tag! By damn ... you're it!" I heard Sonny yell. He and Nancy bounded around the corner of the house and nearly collided with me. Mary was in hot pursuit.

"Stop! Mary, stop!" I reached out to grab her shirttail. "Daddy says come." Immediately, the four of us marched to the edge of the porch where Daddy waited.

"You want to see the new pup?" he asked. The ringlets in Mary's hair bobbed profusely as she nodded. Then she turned and motioned for the rest of us to follow. Dee was already inside. The trace of a mysterious smile that she couldn't hide tugged at the corners of her mouth.

Daddy gently carried the large wicker basket by the arched handle and set it down in front of us. Sonny, Mary, Nancy, and I lined up to see the puppy. Sonny's turn came first, and he looked for a few seconds. Daddy held a finger to his lips, and Sonny moved on without comment.

In turn, my sisters looked in the basket, each following Daddy's don't-tell instruction.

Suddenly, I became the uncomfortable center of attention. Why were all eyes fixed on me? I stepped in close and peeked in the basket, expecting to find a fluffy creature with a wet nose and wagging tail.

"It's a baby!" I squealed. Dee was laughing at my bewilderment while I stared down, stunned by their trickery, at the newborn. I saw the blanket begin to jerk as the tiny bundle from Heaven wiggled and squirmed. Her face turned a bright red, and the little rose bud mouth opened wide and let out a shrill cry. This is my introduction to Carol—our new little pup.

Nothing lasts forever. The ultimate good times and the worst of tragedies are the thoughts that remain etched on my mind.

I am nearly 3 years old, and Carol is the first new baby I have seen. I didn't dare touch her, but my feet were glued to the spot until Daddy shooed me away.

All day long, I was extremely fearful because I couldn't see Mama. I kept coming to the door of the big bedroom, but I was not allowed to go in. Earlier, I had asked if I could see Mama, but Daddy said no. "Mama has to rest. Go outside."

I didn't. I watched the door. Someone finally left it ajar. I wanted to go inside, but I worried that Daddy would be mad so I looked for Mama without crossing the threshold. I found her propped up in bed with pillows bracing her back. I stood in the doorway, hesitating to go further because of Daddy's orders.

She noticed me standing there, and beckoned me to her. I stopped at the foot of her bed—Mama looked so pale. I had been desperate to see her, but now I felt better, relieved. I knew she wasn't going to die because she spoke to me. I could go on and play.

Providing background to my story means retracing my steps back to the beginning. Looking inside a rented two-story house on Oak

Street, in the small, Southern Illinois town of Chester, I find myself along with my intact family gathered there.

In the next vivid recollections from my childhood, I've grown two more years—I'm 5 now. Out pops the sensitive and oftentimes Jack-in-the-box impulsive kid. That's me.

My world is small and secure. Only a wishful dreamer can hang on to this much fun. I try to capture and hold tight each new day. I collect and save memories: the bits and pieces of wonderful times.

All the kids in the neighborhood gather in our yard to play and search for adventure. Sometimes we form a large circle on the shady lot to the right of our house. Pretty close to Heaven sums up the location.

It is a sunny day, and we are laughing out loud as we march around in our circle, singing the chant of the game. Everyone is taking a turn running in, then around and back. I have a baloney sandwich in my hand. I won't quit playing to eat.

How simple and good this is to remember. It is more wondrous how that image of me was so captured in a child's eye that I can draw out the little Shirley still running and holding the sandwich, again and again.

Romance is wonderful; I can hardly wait for my turn. Dee is so lucky to be 12. On this evening, the whole Oak Street gang of us is out for a moonlight stroll.

A couple of blocks up the street, we made use of a stone retaining wall. It was a grand place to sit and star gaze. The Big and Little Dipper, a bear, and a hunter were hiding somewhere high above us. A million tiny diamonds lit up the night sky. How could I hope to locate the right ones?

Dee pointed out the elusive stars and drew an imaginary line in the heavens, directing my eyes to find the Big Dipper. "Oh ... I see it. I see it!" My face brightened as I recognized the Dipper's outline. Caught up in the moment, one of the Schroden boys begins singing

"Oh Buttermilk Sky" to Dee. I stand transfixed as my mind snaps the picture.

Bidding farewell to romance, for now, we set sail for another kind of adventure. Under the tree beside the house, we plot a new course. It is tempting to climb the big oak, so we do. Up we go, the four of us: Sonny, Mary, Nancy, and me. We scamper from the tree's long branches and onto the rooftop. Someone opens a second-story window, so we can crawl in and out of the house. I don't believe Mom knows we do this.

There are three upstairs bedrooms in this rented house, one of which is boarded up. We held a powwow outside the closed room, hashing over a story we heard about a young girl who died in there. Was it true? I was fairly gullible and no match for one older sister who was a "creative" storyteller. More likely, the room was used as storage space by the homeowner.

Curiosity got the better of us, and we looked inside the room by using the narrow cracks between the boards, as peepholes. Not satisfied with an obstructed glimpse, Sonny borrowed a crow bar (we'd better put that back!) from Dad's garage.

Three of us pushed and pulled together on the crowbar. The fourth got cold feet; Mary washed her hands of us, declaring: "You guys are on your own. I'm not taking the rap for this." A few squeaks, squalls and splinters later, we beheld a clear view of the room. Daylight spilled across the bed where, supposedly, the sick girl had lain. We saw outdated clothing and various other fascinating things draped and strewn around the room. All these added spark to our own imagination. To mine it was a solemn experience. We hammered the boards back in place.

We youngsters have the run of the largely unused upper story, and that provides opportunity for mischief making. Usually, one of us would stand lookout while the rest explored.

Mary, Sonny, and I rolled up tight little strips of wallpaper torn from the walls, to make homemade cigarettes. I don't recall any flames, but then it happened so long ago, and I was younger than school age. I do remember that I found the idea of smoking alluring.

Dee could be a wet blanket on our shenanigans so we left her out of some of our more adventurous antics. Nancy was the opposite, and she threw caution to the winds. She developed a liking for roof walking. Nancy wasn't sure footed. Periodically, I would get a stab of worry, and I'd drop what I was doing and run to the window to admonish her. "Nancy, you be careful."

A guardian angel is probably the only reason we didn't fall off the roof or set the house on fire. Boy, was our mom ever a pushover. Dee was still about 12 now, and I think that angel used her part time to look after and civilize the rest of us.

Even though there are two years and eight months between Carol and me, everyone linked us together. It was always "Shirley and Carol," as if we were one person. We were inseparable playmates.

But I was pleased to go on my merry way without her when Grandma Mollie let me tag along for a short stay with her and Grandpa Alf. Loneliness soon gnawed at my insides. I missed Carol something awful.

Nobody is as kind and understanding as Grandma Mollie. The remainder of the day brightened when she offered, "Shirley, honey, we can ride the Dinky and take you home tomorrow."

The next morning, Grandma and I walked to the train station to board the Dinky. After purchasing our tickets, we waited on a wooden platform amid puffs of smoke and the warning clang of a bell, as the little passenger train screeched and squalled to a halt.

It was a wondrous, bumpy ride on worn, sun-faded, red leather seats. George, our friendly and trustworthy conductor, lurched slightly from side to side as he made his way down the narrow center isle to collect our tickets.

We shared one of the train's tattered seats. And Grandma, bless her heart, left the spacious window seat for me. She and I stared out through the glass, taking in the panoramic view as the little train clickety-clacked down the track.

Too soon, our breathtaking ride is over. Grandma and I left the train and set off on foot. Near home, I spotted Carol pedaling her tricycle. My impatient feet begged to run ahead and Grandma knew it. She waved permission for me to run on while she continued at her usual slow pace, taking short, halting steps. Always, her swollen ankles puffed out and spilled over the tops of her shoes.

I raced down the sidewalk to greet Carol. "Did you miss me?" I whispered in her surprised face. "No," she said. "I was busy."

CHAPTER 7

❦

Seeds of Disharmony

Miss Nell was a nice, older lady who for some reason took a special interest in me. She lived just up the road from the farm, which was owned by our paternal grandparents, August Sr. and Pella. I must have spent time with Miss Nell that I can't recall. Why else would she want me for her own?

In the midst of my confusion, a forgotten moment surfaces. Miss Nell is standing beside me. She and I are alone on her long, enclosed side porch. We are in a maze of cactus, all planted in clay pots. There must be a hundred of them. A few are blooming. She is telling me all about them. But Miss Nell is lonely, and she wants something more than cactuses.

Some time ago, while Miss Nell visited Mom, I had walked in on their private conversation. Words trailed off as I entered the room, but there was a hint that Miss Nell was offering to give me the "good life." It became more than a hint when Nancy told me, "Miss Nell will give you anything you want. She wants you."

The next time we meet, we are in Miss Nell's driveway. Reluctantly, I get out of the car and follow Mom. Little Carol and the driver, a woman acquaintance of Mom's wait in the car. Mom and I go inside. Miss Nell has a tray with some dainty little cakes on it. I am too fearful to want the cakes. I search Mom's face.

"Can I go with you?" I already know her answer.

"No, I'll be back soon."

Mom leaves, and I struggle to hide my fear. But I don't cry.

"Look," Miss Nell points at an antique, "it's a big high bed and you can sleep here if you want."

She keeps trying to persuade me to stay; all the while, I am backing away. I keep widening the distance between us because I feel trapped. I'm lightheaded because my breathing is all ragged and funny. If only I can get to the door ...

"I need to go home. I have to go home now," I say.

Miss Nell didn't try to hold onto me. She was not the witch stepping out from the Hansel and Gretel story. She was just lonely and childless. After I had time to reflect, it flattered me in a way. Miss Nell saw something in that quiet, easy-to-overlook little girl that caused her to want me.

So the incident passed. I went home, and Miss Nell faded from our lives. But why was I there? It was a haunting question. Was this just an innocent overnight stay with a lonely old lady, or was it a test to see if Miss Nell could keep me? It puzzled me for a long time. Much later, I learned from one of my sisters what really happened. Grandma Mollie had put a stop to it.

Animosity on the part of Dad's family, along with differences in our parents' upbringing and religion, caused the us-versus-them situation. Grandma Pella, especially, was very controlling. She neither liked nor accepted our mother.

In the beginning, Dad's people openly expressed doubt that the first child Mom was carrying belonged to Dad.

Mom told me her story.

"Dee was nearly due, and I was big as a barrel. We were turned away by several other priests before your daddy went to one who agreed to marry us. The priest was old and lived way out in the sticks. Dee was born shortly afterwards." And Mom assured me, "Dee is a copy of your daddy."

We shuttled back and forth, living in rented houses between the two small communities where the grandparents lived. Our maternal and paternal grandparents were separated by about fifteen miles, geographically, but in all other ways they were hundreds of miles apart.

An old family photo, taken before Carol was born, shows us at a small frame house beside a railroad track. These must have been lean years. Dad reminded us about the poverty. "Holy cow! that was a cold winter. I walked these tracks and picked up lumps of coal that had fallen off train cars. You do what you have to do to stay warm."

A few mineworkers, in sympathy with those who were stuck in hard-times, shoveled off extra chunks of coal for those less fortunate to scoop up. Our family was one of these.

Our next move brought us home to our mom's folks.

"Hit the hay." With that command, Dad would send us scurrying off to bed early. When he wasn't there, Carol and I could listen to our radio program at least an hour longer. I hated going to bed so early, always in the middle of our suspenseful story. What happened to the *Fat Man* or *Inner Sanctum* remained a mystery to us. I thought Dad wanted us out of his way.

Grandpa Alf was less strict. When he was in charge, we always waited for "the signal." The signal was that Grandpa, wearing long johns with the back door flapping, marched into the kitchen after Carol and I ignored his earlier requests.

My siblings have their own stories. The worst I can remember is the sharp stinging rap on the top of the head with Dad's knuckle. That hit can be startling if you don't know it's coming—and I never did.

One cantankerous old man has little patience for another.

It is dark outside but not late. Grandpa usually locks up at 9 p.m., and the clothespin lock device is already in place.

Dee, Sonny, Mary and Nancy are not back from the basketball game yet. Mom went to bed early because a throbbing toothache had kept her awake the previous night. Carol followed, and they are both fast asleep. Grandma is in bed, as well, so Grandpa and I are waiting up for the kids.

Since it's payday at the shoe factory and Dad still isn't home after work, Grandpa assumes he's perched on a barstool. That's why Grandpa is not going to let him in. Dad gets the big mouth from the long-necked bottle.

I am sitting cross-legged on the front room floor, busy playing when the pounding begins. What if he comes to the window? I agonize. I glance up at the glass behind the ivory lace curtain, and I worry I'll see Dad's angry face there and won't know what to do.

Grandpa Alf doesn't move from his chair. He sits there quietly, his face expressionless.

The wooden clothespin rattles and bobs in the latch where a padlock belongs, as the pounding, shouting and swearing continues. My eyes grow round in a fixed stare at Grandpa's face and I think, Grandpa's not scared, but I am. He is old and I picture him falling in a scuffle. If the clothespin breaks, I'm afraid he might get hurt.

A gruff exterior covers that too old body. It seems incredible to me, that the only thing holding back the violence is a single clothespin.

The pounding stops and I look to the window again. No face is between the lace curtains. He could be standing in the shadows. I only see the streetlight. I breathe a sigh of relief. Grandpa chuckles softly to himself.

Dad was back the next morning, sober, to look sharply at me and ask, "Why didn't you let me in?" So, he did see me from through the window. I didn't have an answer.

Dad was not easygoing like Mom. He tended to show his cranky side easily. Divorce seemed inevitable. It's unfair to place blame. I'll choose circumstances and human frailty as the cause. I don't know why we were living with Grandma Mollie and Grandpa Alf before Mom and Dad separated, but theirs was the only place I thought of as home.

Dee is 14 now, and all the girls her age dress alike. The popular style is carefully planned to appear happy-go-lucky. They are all wearing cotton shirts tucked inside blue jeans with the pant legs rolled up to just below the knee. The girls complete their breezy look, as they walk along together, by hooking their thumbs in the side pockets of their jeans. The shoes are squeaky, leather strap sandals from Mexico, called huaraches.

It's 1943 and other than a young girl's style, nothing is cool. But Kilroy is everywhere.

You need to know that Kilroy was the mysterious man who drew a long-nose caricature wherever he went and signed his name. He had many imitators, and his signature appeared on train cars, buses, and storefronts across the land. That sneaky fellow might even autograph your underwear. The "Kilroy was here" phenomenon originated in World War II when Kilroy worked in a munitions factory inspecting bombs.

Dee had more good things going for her than she recognized, including a priceless ability to fix or change any negatives that bothered her. If there was a way out, Dee could find it.

"My hair is straight as a stick," Dee used to fuss over her dark blond hair that she called dishwater blond.

"You're so pretty; none of that matters," I told her.

Every morning before leaving for school, she took out the hairpins, fixed and changed it into beautiful hair full of the curls she always wanted. That was Dee. She threw herself into anything that needed to be fixed or changed.

Some older women from nearby, paid her pocket change to pin curl, comb, and style their grays. Dee could easily have been a beautician.

No matter how many times we played the counting game—reciting "rich man - poor man - beggar man - thief - doctor - lawyer - Indian chief," in 1944, there was really only hairdresser, waitress, or school teacher, for girls. Career choices were limited, and the fairer sex always earned less. An expression I heard often and resented much was "not bad pay—for a woman."

The night that Dad went to drag Dee out of a friend's car was probably one of the last straws. Our parents' marriage turned rockier because of his hot-headed action. He had worked himself up with his usual poor judgment.

Dad didn't realize he was making an ass of himself; he thought he was taking charge of his family, doing the right thing. Dad, stubbornly, had to be right. Mom and he had a terrible fight earlier, when he found out Dee was gone on a date with Delbert.

He must have looked a crazy sight the night Delbert first met him. Dad came charging out the back door like a wild man, hair sticking straight up, eyes daggered. Dee began to cry as soon as she saw him, and Delbert drove away with her. He took her home to his mother's house for the night while Dad cooled off. The next morning, Dee came home to a gentler situation; either Dad had left for work or Mom had put him out. I don't know which, maybe it was both. Dee and Dad's relationship was strained after this episode for quite a while.

A few years earlier, when we still lived near Dad's parents, Grandma Pella pulled all the strings. I remember the oranges.

Dad was driving us back home after a trip to the grocery store when he instructed us, "Hurry and eat your oranges before we get home so Grandma won't know."

Certain food my family took care to eat promptly, or squirrel away from Grandma Pella. She could disapprove of its cost to Mom and insist it was a waste of Dad's hard-earned money. Oranges were one such extravagance. "We got oranges once a year in our Christmas stockings," Dad said.

My rejection of rules and of folks saddling others with their controlling behavior most probably stems from these early childhood impressions of unfairness.

While Mom and Dad were separated, Grandma Pella urged Dad to bury his cash and valuables in her cellar. Uncle Bud, Dad's brother, accidentally dug it up one day when he noticed loose dirt.

Approximately twenty years later, Dad casually mentioned the incident as a funny story. An uneasy tug-of-war went on inside my head. Things were good between us then, and I didn't want to spoil it, but I remembered that while Dad was burying money I was wearing my brother's hand-me-downs.

Yet a still, small voice reminded me that in 1945 it had rained in Dad's life, too.

That day in 1945, we didn't go to court with Mom, but the whole day was gut-wrenching. By early afternoon, I sat glued to the side of Grandma Mollie's rocking chair. There I stayed, asking her impossible questions, watching the clock's hands crawl, and growing old beyond my years from the wait.

The judge ruled in Mom's favor in the legal battle, and she was awarded custody of us plus child support. Our support was infrequent, depending on Dad's mood. He remained grim faced most of the time.

When I next saw Dad, he was giving his account of the day in court. Standing tall, in the doorway of Grandma Mollie's front room, he quoted the judge to everyone within hearing distance. I listened, and it really stuck in my mind when Dad told all of us, "I found out you can hit 'em, but you can't kick 'em." He repeated himself.

I filled in the blanks with the worst thing I could think of. I envisioned Dad standing over my mother, yelling and kicking while she lay crying on the floor. Did I ever see this? It didn't matter; I was mad at Dad, and I wanted him gone.

You can hit 'em, but you can't kick 'em. That's the way it was in 1945. If necessary, equality could be battered away from women.

I think I held on to some cockeyed idea that if he ever changed, he and Mom could get back together.

Mary decided to live with Dad. She and I shared the same household, but how is it possible we didn't live the same sights and sounds? I tried to change her mind, but Mary would not budge. In desperation, I pleaded with Mom, "Don't let her go." I knew I was speaking to a closed mind when Mom answered, "That's her daddy, and she wants to go."

We rarely saw our sister during her stay with Dad and the other grandparents. "Mary's here," were sweet words, but it only meant for an hour or less. I loved her bubbly personality and felt emptiness after she left.

Petey was Dad's pet name for Mary. She lived with him for two years, and he loved her best because she chose him over Mom.

Dad and Mary were missing from our lives, and we really didn't have Mom with us, either. She was working as a barmaid, miles away from home. The owner of the tavern was a woman that our dad disliked, and he referred to her as "Hog's Head." Around the same time, he dropped "Norma" or "your mom," and he named her "the Ol' Gal."

Sometimes Mom came home on Sunday afternoons, but she was gone before I could warm up to her. Carol fits back in quicker than I can.

Mom was a special blessing to me when she sang because happiness is contagious. While she was around, I caught myself singing her songs. "Room Full of Roses," an old Eddie Arnold hit, is the one I remember best.

Mom worked at the knitting mill for a while. The factory produced nylon hosiery. Her job required heavy lifting, and she underwent a partial hysterectomy because of it. After the surgery, she worked at a dress factory.

Mom's next job was at a café. Late one night, she had a very frightening experience there. She had worked the evening shift alone and felt exhausted at closing time. Needing a rest before her walk home, she stretched out on the booth against the far left wall. Mom only meant to close her eyes for a moment. But the long day she had spent on her feet caught up with her, and she promptly fell asleep.

Sometime later, she was startled awake by the sounds of someone bumping against a barstool. She could barely distinguish the outline of a shadowy figure moving around. Her heart began pounding wildly.

The only light was a silvery shaft from the moon, streaming through the wide front window. Paralyzed with fear, she watched as the robber crept around the corner of the bar and opened the cash register. Thankfully, Mom's hiding place was secure in the dark, blocked away from the beams of moonlight by the high back of her end booth.

"After what seemed an eternity," she told us, "the intruder fled through the kitchen and out into a back alley."

We accepted Mom's safety as a miracle. No telling what would have happened if the man had discovered her lying panic stricken in the last, high backed booth. She could not throw off the terror of that night, so she quit her waitress job.

Some happy moments pulled us back up. Dee was still dating Delbert, a wonderful, young man she met on a blind date. His fair complexion was painted a rosy red by wind and sun, and his blue eyes spilled over from a battle with ragweed, but he was sure a welcome sight to us. Delbert took Dee's little tagalong sisters for a ride in his shiny car. Can you beat that?

On some of their dates, they went to a dance contest where couples had been dancing nonstop for days. The dance-a-thon rule was to keep moving, and whichever couple could go without sleep the longest won a cash prize.

As soon as Dee turned 16, they were going to be married. I watched Dee struggle daily to make her dream come true, without any money. Somehow, she bought a new dress and shoes.

God was directing the show now.

It was planned to be a double wedding with the friends who brought them together on that blind date.

It had rained for a solid week. Like Dee, by bedtime I was anxious with the day-before jitters. Lying crossways on the double bed beneath a window, I grabbed my pillow and pushed it onto the wood sill, and I watched the starlight show—my usual ritual to unwind.

With my head cushioned on the pillow in the window, I breathed in the cool night air. My weary bones relaxed. Through partly closed eyes, I surveyed the heavens and I begged God for a sunny tomorrow.

Early next morning, I felt the warmth of sunlight as it filtered through the upper glass pane and spread across my sleepy lids.

The sun was smiling down solely to brighten Dee's wedding day. At their reception, I had my first taste of wedding cake. It was like biting into a slice of frosted magic.

The big sister, the one who patiently taught me how to tie my shoes, even though I learned it backwards and to this day still tie opposite bows, had a new life.

I wanted to be more like Dee, but I couldn't; I had to stay Shirley. Around my sister, the little girl I pretended to be could put on a super active performance, hoping for attention. The sensitive 9-year-old that I was stuck with, outside of my small circle of siblings, more often tried to become invisible and "fade into the woodwork" to hide her insecurities.

For a short time, Mom and Dad were close to reconciliation; sadly, it did not get the push it needed from any of us. Mom never found a better man. She went from one fault-filled man to another.

As far back as memory will take me, to Oak Street, there was always these nagging hints that Mom was not well; something, I noticed, was amiss with our eye contact. She looked at me, yet she was somewhere far off.

She laughed too loudly, too long at things that weren't that funny. I could tell from her actions that sometimes her thoughts did not follow a plan of logic. Mom just couldn't help herself. Did anyone else in our household observe the same things as I?

It was Christmas time, after Mary and Dad's second year together, when the awful thing happened.

Mary is home with us for the holidays, and a change is taking place. My heart is carrying a heavy burden for Dad. Mary is all he has, and she is not going back to him after the holiday. I dreaded Dad's coming for Mary, on the last day of her visit. Back when Mary left us and I begged, "Don't go," I knew it might end this way.

Late that evening, he stepped from the back porch and into Grandma's kitchen. Mary had earlier decided how to break the bad news. "It'll be all right," she promised. I knew it wouldn't be.

The rest of the household had gone to bed. I moved mechanically to the window in the far corner of the kitchen and stood motionless, looking out into the darkness as Mary led Dad to the front room for privacy.

There could be no secrets in this old house. Years earlier, Grandpa had built on the kitchen from any scrap available. The floor was set on top of discarded railroad ties. The walls were not plastered—simply rough boards smoothed over with mismatched patterns of yellowed wallpaper.

Every hard rain caused a stir of activity. We scrambled to fetch and set out buckets and metal pans to catch the drips. I found it soothing: the murmuring "din-din-splat" rhythm from the water droplets hitting our old tin buckets. The rain sounds always gave me a comforting back rub feeling—and I wanted more. Predictably, I hoped nobody would mend the roof before the next downpour.

There was going to be no easy way out of this storm for Dad. I tried to put my feelings on hold. If only Mary had turned on a light in the room. It seemed worse for Dad to be hurt in the dark. It was bad; I could hear her crying. Their hushed whispers leaked through the paper-thin kitchen wall. It was an emotional massacre for all three of us. Dad pleaded with his Petey. He asked her why.

Mary had shared with me that Dad had given her a radio for Christmas to listen to in bed. As soon as Dad left for his nightly trip to town, Grandma Pella marched into Mary's room and switched it off.

I think Mary wanted to get out from under Grandma Pella's thumb. Grandma Pella barely stood five feet tall and weighed less than eighty pounds, but that didn't stop that wiry lady from owning everyone around her.

Mary resembled a darling little paper doll. She was born with the dark brown ringlets that framed her face, the naturally curly hair that Dee would die for. Mary's thorn was that she could not cope. By the young age of 13, she was already a bundle of nerves.

Finally, Dad gave it up. I heard his footsteps coming and wished I could disappear. As he walked through the kitchen, I caught a glimpse of him; his shoulders slumped, and his long face hung even longer. What sounded like my voice managed a quiet "Bye."

Dad answered, "Bye," without looking my way. The silence that followed was as crushing as the sound of Mary's crying. I carried sadness to bed with me that night.

After the divorce, Dad came to take us for a drive with him for our visits. Nancy and Mary went infrequently. Dee and Sonny refused to go at all. Dad coaxed Carol and me to go back in the house and bring Mom along for the ride. He wanted Mom, badly!

At the same time, he would warn us, "Don't ever tell Grandma Pella that your mom goes with us." I guess it was too hard to upset his mother, so he kept ours hidden.

If Mom had decided to be with Dad, I think he could have gotten around Grandma Pella's objections. She was not the cause of their divorce. Grandma Pella was just stingy and set in her ways.

Mom consented to join us on these drives with Dad because she wanted the support money. The last time they were together, it went sour. After Daddy leaned against Mom and whispered something in her ear, a spat followed.

"No," she told him, angrily. "You can just take me home ... right now. Don't you start it." He whispered some more to her. She shook her head, emphasizing her words. "Now, Wib, I'll not do any such a thing. I'll not. No ... No."

On these short drives, Carol and I were in the car with them every time, but I was left in the dark about their quiet conversations. It wasn't long before Mom decided not to see Dad again. She told me, "I'm not puttin' up with his old crap anymore." Whatever that meant.

I'm a 9-year-old "green" kid who is trying to play cupid to my stubborn parents. As much as I once wanted Dad gone, I now wanted him back. But nothing I said made any difference to Mom. She gave me a word of warning: my middle name. "Now Shirley Ann, you better leave it alone."

Things were never quite like Mom believed they were. Constant change was her path of escape, and she was always leaving her troubles behind.

After Mom refused to go for our drives, it got really ugly. Dad would go into a stormy rage for the first few minutes when he found this out. He couldn't settle down until after he called her all the bad names he could think of.

"You bitch! You whore!" He exploded, his fist banging on the steering wheel.

During Dad's outburst, Carol glanced at me and then shifted her gaze to the floorboard. She was watching me out of the corner of her eye. Patiently, she seemed to wait it out and throw it off easier than I could.

I learned to prefer the back seat, so Dad wouldn't see me cover my ears and block him out. Those fits of anger spoiled our time together. It made our ice-cream treat a little less sweet.

Daddy boycotted Mom's hometown. Our visitation had evolved into his driving just the three of us (himself, Carol, and me) to the next town. Once there, we patronized the café. We'd sit in our usual booth, while Daddy ordered a treat for us. Carol and I spooned down a dish of vanilla ice cream. Every time it was vanilla. But all along, I secretly craved chocolate.

Having it scooped into a cone was out of the question, as well. Daddy ordered the treat for us. He had already decided, "Cones are too messy." Earlier, I had wasted my best wheedling on Carol. Daddy seemed more patient with her, so I tried to persuade her into asking for some chocolate ice cream, or else a bottle of Coke.

Darn the luck! Carol turned me down flat, and she warned, "Daddy won't like that. Besides, I want white ice cream."

It appears as though we have choices—but we really don't. When the matronly owner and waitress came to our booth and stood ready, pen and ticket pad in her hand, I was dying to say to her, I'll have a Coke—or make mine chocolate ice cream.

One day, after having given up on Carol, I decided to take the risk. But to avoid a worse embarrassment, I worked up my nerve before the waitress appeared at our table. In front of Daddy and Carol, I blurted out, "Can I have chocolate instead of vanilla?"

He frowned at me, really hard, and he thought that wasn't a good idea. Carol guessed right; my asking had annoyed him. There I sat, with my foot in my mouth.

"If you don't want any," Daddy snapped, "we'll just skip it." Then, as if that made it all right, his attitude softened, and he shared his objections. "Chocolate will stain; you might spill it on your clothes; it could spoil your pretty dress."

He touched my collar to indicate where the chocolate could drip. But it was too late to smooth everything over. My feelings were hurt, and I would rather be anywhere other than this miserable booth. Carol fell unusually silent. At her first opportunity, she gave me the look, rolling her wizened eyes and mouthing, "I told you so."

Although Daddy never gave it a second thought, I was mortified. A lump formed in my throat, and the vanilla ice cream was tasteless. I was obliged to eat it anyway, and to pretend that it was as good as what I really wanted.

I admit to being sensitive. I was still in the delicate process of becoming—of sorting out who I am meant to be. In this procession called life, all the turmoil over ice cream flavors seems petty at first glance, and it may not have amounted to much if I had seen my father every day and had, therefore, been used to being frowned at over trivial things.

Daddy's absence made him almost a stranger to me, and everything he did or said stood out. Divorce is too complicated for children to understand, and yet they want to know why it happened and to feel it wasn't somehow, their fault.

After the dust settled, Dad began to mellow. He did reach out, especially to his Dee. Things gradually improved between them. He visited often with her and Delbert at their farm. She would let Dad be right more often to avoid conflict, I noticed, than Delbert would.

Spring was just around the corner. Carol and I crossed out each new day on the calendar that hung on the wall in Grandma's kitchen. Dad promised to take us to Dee's house so we could order Easter outfits. Today, we marked across our last number.

The four of us sat at Dee's kitchen table, poring over the Sears catalog, turning the pages filled with pretty little girls all dressed up in my and Carol's new clothes. Then I saw it, the perfect hat. I wanted this one. But alas, everyone else liked the wide-brimmed straw hats with the blue or red grosgrain ribbon dangling in the back. I was being overruled, but I wasn't going to give up easily.

"Couldn't I get this one and Carol have the straw hat? I really do want this one."

Today was supposed to be a happy day, but right in the middle of a sentence I felt the sharp point of Dad's knuckle hit the back of my head. He got my attention. I blinked once, hard. Dee tried to smooth it over. I know she saw how devastated I was. I said it was all right, but it wasn't. It was ruined.

Was this practice an acceptable punishment that Dad learned from his childhood? At that moment, I made a conscious decision that this would never happen to me again because I would keep a safe distance and never again turn my back on Dad.

On Easter morning, Dee came to Grandma's house to help Carol and me get dressed for church. As she positioned the straw bonnet on the top of my head, she asked me, "Do you like it?" I lied. Every time I saw that hat, I was reminded.

Temporarily, I ended my hour visits with Dad because I was still mad about his outbursts over Mom. Maybe his head figured out what his mouth was doing.

"My daddy quit that," Carol said, and then, using her best 5-year-old logic, she added: "Besides, "I want the ice cream."

I felt that I was invisible to Dad throughout my childhood, and I grieved every unmentioned loss. I don't believe we knew each other until we were given a second chance. A decade later, Dad wanted to be included, and I wanted to be wanted. What might have been will never be, but hearts can heal when people change.

Sonny only does whatever pleases Sonny, but he is my brother, and family loyalty runs deep. I care about that bossy character.

It just so happened that Daddy's unexpected visitation, on that evening, came with bad timing; my spoiled brother and I were the only youngsters at home. Daddy's black Plymouth slowed, but it didn't stop. After he drove on past the house, I continued to stand watch through the front room window, waiting for him to cruise back to us.

"Are you going out to see Daddy?" I asked Sonny.

"Shir'we, are you out of your rabbit ass mind?" Sonny had a speech impediment; he could not form the L sound and make it come out right. His L's always had the W sound. He pronounced the color blue as bwoo.

No. I was just feeling anxious over the prospect of having to entertain our daddy, all alone.

After a final circling of our block, the car returned and stopped. Daddy deliberately parked at least one car length away from our front door, never exactly in front of the house. That avoidance bothered me to no end. I was certain that he purposely chose a parking spot where he was tucked away from the front window and from eye contact with anyone inside.

Daddy didn't risk exchanging glances with any of his former in-laws. Parking farther away from the house is another way to express his resentment of these "heathens." Grandpa would peer out at him from the window and chuckle.

The last exchange between the two hotheaded men ended at an impasse—with Daddy vowing he would never give Mom a red cent. Grandpa chuckled at him under his breath. "Never's quite a spell, Wib. 'Ery you squat on your haunches in the jail house till your beard is growed long and white, you might commence to change your idea." Dad was not going to get the best of that sarcastic old man.

How can I know anything else, except what I see with my own eyes? Daddy's face was an open book; every emotion he felt was visible there. He looked grim. My eyes traced the furrowed lines of an unhappy mood crossing Dad's brow. I wished I didn't feel the effect from all of this. Daddy was waiting in the car, and Sonny wouldn't go out there with me to meet him. He was being his usual independent self. If Sonny even gives a care whether anyone loves him or not, he doesn't let it show. And since our sisters were out gallivanting, that left Daddy and me thrown together on this visitation.

It is an insecurity issue I am saddled with: forever needing to be reassured that I matter, and I searched for approval in the reflection of my father's eyes.

During our visit, Daddy is unusually quiet. When he cuts short the drive, I ask myself: Would he leave early, this way, if one of the others were here with us? Being the only one is not nearly as great as I thought it could be. Fumbling for the door handle, I'm ready to escape the difficult art of small talk. I just can't take the pressure of socializing on an adult level.

"You don't have to shut it hard—just pull it to," Daddy says. "It doesn't take much force to close it."

I've been reminded of this before. By now, I am pretty conscientious about the way I handle Daddy's car doors. I'm used to tugging on ancient, warped house doors that demand persuasion.

I beat myself up some more. You're plain and dull, and that is why Daddy is leaving early. Galvanizing self-doubt is as confining as iron bars: an invisible prison of my own making.

I listened to the whispers from my heart, and although I wanted everything to be different, I couldn't understand myself any better than I understood Daddy. When I finally—ease—the car door shut behind me, I feel liberated.

Although Sonny, in his wanton teens, doesn't have much respect for our father, in another age, they will finally get it right. When the hour seems late: the bond between father and son grows strong. It doesn't happen in the blink of an eye. Hope groaned through a generation.

But that is a giant leap from where my story is now. First there is a string of tries and failures, an every-man-for-himself attitude, extreme poverty, and saddest of all—prison time. As Grandpa predicted, Sonny was jailed for theft, along with the same group of boys that Grandpa had warned him about.

Through Mom's "vacations," which is how she described her stays in mental hospitals, we bled individually, unable to share our misery.

Spread out on paper, my childhood looks worse than it actually was.

Everyone has a story.

CHAPTER 8

—— ✂ ——

Unforgettable Play

NONE OF US had many playthings; we improvised by making our own entertainment. Grandma taught the little ones a simple game of folded hands that we called "button, button who's got the button."

It was a sign of the times: young boys moved around on hands and knees in the dirt, crowding over a crudely drawn circle on the ground.

Competing for marbles was Sonny's favorite pastime. His group of buddies occasionally played just for the fun of it, but usually the rivalry turned serious, and then they would agree among themselves to match skills in a game called "keepers."

Sonny's hand was steady and his aim true, and he earned the name "top dog." He had amassed a kitchen cupboard drawer full of sparkling glass marbles. This special drawer belonged to him alone, and I think he dusted it regularly for fingerprints.

Curiosity got the better of me, and I risked a scolding from my brother. "Shir'we, you shut that drawer and weave my dang stuff awone." It was daunting to look inside Sonny's drawer without making noise. I used to slide it open by carefully inching it along so that his marbles didn't jostle. The slightest movement caused rolling and telltale clicking sounds. After quickly noting Sonny's newest winnings, and admiring his priceless lucky shooter, I eased the drawer shut.

During the winter months, it was a challenge for Grandpa to keep the drafty old place heated. The sharp sound of his breathless "huff-huff," from 1944 comes back to me, and I hear, again, Grandpa's labored breathing.

Grandpa tires out easily, and he must stop twice as he carries a bucket of coal from the shed out back. After each short rest, his gloved fingers, repeatedly, wrap around the wire handle of the heavy bucket. I hear him grunt as he leans his stocky frame slightly to steady the load.

As he walks up the ash-strewn path, Grandpa holds a one-sided conversation. It's always the same, "I work my fingers to the bone (huff huff), and nobody appreciates it."

Grandpa is wrong about that. I saw his struggle and wanted to help. I wasn't strong enough to carry the heavy bucket, and if I dragged it, I lost half of the coal. Grandpa asserted, "You're too little; you'll wear a hole in my bucket."

On frosty winter evenings, we would huddle next to the iron coal stove in the front room. This potbellied monstrosity was fixed to the back wall with curved sections of dull black stovepipe and lengths of sturdy wire. Shortly after Grandpa fires up, both stove and black pipe turn a searing deep scarlet.

It was there, on the front room floor, that I honed my jacks playing skill to the utmost by practicing the game religiously. Nevertheless, I was not the best player.

I perform poorly under stress. When I missed, I would console myself by thinking that I must have a hidden talent. All I can come up with is that I have a vivid imagination, so I spin my dreams and deepest longings into a make-believe world.

On the scrubbed out surface of a grayish, floral linoleum, I while away my time. The warmth from the stove, spreads over my back as I lay out my paper dolls.

In my chosen corner of the room, I was oblivious to everything else around me. The paper doll game was spellbinding. I got carried away in let's pretend, lost in my thoughtful, intricate play, until an hour could seem like minutes. I fabricated a complete personality to match every paper person, and I knew each character by heart.

We dress up in costumes for glamorous performances. I fall in love, too, with each glowing, imaginary romance. In exotic, faraway lands, we battle against evil in terrible wars. We laugh together in happy moments and share our sadness in times of tragedy. Their fragile lives seesaw back and forth with loves and hates that parallel my own.

I used to wish that Dee and our neighbor, Gary, another older man of 16, would get together romantically.

Gary was a man of many talents. I had, on occasion, seen him wring a chicken's neck; on another, he hallowed out a pumpkin, carved a face in it, and then wore it over his head on Halloween night. Later he told me, "The stink was awful."

One day, while in his back yard, which adjoined ours, Gary was busy sawing and pounding nails into some boards. He let me hang around and watch him build, and when he finished, he handed me the pair of stilts. This was the proof I needed to confirm my belief in a Prince Charming.

The gift caught me by surprise. I was glad that Dee found her own man, now. I named a paper doll after Gary, and a fantasy romance with my older man blossomed in paper land.

Traces of time: Gary enjoyed writing as a pastime. The short story of our "paper doll" romance would have made him smile. Fate had kicked him around for most of his earthly days—he could have used more reasons to smile.

Although Gary married, he remained a lonely man. And after a bitter divorce, I saw the hunger for an elusive true love, still in his eyes.

He will never read the memories of the little girl next door, who had a crush on him, from afar. Yet heaven knows that Gary was a kind young man who once gifted a poor child with a pair of homemade stilts.

Carol hugs Sally, her favorite baby doll, closely. Poor Sally; she gets lost in one of our moving shuffles along with my paper dolls, a loss that crushed me. Our mom mistakenly believed that everything is replaceable. Grandma Mollie angrily disagreed.

Once, in a vulnerable mood, I looked around at the somber, serious folks in my life and promised myself that I would never forget how it feels to be a kid. It's scary to think about changing to old, and I dreaded the day I might cease to run. So I ran all the harder.

By and by, Grandma's sister Emily and nephew Everett came to visit her. Everett was an old man of 28, yet he seemed like one of the kids because he chased and romped outside with the best of us.

What a relief it was to understand that age is a state of mind. If I hold tight to young, it can't go away; if I run every day, old can't jump on.

At dusk, we followed Everett inside. Grandma's crowded kitchen was bursting at the seams, full of the fun I was so desperate to keep.

Laughter rang out when Emily goaded Grandma, "Mollie, do you think we need some face washing?" Everett exploded, laughing uproariously.

The lighthearted side of my serious family is showing. "Got your goat, Mollie," someone teased. What was so funny? I would ask Grandma Mollie later at her rocking chair time.

Grandpa always wore white long johns, the kind that has the button back trap door. He traded off his summer pair for the heavier winter ones at the first cold snap. In between, usually monthly, he pulled off the underwear and gave it a good wash by hand. He hung the long johns on a line stretched across one corner of the kitchen, beside the coal stove, until they dried.

It pained Lena, one rather gossipy daughter-in-law, considerably, that Grandpa didn't change his long johns often enough to suit her, and she harped on it.

One winter, Grandpa had a bad spell and took to his bed for several days. He looked ghostly pale and couldn't hold anything down. "The pained one" heard the news that Grandpa was sick. She rushed to our house, ready to aid him and to help strip Grandpa's underwear right off of his body.

She fumed and fussed about her shame if he should be carried off to the hospital, in dirty long johns. Well, it took a titanic effort to hold her back; Lena was queen sized and very opinionated.

Soon Grandpa began to improve; he swallowed some broth, and nobody was a takin' his underwear.

Lena exited in a fury, sulking, without her trophy; she reminded us, "I've done all I can do."

Every once in a while, Grandpa limps quietly away to the local pub, and he is still missing past our 9 p.m. curfew.

He returns home a little unsteady on his feet and very merry. Grandma and we kids are waiting up as he comes wobbling through the doorway. Grandma is as fragile as a china doll, but she has never turned over her own power to anyone. She still has it and doesn't put up with any monkey business. She ignores Grandpa's unusually affectionate gestures.

Playfully, Grandpa rubs the top of her head, "How ya doin' there ol' lady?" He repeats it several times, slurring a bit.

Grandma pushes his hand away, "Now Alf, you go on—go on and let me alone." Finally, he does. He gives it up and heads straight for his bedroom to sleep it off. "Your grandpa's got a snoot full," she tells us.

Many times, I have heard my Grandma say, "I think your Grandpa's out on a toot." Although he is a binge drinker, he doesn't drink every day. After months of sobriety, Grandpa might wander down to the local tavern and overindulge. In his younger days he might be gone a week at a time but not anymore. He makes his wobbly way home, resting on doorsteps along the route. Sometimes, Grandma would send one of us kids to find him; at other times he would be delivered to us by a good-hearted neighbor.

Some of our relatives are down on him because of his alcohol addiction; lots of arrows fly my Grandpa's way. They blame him, and maybe rightly so, but I throw it off anyway. I know that Grandpa has another side.

I see through the tough guy exterior to the old man's soft heart even if no one else can, and I notice he always leaves the best portion of everything for my grandma.

Grandma works to keep the rest of us in line. "Don't make a pest of yourself, Nancy," Grandma warned my sister. And I don't think she ever did; mostly her little visits were kept short. Today was not ordinary, though—Nancy had something new. "I have to go show Doris my shoes," she explained to Grandma as she was leaving.

"I have new shoes … I have new shoes." Nancy walked away rehearsing the words she intended to say to our neighbor, Doris. She crossed over the front yard, looking down and stepping high, oblivious to everything except her pretty feet. Nancy has a hole in her heart that she keeps trying to fill with new things. It's an emptiness that we shared.

Doris was a kindhearted woman who took Nancy under her wing, befriending her when she so desperately craved attention. God mysteriously places angels in unlikely dwellings, sometimes even in the house across the road.

Back home, and at the end of a satisfying day, Nancy reluctantly unbuckled the straps and removed the dainty leather shoes from her small feet. She climbed onto the narrow bed beside the kitchen stove and placed those wonderful shoes close by her side. Nancy's mouth stretched open with a wide sleepy yawn that she hid behind the back of her hand. All curled up on Sonny's bed, she reminded me of a contented kitten.

The back screen door slammed shut behind Sonny, sounding a loud bang! "Get off my bed," he snapped at Nancy. "I gotta get to sweep."

Sonny and his small beagle, Spotty, slept together on the daybed that Nancy was presently, so rudely being evicted from. The cot-sized bed was beneath a kitchen window that faced our back porch. A soft feather mattress, a body could sink into, cushioned the coiled metal springs. It was the coveted sleeping place in the house—I know I wanted it.

Nancy glared scornfully at "sweepy" Sonny, gathered up the new shoes, and hugged them tightly against her chest as she exited his bed.

Tomorrow morning, before school, I will be whining around as usual and searching high and low for my own misplaced shoes. Nancy's shoes will be easily located, neatly parked side by side, just under her side of the bed.

CHAPTER 9

⚹

Face Washing

"SQUEAK—SQUAWK—SCREECH!" The old wooden rocker sings out its noisy lullaby.

Grandma's rocking chair had pacified two generations of fussy babies with its soothing rock-a-bye song, and it was beginning to show its age.

Shortly, the rickety sounds emanating from her rocker's nightly chorus comes come to an end. Grandma is at ease now, sitting quietly in her usual place beside the lone, darkened front room window.

A shadowy night scene fills the window as she draws aside the lace curtain. The sidewalk going past our house is lit up by a streetlight across the road. Now and then, Grandma comments when she recognizes someone walking there, under the light.

Inside the house, a single bare light bulb dangling from the ceiling, on the end of a wire, illuminates our front room. "Shirley, pull the chain before you turn in," Grandpa reminds me. He doesn't make me go to bed; he only insists that the last one up shuts off the light.

Sometimes I am a night owl. Thankfully, Grandpa understands; he doesn't push me off to bed, all wide-eyed and restless. These grandparents of ours are easy to be around. There are a few boundaries but not any strict or trivial rules to follow. You can breathe here.

Grandma and I are the only ones awake now, and she is getting ready to call it a night. As she begins to loosen the bun fastened at the nape of her neck, I notice how uncommonly rough her hands are for such a vulnerable looking old woman. Household chores have taken a toll on her hands.

During the heat of summer, Grandma ties on a faded print sunbonnet before she ventures outside, and she always wears a bib apron to cover her dress. She never bothers to pull on gloves to protect her hands: not even in the cold of winter when she picks up a lump of coal to add to the fire or uses the heavy iron stove poker.

Everyone here lingers next to the fire, even Grandma. She finds some comfort in its dazzling warmth. Like moths to the flame, we are drawn to play near the fire; there is something mesmerizing about watching it burn and feeling the heat from the yellow and crimson blaze. Once, I stood too close to the open stove door, and my eyebrows were singed.

Occasionally, while Grandma is using a poker to break apart the red-hot clumps of burning coal, a large ember tumbles out of the stove and crashes to the floor guard below. When I first witnessed her bend down and whisk up a smoldering chunk of coal—bare handed—and toss it back into the fire, I thought she forgot herself and grabbed it accidentally.

"Grandma!" I gasped, scared out of my wits and expecting to see scorched flesh. Calmly, she stuck out her calloused unharmed hand for me to examine.

Tonight, Grandma is lingering in her rocking chair later than usual to keep me company, and also because "little pitchers have big ears." I am still curious about the "face-washing" incident from Grandma's past, the reminder that cracked everybody up a few days earlier, and I have been anxiously waiting to hear the story.

After Grandma undid the bun that held her long twist of snow-white hair in place, it unwound swiftly and cascaded down her back. She leaned her head to the side and closed her eyes; the slow and steady rocking motion enticed the sandman to come, and he closed in fast. Cradling her aged face between coarse hands, she dozed off.

56

"Grandma, can I brush your hair?" I asked. Her whole body jerked defensively from being startled awake by the sound of my voice.

Her eyes fluttered open and she nodded, "Yes."

I hurried to Grandma's small bedroom and grabbed the hairbrush off the dresser. Since I was the kid who cried every morning because I couldn't find my shoes, it was a good idea to let Grandma take charge of the hairbrush.

I stood behind her, brushing and fixing her hair. Sometimes I braided small strands that stuck out all over her head; she looked really funny that way because she was so old. But when I handed her our hand mirror, to see her image and to capture her look of surprise, she was amused.

Hair fix time was beneficial for both of us; Grandma enjoyed my brushing her hair, and I was hooked on the stories from her past.

"Grandma, will you tell me the face washing secret?" I asked. She didn't answer for a minute. Then she turned to face me. Grandma looked me over as if she was measuring my size to decide whether I was old enough to be let in on her family's joke. After the long scrutinizing, I thought: She's not going to leave me hanging. We're so close that she can tell me anything.

Grandma began to unravel the mystery by explaining the circumstances and surroundings.

"Beginning every fall, when the weather permitted, my brothers, sisters, and I trudged several miles back and forth to our country school."

She said their attendance was sporadic, only when their pappy could spare them from farm chores. I know that Grandma quit school after sixth grade, so that dated the story she was about to tell me, and also her age. She was probably only about 10 years old then. And that explains the impulsive and reckless thing that happened—it just seemed like a good idea at the time, to silly young girls.

I was listening intently to her every word. "Our school was a one-room log cabin in the woods. In these times," she recalled, "we were backward; the school didn't yet have an outhouse. When we had to go out, we went anywhere in the woods. As soon as the school master gave us permission, we lit out for the bushes."

I shuddered to think about the schoolmaster. The stern fellow that Grandma had described, taught his pupils by means of a threatening hickory switch and the dunce cap.

I was mortified, and I asked if she saw anyone beaten. Grandma could not recall any incident with the hickory stick, but its very presence ensured discipline.

In a corner of the classroom, the tall, pointed dunce cap lay on a three-legged stool, waiting to be occupied by some wretched child. It served as a grim reminder to the children to learn—or else.

Grandma picked up the story where my question about the stick had interrupted her. "We separated; the boys all went their way into the woods, and the girls ran down an opposite path to a secluded area that was screened by a thicket. It was just a hop, skip, and a jump away from the school yard."

Grandma explained their normal routine. "At first we could make ourselves at home, and after we finished buttoning up our bloomers and straightening our rumpled skirts, we headed back toward the clearing to meet with the boys again."

"Lo and behold, one mischievous older boy wouldn't stay where he belonged, but instead he slipped away from his chums. The bully circled around through the woods, sneaking up behind us to gawk. He meant to surprise us with our bloomers down around our ankles."

The girls could hear footsteps as he wandered nearby, in the woods. Grandma described the faint rustling sounds coming from disturbed leaves, and the sharp crackling noises caused by dry underbrush snapping beneath his clumsy feet. The noises gave him away.

Their "Peeping Tom" hid among the trees, taunting them. He crept forward, and then fled. But he always left enough safe ground between himself and the girls' group so that he could escape, even if they saw him.

"That's how it was on the day of the face washing," she told me. "He was roaming again in our part of the woods, zipping from one hiding place to another—only this time he got careless and came too near us."

I paid rapt attention as Grandma paused.

"Well, gol doggies!" She declared. "We caught the scoundrel and all five of us piled on top and pinned him to the ground. We sat on his arms and legs to keep him from hittin' and kickin' us. While they held him flat on his back against the ground, I tied my bandana to cover his eyes so he couldn't peek."

"Once we got the best of him, we decided he needed a good scourin'." She giggled, slightly embarrassed, and then continued. "We yanked up our petticoat, squatted low, and washed his face. He whooped and hollered and carried on, all red faced and mad, swearing to get even!"

I am stunned by her bold confession. "I can't believe you did that!" The sound of her laughter was contagious, and I laughed too. It's funny to me because I'm thinking, she must have been someone else when she was young.

Mary Cerena—that's her real name—is completely out of character as the instigator, or heroine if you choose it, of the interesting face-washing plot. Although Grandma reminisced frequently about her school days, the face-washing incident went unsurpassed.

"Did he tell on you?" I asked, knowing full well he likely couldn't, without the whole story surfacing. The bully's punishment from their strict school master could have been almost as severe as the face washing.

"No, he never told on us," Grandma answered, "and he didn't come a slippin' around and followin' us anymore, either."

Grandma let me draw my own conclusion as to how the face washing was actually accomplished. I supposed that there was only one way to do it, and I held that picture in my head for all of these years.

Forever and a day later, I have begun to wonder if Grandma and her school chums may have done the scourin' (washed his face) with a bandana or handkerchief that they had unceremoniously "soaked" themselves. Similar to Grandma, I leave this ages-old puzzle for you to solve.

Grandma's candid reflections cause me to remember and brood over my own unnerving outhouse trauma from last summer.

It's on the tip of my tongue to tell her about it, but I quash the urge because I am afraid I will feel sorry that I spoke so rashly. Besides, if I spill my guts tonight, come tomorrow, Grandma will worry over my close friendship with Bobby.

She doesn't know every bit of mischief I get into; I try to conceal my little shortcomings from her because I can't bear to see her look at me with disappointment in her eyes. Our Grandma is too darn trusting; she defends each of us down to the last possibility of our innocence. Try living up to that!

Grandpa is another story; he always assumes the worst and threatens, "I'll whip the lot of ya—then I'll be sure to get the right one."

When Grandpa gets riled up, he hobbles into the kitchen and takes the wire fly swatter down off its nail. He waves it menacingly close in front of the lot of us, and it makes a scary swishing noise as it cuts through midair, clutched in the old man's hand. I've felt the breeze—but never the whack.

CHAPTER 10

❦

Bobby and Me

IT IS SUMMER vacation. Carol and I play most of the daylight hours two blocks away, in my friend, Bobby's, backyard. Carol and Bobby's young brother, Teddy, are playmates. If our playtime runs into the supper hour, Grandma sends Nancy to fetch us. Otherwise, we hurry home after Bobby and Teddy have to go inside. Every evening, as we part, Bobby reminds me, "Come again tomorrow morning—early. Come earlier!"

My eighth year on this earth would have been awfully boring without him. Bobby was my only friend that summer.

He and Teddy lived with their grandmother, too. Both she and her daughter-in-law, the boys' mother, were widows.

Bobby told me the story of how his father died in the twisted metal of a car crash. "They found him too late," he lamented. Bobby's dad had tried in vain to apply a tourniquet to his nearly severed leg, after dragging himself free of the wreck. "He bled to death, laying only a couple of short feet away from the car."

Bobby missed his dad something awful.

I recall their mother as an attractive, dark haired, slender woman who worked far away. Sometimes she came to visit with the boys on Sundays (as our mom did). We had a lot in common, but there was one major exception: I would not have traded grannies with Bobby, no matter what he threw in to boot! Even though I am sure she loved them, their grandma was extremely old-fashioned and controlling. Bobby explained his predicament: "Mom can't change anything because we have to live here." I hugged my freedom, like a solemn object, close to my heart. I felt sorry for Bobby because his world seemed so small. A body could smother in there.

His grandma's rules were "etched in stone," and one rule was that Bobby could never leave the yard. So … every morning, he and Teddy waited for Carol and me to arrive. Then the four of us pooled our ideas and let our imaginations run wild—in the confines of the backyard.

I remember once, Bobby and I were standing alongside his grandma's property line at the edge of her yard. As I straddled the ditch that we considered "no man's land," I teased him. "Can you just take one little baby step over it?"

He looked toward the house and shook his head warily. I thought to myself, I swear that old battle ax has eyes in the back of her head.

"No," Bobby answered. Then those beautiful brown eyes grew serious. "I'll get in trouble."

Bobby was more than nice looking. He was an enthrallingly handsome young boy, and he knew how to use those soft, dark eyes to his advantage.

My heart always melted under the pleading of his soulful gaze, and I often stayed beside him beyond hunger or anything else. I would have done almost anything to please him … almost.

Bobby and I had been outside in his backyard for several hours that afternoon when I needed to run home for a second. "I'll be right back, Bobby," I told him. "Gotta go."

"Oh, don't go home; I'll have to go inside pretty soon." He insisted. "Just use ours."

I didn't want to, so I said, "No, I'm going home."

We batted "yes" and "no" back and forth until it got silly, and we both laughed. "Stay here. Please," Bobby begged. He pointed to the large maple across the yard from us and away from the outhouse. "I'll stand way over there. I won't peek. Honest. I promise."

He crossed his heart to reinforce his sincerity. Bobby seemed so angelic right then. I was convinced I could trust him. He ran over and stood by the maple tree, and I went inside their WPA outhouse.

When I unhooked the door and stepped back outside, there stood Bobby—not by the tree as he had promised. He wore a mischievous grin from ear to ear.

His face lit up in a smug expression. "I looked," he said. Those dark, compelling eyes sparkled with a sick, teasing humor.

Wounded beyond the measure of mere words, I stormed off silently, leaving a quickly withering Bobby being consumed and crumbling into a smoldering heap of ashes beneath my fiery glare. Or so I hoped.

As I crossed the alley, I could hear Bobby's protests. "No, I didn't. I didn't look. I was just kidding. Shirley! Come back!"

I vowed to never more return. It took several lonely days before I cooled off enough to make up with the little creep.

I learned early from Bobby that boys will cross their hearts and promise anything, and sometimes they cross their fingers at the same moment behind their backs. And that is a handy thing to know before the age of love begins. It was still early springtime in my life, and I had a ways to go before the season of first kiss arrived.

After all was forgiven, Bobby wanted to seal our friendship the way we thought the Indians used to do it, with a blood oath.

He gave me a brief explanation and hurried inside. He came out a few minutes later with some butcher's twine. Next, I followed him over to the infamous maple and watched as he broke off a short twig from it.

Bobby knew many interesting Indian rituals that I didn't, and he assured me that the mixing of our blood would bind us together forever and ever.

Several times that day, Bobby wrapped the grocer's string around our arms and legs and tightened it with a stick. He wanted to see how quickly he could apply a tourniquet—if ever he had to.

We rummaged through the trash barrel next to the tall stalks of flowering hollyhocks that grew along the alley. While we poked around in Bobby's household rubbish, I warily kept one eye on the fat bumblebees that zoomed past us and landed on these giant yellow blossoms with dark brown centers.

We did a weird sort of waltzing around there in the alley, dodging and cringing in fright, as those nasty buzzing invaders threatened us from every direction. My head reeled with an unreasonable terror of these winged creatures. It is another phobia that Carol and I share, and it's one I wish I wasn't responsible for passing on to her.

As much as I intended to stand firmly beside Bobby, my feet took on a mind of their own and automatically deposited themselves yards away. I left Bobby, the brave leader in command, to stand and search his trash barrel alone. He quickly backtracked clutching a dirty pottery cup with its handle broken off.

Using a dull chip from the discarded dish, we scraped across our left hands just below the pinkie finger to prepare a slight but stinging wound: a welt from which not a drop of our blood flowed.

After our dry run, Bobby and I struck up a compromise, we agreed that rubbing our angry red scratches together created an indelible pact as true and lasting as a bloody cut could. Our bloodless oath was finished.

Grandma stirred in her chair beside the front room window. I moved from the back of the rocker around to Grandma's side and waited in case she needed help to get up. When she sat too long in one place the stiffness set in.

She eased her frail body forward, posturing on the edge of her seat and looked up at me. Behind that pleasant, toothless grin sat an old and withered woman that I felt very protective of.

"No … I can get up all right." Grandma reassured me, and leaning on the arm of the rocker for leverage, she helped herself rise.

"My old head goes whir, whir, whir," she told me, describing the tinnitus that plagued her almost constantly. Sometimes, though, she stroked her forehead, feather lightly with her fingertips, to ease the loud and equally bothersome "roar, roar, roar" from a colossal seashell that only she could hear.

With halting footsteps and treading lightly to coddle night-swollen ankles, Grandma crossed the room. She paused, as usual, inside the threshold to her bedroom and turned to murmur, "Well, goodnight."

She painstakingly climbed aboard the single bed, and then something alarming happened. She got up on all fours in the middle of it and started to struggle with something. Her whole body trembled from the strain of trying to balance her weight between a quivering right arm and two wobbling knees. I watched her for a moment, puzzled speechless. Teetering precariously near the edge, Grandma yanked and tugged at the long gown with her free left hand. I couldn't believe my eyes.

It's strange how moonlight can play tricks on sight. Even though I know better, my blurred vision showed me the outrageous form of a swaying baby elephant.

"Grandma! What are you doing?"

"I'm tangled up in the gol blessed thing!" She gasped, out of breath.

A step closer brings a completely different sight. Grandma was fighting a battle, up on all fours, held prisoner by a flannel nightgown tangled up under a white bed sheet. I smile again at the thought of it. I stood there until she stretched out, making sure she wasn't going to tumble off the brink during all that nightgown rigmarole.

I planted my anxious, skinny carcass just inside Grandma's doorway and waited for her to finish unwinding the long flannel nuisance that bound her. From the threshold, these eyes only guessed at an outline of shadowy things in Grandma's bedroom.

Dee once called me a worrywart, and I guess the name fits because my thinking is often cluttered with some vague, foreseeable event that I try to fix before it happens.

The metal bedsprings ceased their squeaking, and I returned to the front room. My hand reached for the bare light bulb, and my fingers dutifully pulled the chain. The house went black. I felt my way along the wall toward the bed. Another memorable day in our whimsical, faded yellow house came to a peaceful end.

CHAPTER 11

Great Spirit of Flight

STORM CLOUDS GATHERED and turned the skies an angry gray. Trees on either side of Bobby and me bowed earthward; their cumbersome branches swayed and crackled under the force of nature's scolding.

We braced ourselves against the gusts; my bare toes hung over, curled under, and hugged the slanted ledge of the high place. A rush of adrenalin quickly followed. I let my fired-up imagination run wild, and I half expected to feel my uplifted arms change and unfold into miraculous feathery wings.

Get ready—get set!

Bobby and I wavered on the verge of an eight-foot drop. Tangled and wind driven, my baby fine hair beat at my face. I brushed aside the unruly, blond strands of hair that were tightly glued to my stinging eyes. The wind pushed our backs, adding reckless buoyancy to our daring stunt and urging us to go on and jump.

Bobby's shirttail was loosened by invisible fingers in the gale, and it sounded like gunfire as it was caught up and sent flapping wildly. "Pop, pop, crack!"

The same irritating wisps of flying hair that made my eyes water, left me with a dirt streaked face. A fresh burst of air fanned beneath my dress and sailed the hem above my knobby, skinned-up knees, and I felt handicapped by it. It's impossible to behave in a ladylike manner and have fun, too. The social restraints little women have to bear and wear! I suddenly felt cheated and impulsively wished I had been born a boy.

We clasped hands, filled our lungs, and shouted, "Geronimo!" We vaulted off into space from the rooftop of the old tool shed.

Never count on the legendary, Indian "Great Spirit of Flight" to help one stay airborne. Despite his dramatic appearance in the form of an eagle circling far above us—or was it a large hawk—we plummeted like rocks to the earth.

But in that weightless split second before our feet slammed against the hard ground, we pretended we could fly. In my willing fantasy, we soared—there in the alley … and later again that night in my dream.

A smidgen of worry, a sprinkle of daring, a full measure of shyness: God rolled up all these, simultaneously, to make me. I wish I knew how He made Bobby.

Often weeks slid by without a disagreement between us. When we did quarrel, the earth shook, and it was always Bobby's fault because he couldn't play nice. Although we shared an important phase of our growing up together, our thoughts were not exactly the same; Bobby was miles ahead of me in the boy/girl stuff.

For instance, I wanted Bobby to carve a heart with our initials inside it into the trunk of the maple. But alas, he should think of that himself because to my idealistic, young mind, a heart must be given away unasked for and without strings attached before it feels real.

Bobby was more temporal. On a hot and sultry afternoon, the sort that southern Illinois is known for in mid-August, Bobby and I clashed.

His sudden and unusual chivalry, as we stood in the cool shade at the base of our tree, was unexpected.

"You climb up first, Shirley," Bobby offered, and he gallantly backed away to make room for me to step up into the ample crook that we used for the first foothold. "I'll let you go ahead of me this time. Go on."

He motioned politely using his right arm, stretching it out palm side up in front of me. He elbowed my hip with a gentle nudge, "ladies before gentlemen." Bobby clicked his heels and stiffly raised his right hand to his forehead in a sharp salute.

I smoothed my dress in an uneasy gesture.

"Nuh-uh," I shook my head. "Age before beauty."

We did the monotonous "yes-no" thing again, and nothing was solved. It was one of those unwinnable arguments with him that made me want to tear my hair out. I was always the worst off for it.

I thought, with increasing trepidation, about my last feud with Bobby and the bumpy ride after he sweet-talked me into warming the other end of the seesaw board.

"Teeter-totter with me," he coaxed. "Give me one more chance. I swear, I won't jump off. I'll tell you first. Please!"

I had heard that before, and I frowned at him. "I don't trust you anymore, Bobby!" How many times had he bailed out on me?

Soft brown eyes pleaded his case. "Come on, Shirley. I promise I'm not lying. If I lie you can dump me, too." I liked the sound of that, and so the last of my iron resolve ebbed away.

Minutes later, as soon as I let my guard down, the feminine end of the seesaw board plunged to the ground with an unexpected thud. The wallop jarred my head so hard my brains rattled.

Bobby had not followed the golden rule; he would do it unto me, again, unless it happened to him next. I bided my time until I was given another invitation to seesaw with Bobby. I nonchalantly baited the hook, and an unsuspecting Bobby got the seesaw drop of his life.

Now Bobby was being too nice again, to be true. Our war beneath the tree continued. We were standing so close together that I felt his warm breath on my face when he whispered, "I dare you to go first!"

Our eyes met and locked, plainly it was a duel to the death over who would climb up last. We both scrambled to shove the other forward and get behind. And the touching began. With the heel part of my hand, I whacked his shoulder. While I could possibly take him in a fair fight, I felt handicapped by this gosh awful dress.

Bobby didn't want to play nice, and trying to engulf me inside those wounded, dark eyes was wasted. The chances of my shinnying up our tree ahead of him were twofold—slim and none.

I yelled at him, "You—old—Bobby—you!" Giving him one last shove for good measure, I bolted from his backyard and hit the alley in a dead run, shouting, "I'll be back."

The crippling dress had to go. Back at home, in the bedroom I shared with three of my sisters, I picked through our basket of meager, community belongings, "making do" again. Before a mysterious and possibly irate owner showed up, I quickly claimed them.

I lifted my faded print dress over my head. Counting the one I had just taken off, I owned all of two threadbare dresses. I pulled on the soft, washed out pair of comfortable denim jeans over my cotton undies. I discovered that jeans are the next best thing to wrapping up snugly in a security blanket. The basket also had yielded one loose pullover shirt. And I hurried back to meet Bobby beneath the uncarved tree. His interest in climbing had waned after I traded my dress for the jeans.

I think all of us have an angel that waits at every crossroad. Mine beat me home that day and left a set of modest, borrowed clothes in our community basket.

One thing I am sure of: childhood innocence is a spirit that belongs to the heart. It would be too sad to let one go without the other. Children deserve an unjaded growing-up time, but they need a guardian angel—and snug fitting jeans—to accomplish it.

Shortly after the tree-climbing episode, I initiated a casual discussion with Grandma. Without giving anything away, I wanted to get at the honest-to-goodness truth concerning Bobby's peculiar knowledge of Native American customs.

Grandma's people, on her mother's side, came to Illinois from Kentucky by covered wagon in the late 1700s. Therefore, I concluded:

the family must have encountered Indians along their arduous trek to a new homestead.

Her mother, Margaret, was born in 1850. She fell in love with (I wouldn't have it any other way.) and married my great grandfather, Marion, who was orphaned when his family was slaughtered by Indians when he was a youngster.

Grandma was an exceptional storyteller, and she could make the past come alive. Sometimes I found myself exchanging places with her, and I became that sturdy pioneer girl who had all these strange, yet wonderful experiences. As I listened, I would walk spellbound in her very footsteps.

"Grandma, do you know if Indians cut themselves and mix their bloods together?" There! The dreadful practice was spoken about.

All I knew about Indian lore came from the movies and picture books, and it was hard to let go of an enduring dream all at once. I pictured a magnificent bronzed warrior—naked, except for the scant covering of a deerskin loincloth—standing on the crest of a mound in breathtaking silhouette and blazing ruby red against an old West, setting sun.

"Not as I know of." Grandma's differing comment brought me back down to earth. "The Indians I used to see, passed by late of an evening when it was all woods through here. I don't know about a blood ritual. The ragged clothes they had on were caked with dirt—and stink! Law—I didn't think they ever took a bath. They smelled like a bear. Once in a while, I'd see a few drunken ones goin' home, hangin' off their horses with a whiskey bottle in tow."

"Bobby told me it was against the law to sell whiskey to an Indian." I said.

"I don't know where they got the bottle," she answered. "Anyhow, the horses had to lead 'em home."

I was disappointed at needing to erase the flawed image I had romantically sketched on my mind. "What about the Indian women?" I was curious about them also.

Grandma did not remember seeing any, and she supposed that they were never allowed to leave camp. I felt an immediate, feminine kinship with the Indian women and was saddened that they were so hindered. I could not even be persuaded to stay in our end of town.

CHAPTER 12

❧

The Cave

I SUDDENLY THOUGHT about the cave, the darkness inside it, the damp slippery goo that clung to the rocks, and the gritty feel of sand between my toes.

The day that we sneaked off to Indian Cave was still there, waiting for me to come back and reclaim it. Old memories surface in uneven baby steps. Gradually, I remembered it all. I was catapulted across the decades and once again smelled the pungent, dank air. Once again I felt the slick walls in the darkness and tuned my ears for the sound of slithering snakes. Once again I felt an overpowering premonition of danger.

Our family is still intact. Ancient history finds all six of us little ruffians visiting our paternal grandparents ... well, sort of. Actually, five of us (Carol being too young to run with us) are up to no good.

Momentarily, Mom and Dad's attention is off of us, and dinner preparations are getting under way in the kitchen. Our absence won't be missed for quite a while, and if we don't answer Daddy when he calls us, he will assume that we are gallivanting deep in the woods out back.

Sonny doesn't let any grass grow under his feet. He has already sneaked down to the cellar and swiped a couple of candle stumps. Grandma Pella keeps a supply of these on a ledge at the bottom of the steps because their electricity does not reach the cellar.

Twin weather-beaten doors at ground level shield the steps that lead down there. Whenever I see Daddy come outside and tug one of these open, I am right on his heels.

The dirt cellar is a novelty for me, and I like going down there. Its natural earth floor, tightly packed from steady use, feels powdery smooth under my feet. Spiders string their webs in every conceivable place; they angle across the room's four corners, fasten over the door posts, and spin their way on into the second room. Their clusters of eggs are intriguing but creepy, too, reminding me of Halloween. I bend low and carefully duck to avoid them. Almost as quickly as someone brushes a web down, another will appear.

Threatening winds from the west always send everyone scurrying to the cellar. Besides providing a haven against tornadoes, it is also a place to store food for the winter. Jars of tomatoes and pickles line the walls. A potato bin at the far end adds to the unique aroma that the rooms hold.

I'm hooked on the earthy, musky scent of it all; every chance I get, I breathe deeply of the fragrant dirt-laced potatoes, sucking it in like a cat going after catnip.

The fall harvest is quite an accomplishment around here. The put-up vegetables and jellies are displayed proudly for every visitor.

Some things go over a kid's head. I can't arm myself against bewildering confrontations. Out on the farm, there just wasn't any wiggle room in Grandma Pella's endless rules. My thoughts wandered back to a previous short stay with her, one that found me wishing that I was anywhere else but there.

The evening began ordinarily enough, at our house on Oak Street. I was playing outside alone when I looked through the big oval glass window of our front door and saw Daddy. He came out onto the porch, closing the door behind him. He made me think of a grand daddy longlegs, as he went quickly across the front lawn, striding comfortably in giant steps.

I knew where he was going. It was a set pattern. Directly after supper, Daddy would hop in his car and head for the farm.

I ran to catch up with him so that he couldn't get away from me before I could ask him. Otherwise, I would be left, as usual, standing and waving bye-bye to him from the curb.

"Where you goin' Daddy?" I pretended not to know. I was tempted, but I couldn't bring myself to ask Daddy if I could go, too. Maybe though, he would take a hint and invite me.

"Daddy's going to the farm," he said. With his hand poised on the car door handle, and almost like an afterthought, he said the words I was waiting for, "Do you want to go?"

"Yes, I do!" There was nothing I liked better than a ride in Daddy's car. I climbed in next to him, delighted with my good luck.

Across from Daddy, scrunched up by the window, was the best place to sit. There, I could rest my elbow on the window ledge and feel the wind blowing in my face. The passing landscape was entertaining. It was almost like watching a moving picture show.

Daddy started the motor of his 1929 Model A sedan and let it idle. I was so antsy for Daddy to pull away that I could barely sit still. "Oh hurry!" I tried to rush him with my thoughts, as I impatiently held my breath and counted off the seconds.

If one of the others happened to join us, they would most likely scoot me over, take my place beside the open window, talk over me, and drown me out.

Once we drove away, I ate up the time that I had Daddy all to myself, but it was short lived. A few minutes later, he and I stepped into the lair of the dragon, Grandma Pella's kitchen. She eyed me up like an intruder, and I felt like one. I felt afraid to take a breath without her approval.

Grandma's face bears a look of displeasure, and I think she's unhappy because Daddy brought me. Daddy didn't seem to notice it.

He let me follow him down to the cellar. Grandma descended directly behind us to oversee every little thing.

After he collected a spading fork, the three of us climbed the steps together, and then Daddy left me with Grandma while he finished chores.

In every room of her house, the fingers of a child were not allowed to touch anything. I kept my arms clamped tightly against my sides to avoid a scolding over marring Grandma's polished furniture with handprints.

In a futile attempt to narrow the gap between us, I tried to begin a polite conversation with her. From what I thought was surely a safe distance, I pointed to and admired one of Grandma's nice things. I told her, "Your vase is so pretty." I meant it as a compliment to try to get on her good side.

Without raising her voice one iota, Grandma sternly warned me, "Don't touch that, you'll leave fingerprints."

"Oh! I wasn't going to touch it," I apologized.

Her look said, "I don't believe you."

The moment was spoiled, and the same dejected thought I had had back in the kitchen clicked inside my head again. The reason Grandma Pella was so unapproachable was because she didn't want me here. Maybe she misunderstood what I wanted.

Grandma Pella had the annoying habit of calling everything a "whatchamacallit." Even simple, easy-to-remember items such as a comb, knife, dipper or broom. That seemed odd to me.

"Don't sit on the whatchamacallit," she told me. I moved obediently across her parlor to another seat, only to have her tell me, "Not there either."

"Where?" I asked, growing more ill at ease. Grandma looked doubtfully at the last option, a straight back chair.

It was better to go outside. There, I sat down on the front porch swing, although I didn't dare set it in motion. Shortly, Grandma materialized in the front doorway, scrutinized me, and silently withdrew inside the house. I thought it would never be time to leave this rigid place.

My subsequent visits to the farm were few and far between. After Mom and Dad were divorced, I rarely visited there. When I was trapped there for an occasional afternoon, I felt more at ease around Grandpa August, and so I tagged along beside him as he worked outside. He didn't mind hearing little girl chatter, and he answered me back. I wasn't used to that. After all, this was still an era when many believed children should be seen and not heard.

Grandpa August could have stood in for Uncle Sam without walking on stilts. Besides being tall, he had that wonderful full head of hair, so snow white that it was shocking.

Dad inherited Grandpa's slender frame, but conversely, Dad was balding early. And he had Grandma's unbending disposition.

For better or worse, no one can choose the order of such things, or choose the ancestor they most want to resemble. I most wanted to step into Mollie's shadow.

This is the way things were at the beginning of our cave adventure. Our day at the farm started out innocently enough; we romped out in the cold until my older siblings decided to sneak off to the cave.

Back in the kitchen, Mary is keeping a watchful eye on the comings and goings of the adults. Nancy is nonchalantly hanging out in there also, she is trying to smuggle out a handful of jumbo country matches.

It's really cold; I can see the fog of my breath in the frigid air. I begin to agonize over our plunder. I'm not feeling remorseful because we are getting the matches and bits of wax; oh no, I'm fretting about our risk of getting caught with the stuff.

Suppose Grandma goes down to the cellar for a jar of something and discovers a few of her candles are missing; it's believable she's counted them. Then what? I wondered. My conscience was starting to bother me.

Joined by Mary, Nancy, and their cache of matches, the five of us meander casually off the property. We rein ourselves in until we're out of parental sight and hearing. Then, we scurry away like field mice to the cover of the woods.

Our secret destination is about thirty minutes away from the farm, by short cut, beginning and ending over and under a barbed wire fence.

"Heywoes, beywoes!" (Hell's bells). Sonny just thought of something, and this was his own colorful expression of amazement. "Is anybody wearing red? Check it out," he warned us.

Even though I don't understand the emphasis on the color red, I take Sonny's word for it, and I quickly scan what I'm wearing from head to toe.

I lost pace with them and fell behind when I slowed to look at my clothes, and Sonny griped. "Get the wed out, Shir'we."

I'm trying hard to equate our fear with red clothes, and it's upsetting me: the not knowing. "What's wrong with red?" I ask.

How peculiar it is, that nobody seems to hear me the first time I say something. They presume that I am just too young and insignificant to be taken seriously. I have to repeat often and sound extra mean before they pay me any attention. I wish I could trade my easily strained voice for a stronger one. Even baby sister, Carol, can outshout me.

Because they are ignoring me again, I stubbornly pull back and yank my hand away from Dee's protective tugging. "No!" I skidded to a halt and dug in my heels. Not another step further until one of them listens to me. I am desperate to know the truth. "Tell me why we're scared of red!"

"It's because of the bull." Dee is hesitant to include me in everything. "Red makes him mad, and he will charge us if he sees it."

Before we left the farm, nobody mentioned a bull, or that the color red incites him. It was just a fluke that I had not worn something red and stood out like a matador's cape. None of us knew at the time that bulls are color blind.

We are crossing open ground now, throwing caution to the winds and leaving the shelter of the woods behind us. The winter-bare trees we might have climbed to escape a rampaging bull are distant.

The crisp air is taking its toll. In Grandma Mollie's own words, "Dog gone it, my old nose!" It is a thing she and I have in common. At the first cold snap, our noses turn into leaky faucets. Grandma's apron pockets bulge with hankies all winter long—unlike her forgetful grand-kid, who never has one when she needs it most.

My pockets are empty as usual, so I have to make do with my coat sleeve. Dee is pulling me along by the drier sleeve, making me go faster. She keeps twisting her neck around and looking back to make sure that the bull is not chasing us.

"Let's hurry," Dee calls out breathlessly. "Run, Shirley, run!" Her cries of urgency coax a renewed burst of energy, spurring me on, and my feet pound the ground at her heels. I search her face with hungry eyes, seeking assurance there that everything is going to be all right; instead, Dee has the look of terror, and that scares me even more.

The sensible part of me wants to turn back before it's too late—before I'm gored to death. In my present state, I can well picture myself at the mercy of the bull.

I know it won't do any good to run; he'd be on me in a jiffy. What if? Old habits die hard. Conjecture fueled my imagination, and I was swept along in a daydream: I heard his thundering hoof beats coming for me; the noisy sound of exhaled air snorting from his nostrils, in huff-huffing blasts of anger, seem real.

My thoughts raced on toward a bitter end ... the enraged 900-pound bull had me pinned between his terrible horns. He dragged my limp, rag doll body across the pasture and trampled my short life beneath his spiked hooves.

There is no sign of the bull. I am still running. With every backward glance, I half expect to see the raging beast madly pawing at the ground, kicking up dirt clods, and building more fury for his charge. Recklessly, our little band of rebels dashes on, and this child is scared out of her wits.

In the other extreme is Sonny, who is not afraid of any living thing. He is the bravest boy I ever knew. He would, I decided, without a second thought, yank off his jacket and shake it at the fearsome animal if it came toward us. Like a matador, Sonny would fight that bull while his sisters escaped. Sometimes, that smart aleck little dictator is handy to have on our side.

We converge at the fence. Sonny scrambles over the wire and holds it up for us girls to crawl under. The lead weights, that I was sure were strapped to my feet, drop off immediately when I realize a string of barbed wire hangs between the bull's range and us.

Despite all of these fears and grandiose worries, the idea of being included on their journey to the cave thrilled me beyond measure. I wanted to belong, even if it meant sneaking supplies from the farmhouse and braving a bull in the field. In the end, I would rather face that ugly, snorting beastie and stand eyeball to bloodshot eyeball with him before I would miss out on Indian Cave with the rest of them.

But it was a weighty matter—to think about consequences for the first time. How bad had I been? I took a slightly biased peek into the depths of my newly found conscience, and I wanted to mend my ways. I hastily composed a list of faults, right off the top of my head, to impress God—if He was listening. It came straight from my heart, complete with the wild promises of a child in trouble—with a faith noticeably wavering because I couldn't help looking back over my shoulder.

We tramp a little further on, and there it is. My eyes round into circles of disbelief. This couldn't be right! In the cave that I imagined, an enormous brown bear stood upright, with room to spare, in the massive cave entryway. The opening to Indian Cave looks all wrong! Where is the gaping hole that is broad enough to admit a full-grown bear?

The terrain approaching the cave is pristine, and the passageway itself is well camouflaged. Hidden by natural surroundings and unchanged by time, this is how it must have looked generations ago when Native Americans inhabited these lands. A roving hunting party might easily have stalked right past the cave and missed seeing it. The mouth of the cave is so small and narrow—just a slot really—a hole that nosey, skinny brats could barely turn sideways and slip through.

Sonny stretches himself thin and eases through first, because he always assumes that he is the boss. And if you didn't want a sock in your eye, you'd best let that idea be, too. You didn't mess with our brother; he was a bossy little Wib.

A tough, small boy hand reaches out of the cave opening. "Nancy, gimme them matches!"

Daylight seeps through the small hole, but it only penetrates a couple of feet inside the cave. Sonny pauses there in the light, and fishes out the candles he had earlier pocketed. He lights one and moves deeper into the cave.

My sisters follow suit. They quickly disappear, too—gone, like phantoms into nowhere. Out of that suspenseful, unknown hollow, Dee calls, "Shirley! It's warmer in here. Come on in."

The wiggle place, where the others had vanished, was just a hole at my eye level. I edged up closer and stood on tippy toes with my face pressed against the cave opening. Inside, it takes a couple of minutes before my eyes adjust to the dim candlelight. In the soft glow, my brother and sisters cast eerie shadows; their giant reflections leap and sprawl against the cave walls and ceiling.

Little shivers play up and down my spine. Not even Nancy's ghostly bedtime stories, haunted moaning and all, could top the weird spectacle I was witnessing. But as I match each spooky shadow to the outline of its owner, my fear partially subsides.

I look ahead of them, on past the candlelight, and it is pitch black. Quickly, and before I would change my mind, I whirl sideways—shut my eyes to create my own but better, more tolerable darkness—and steel and bluff my body through a hypothetical thousand deaths to emerge inside the hollow of Indian Cave.

At the outset, we had bundled up against the icy wind. I expected more, bitter cold inside the cave, but when I opened my eyes again, I was surprised and relieved to find it almost cozy.

"Hey," I whisper, "are there any snakes in here?"

"Yes!"

Shouted in unison and echoing here in the dark, their answer catches me off guard. It's strange, how they can all hear my faint mumbling about snakes, when scant minutes ago, as we crossed the pasture in broad daylight, my words fell on deaf ears.

"Oh no, not snakes!" Panic clamps my throat like a powerful hand. I am scared stiff by the thought of things crawling around next to me in the dark. I swallow hard to push my heart back down in my chest where it belongs.

A sudden, overwhelming need to see all of my body parts connected and intact—with nothing coiled near them—is greater than my first impulse, which was to stand still, shut out, and rather not know what goes bumpity in the dark.

As soon as I clear the lump from my throat, I ask, "Can I have some matches? It's real dark over here."

Immediately, Mary's face is beside mine and she transfers a stubby, lit candle to my quivering hands. "Shirley, did you see the dugout?"

"No. What's a dugout?"

Mary lights a new match from my candle flame; it flares up between our faces, illuminating her features and making the cave less scary. She explains the dugout to me. "Why, that's our canoe."

"Where?" I look about without seeing any such thing. Once again, my lack of understanding makes me feel like an outsider.

Mary is not answering me. Either there is something drastically wrong with the way I talk, or my poor siblings all have dull hearing.

Once, when we were crowded around the kitchen table, I raised my voice, to get their attention; Daddy conked my head with his knuckle. He gave me a mean look and told me, "Quiet down." Too much noise makes Daddy mad. Outside, I practice making my voice go high and low, soft and loud.

I can't use my loud voice here, in the dark cave, because I'm too scared. Now, I watch Mary walk away toward the bend that curves into the black hole where Sonny and Dee had vanished. She hunches low to squeeze into the hole.

The tunnel shrunk smaller until they had to crawl on their bellies. In my thoughts, I crawled with them. I am slightly claustrophobic ever after, and I have a habitual fear of being trapped or lost.

By the light of Mary's dwindling flame, I survey the steadily narrowing passageway until her long match burns down to her fingertips. She drops the hot matchstick, and it fizzles out in the stream that trickles near our feet on the ancient cave floor.

I wonder if the tunnel leads to more rooms or, inconceivably, bottomless pits where they might accidentally tumble forever downward like a sort of Alice in Wonderland fall—only without a landing.

From beyond the bend and out of the black nothingness, their scrambled voices echo around me; the three of them sound both near and far all at once.

I am beset with tragedies that might occur: they could get lost back there, and I'll never see them again: the air could turn poison or evaporate: a sudden torrent of water could trap and drown them. I am riddled with worry, and the dismal thoughts keep coming.

Standing on the left side of the cave, I nervously shift from one foot to another. With my back pressed firmly against the damp, sandpapery wall, I lock myself into the best possible position to spot a snake if one should come slithering by.

An additional thought pops into my head: long ago, hostile Indians must have stood in my place against the wall, albeit skinny ones—if they could wiggle through the crack to get here. Maybe the savages are still here—forgotten about, hidden. I look around warily. They could be crouching in the shadows, set to pounce upon and scalp me at their whim.

Nancy lags behind, and she is all I have. She is a busybody. I am watching her hop back and forth across a wide puddle of water.

I expect a crash and splash at any moment. With each round over the stream, she stoops down, gathers up a few more pebbles, and adds these to her growing stack.

Using one of her stones, she begins to scratch something on the cave wall opposite from me. Nancy presses hard to make her mark, while she can, on everything she leaves behind. Everywhere she goes, nothing will ever come easily. Her future lies before her; it hints of happiness and heartache. But we can't know this yet. God alone sees Nancy's destiny.

I want out of the cave, but I'm too afraid to move from my snake-free spot against the wall. "It'll be all right," I crooned softly to myself, over and over. To collect my thoughts, I clasp my head between my hands and squeeze it in a viselike grip. I mull over the words to tell Nancy. I hesitate to sound too needy, because she might do the opposite of what I want, just to tease me.

"Nancy, let's not go back there by them, okay?"

"I ain't goin' back there with no snakes," she says.

Whew! I breathed out a chest full of anxiety. The ultimate fear of being left all alone in the dark, faded.

Coming from the belly of the cave, I hear the indistinct ripples of their jabber. Soon the voices are clearer.

I see their shadows first, black monsters racing ahead of them in the wavy glimmer of candlelight, striking in their ghostly shapes against the cave wall, and winning the race.

They emerge from the narrow passage in single file, with Sonny in the lead. He hobbles forward, awkwardly, holding his legs straight and stiff and wide apart, one foot on either side of the water puddles as he straddles the tiny river that must have carved out Indian Cave in its very beginning.

I am downhearted because everyone except me saw the canoe. They spoke of it as though it was under our very noses. I can't let it go by. I insistently hang on Dee's arm and beg her, "Show me the canoe. I can't see it."

"It's right here!" She says crossly.

Was the darn thing invisible? Why couldn't I see the canoe, too? It didn't make any sense that they, obviously, were all seeing something I missed, and it rattled me. "Where?"

"Look down!" Dee points at my feet. "You're standing on it."

I'm dumbfounded. "That's a rock!"

My whole confusing search trauma was for nothing. Where was the ancient vessel, hewn from a tree, waiting for my siblings and me to climb aboard? In my mind, I saw bows and arrows and tomahawks that the savages had left behind. Would we need these to protect ourselves from attack?

"Yes," Dee agreed. "It's a rock, but it's shaped like a canoe!"

They tricked me, and I can't think of a good answer. "Oh," I finally choke out. Dee had just squashed my last hope of seeing a genuine Indian relic. Why didn't they tell me it was a rock?

Sonny pocketed the leftover matches to use later. He would build a fire at the edge of our yard at nightfall. We followed him back to the farm by the same treacherous route. The cave experience was so shocking for me that the road home was an uneventful piece of cake. As always, when we arrived, we looked as innocent as the day we were born.

CHAPTER 13

A Mystifying Walk Through Time

GRANDMA MOLLIE ANSWERED my questions concerning Indian lore the best way she knew how. "We were scared of 'em." Her eyes grew round in conditioned fear. "And we kept our distance. A time or two, I remember, the Indians came by our farm a wantin' to make a trade with Pappy for horses. That's all I know of."

"It sounds funny to hear you call your daddy, 'Pappy.'" That came out of my mouth more critical of her era than I meant it to be.

"Well," Grandma began to rationalize, "we'd have thought saying 'daddy' was baby talk. Nobody would have went around a babblin', 'Da-dee! Da-dee! Da-dee!'"

"You're right," I corrected myself. "'Daddy' does sound like baby gibberish."

"After we were bigger girls, hmm ... 'bout like you, you know," Grandma explained, "we shortened it and just called our father 'Pap'."

Blue thoughts of home and of her long ago youth brought Grandma a yearning to retrace a piece of her history. As she began her journey into the past, she took me with her.

Grandma stretched and pinched the center of her upper lip between her thumb and forefinger, making it pucker, as I had seen her do a thousand times before when she was deep in thought.

At the outset, she introduced me to her beloved pappy. "His given name is Marion."

"My, my," Grandma lamented. Her pining hands met and sealed her lips shut after she spoke the name of the lonely tyke who became her father. A look of deep regret, for what might have been, showed in her sad eyes. A surge of pity welled up inside me in sympathy with her loss.

"Pap surely had a poor start," Grandma revealed. "He commenced to grieve so soon, you know."

I wished right then that I had known her mama and pappy. Which of them did Grandma most favor? All I really knew about her family members came from a vague description of them, and she hadn't included much detail about their physical appearance. "I inherited my pap's nose," Grandma admitted, "from the Slusher side of the family. Folks say, 'the Slusher nose'."

After our previous adventure crossing dangerous bull territory and wading through a cave of imagined snakes, I just felt lucky to be in one piece and look normal.

How awful it is to be different. A mid-summer stroll through our community park confronted me with a shocking view of diverse humankind. Two of the special attractions of the carnival's freak show, the fat lady and her counterpart, the thin man, were seated outside their tents in the heat of the day. Without much success, the woman's chubby hand waved a paper fan in front of her face. She looked miserable, and I felt sorry for her.

The oddity of the carnival sideshows is still fresh in my mind. The small town of Percy, Illinois was not their intended destination. Through a cancellation and a further mix-up in scheduling, this strange looking group became stranded here. With no funds to move on, they opened for business. They were most unwelcome visitors in our town.

In elongated letters, the billboard enticed "Is It Animal or Human?" It featured a caricature that resembled a Ripley's Believe It or Not advertisement. I am not certain what the—something—that lay hidden behind the canvas door flap was, but it drew the curious onlookers inside the tent. You had to be at least 16 to find out.

Sonny helped out on the grounds and that got him a free pass to everything. He told us that he didn't know what it was either—and he saw! "I guess it's a man. They feed him twice day'we, and he bites the head off a wive chicken each time." Sonny described how the obscene chase turned into a blood bath.

This was the heyday of carnival freak shows, and the unusual could hold a fairgoers' attention. Grandma surmised, "For shame on that goin's on." She didn't dwell on a person's outward form, although she had spoken about two very unique individuals to a rather bewildered me.

One of these was Joseph Merrick, the pitiable elephant man. Grotesque tumors deformed him and alarmed others who saw him, causing them to turn their heads and look away, in effect shunning him.

The other unfortunate person was famed Robert Wadlow, the world's tallest man. So that I visualized his stature, Grandma told me, "Robert Wadlow had to walk using a cane to steady his great height. When he died, he was put away in a piano crate because the caskets were too small." I carried these images forward.

A photo of my great grandparents Marion and Margaret would have been helpful. Before I could really form a vision of the little boy Pappy, from her haunting story, I needed to give him a face. To make Marion come to life in Grandma's words, I fashioned his likeness from high expectations and from my own notions about him. Using an imaginary ideal, I built Marion into a brave and compelling looking young man.

Grandma's poignant memoir begins with the tragic massacre of her paternal grandparents. There was no open Indian fighting at that time in Kentucky, this was an isolated occurrence.

Somewhere in Kentucky, a wandering group of hostile Indians came across the family's isolated cabin. Without any warning, (the shrill warble of a warrior is indistinguishable from the cry of a wild creature.) the savages swarmed over the cabin.

In the pandemonium that followed, the parents were murdered by the cruel marauders, who had stumbled upon the homestead, quite by chance.

None can say how merciless they perished; only the sky above and the earth below witnessed the shattering of their lives—and of the children's misfortune.

By the same twist of fate, their sons were left orphaned. The lads escaped death, only because they were away from home on that terrible day. The boys had no close relatives, consequently they were separated. A local self-proclaimed preacher and his wife took in Grandma's pappy, as an act of charity.

Grandma learned of his sad lot from someone who knew well these difficult to please foster parents. In the process of giving him a good home, the orphaned boy had to earn his keep.

"Preacher wasn't a bad sort," Grandma said, "mean or nothing like that-a-way, just work brittle." Speaking of Marion, Grandma said, "He was nothing but a little boy doing a grown man's chores. Their strict upbringing caused Pap to lose his childhood altogether. Lo and behold, the old preacher used him for free labor until he was grown enough to strike out on his own and leave these harsh doin's."

As she spoke, her fingers tugged at a piece of balled up lint that was fastened to the bib of her print apron. She rubbed over her stomach in a circular motion and then patted the lump of hanky in the apron pocket.

She willed back the damp intrusion of sadness that threatened to form in those expressive, bluest of eyes.

I'm not certain that I ever saw Grandma cry. Maybe once, after she had called me to her bedside and asked me to fill her ice pack, I thought I noticed a tear. "Get the ice pack, honey," Grandma requested, "and chip off enough ice to fill the bag about halfway. Be careful, though, of your little fingers," she warned me twice.

Occasionally, she would tie a ragged strip of towel snugly around her head to help alleviate the splitting pain in her temples. I never could see how that would work. Even wearing a loose headband to hold my hair in place feels uncomfortable.

Earlier, before Grandma went to lie down, I had heard her moaning softly to herself. Alone in the front room, with her flushed face buried in her hands, she looked forlorn. Darting on the tips of my toes, I whizzed right by her chair on my way to the kitchen. I was still in there when she called me. "Shirley ... aw, Shirley! Won't you come in here to me? I need you to do something."

Grandma's face would turn quite red when her blood pressure rose, and sometimes an extreme headache followed. For this ailment, she took several brightly colored pills daily.

It's odd, the mundane things that can really stick in a person's mind. I remember, so clearly, standing in front of Grandma's black dresser and looking up doubtfully at the impressive rows of small medicine bottles. These tantalizingly deceptive keepers of Grandma's health stood in formation, like plastic soldiers, on the back corner of her dresser top.

"What are they for?" I asked.

Grandma cautioned me. "Don't ever swallow any. If you don't need these, they will make you sick. They're Grandma's pills."

I often went into Grandma's room and gazed at myself in her dresser's big mirror. I was barely tall enough to see my whole head. The wee child making those funny faces back at me had lots of confidence; I hoped she would lend me some.

While I was staring at the likening reflection and mimicking the little girl's smile, Dee walked in. She had to laugh. In the moment that took forever to pass, I stopped prancing mid-step. The floor refused to swallow me. I had made a monkey out of myself, and I was stuck with it.

I am living proof that closing eyes only makes a kid invisible to herself. Others can see us "saving face."

I wondered if the column of pills did Grandma any good. Grandpa didn't take any, although there was that time when he treated himself with a dangerous home remedy.

I just happened to be sitting outdoors on the well curb, that morning when Grandpa dragged the can from its place at the edge of the porch. I saw him lean the spout forward and pour a dab of the foul smelling coal oil into a teacup.

He brought the cup to his lips. "Hey!" I gasped, not believing my eyes. A startled Grandpa froze with the suspended cup near his open mouth.

I'm certain it was an absent-minded mistake. I thought to myself: that goofy, old man must have gotten mixed up and forgot what he was doing.

"Grandpa, that ain't a cup of coffee." I reminded him.

"I'm not a drinkin' it," he answered, "just wallerin' it around in m' mouth and spittin' it back out. I got a sore throat."

"Grandpa," I spoke tactfully at first, "it isn't a good idea to do that." I carefully added, "I wouldn't do that if I was you; I think that might be poison." My warnings got stronger. "You might get real sick. It could make you die." I went as far as I dared. "You're gonna kill yourself!"

My words fell on senile, deaf ears. I grew frustrated from my own feelings of helplessness, and I was mad at Grandpa, too, because he wouldn't listen to me. I felt an overpowering urge to grab his elbow and knock that cup of smelly liquid right out of his hand.

Grandpa ignored my powerless whining, took a sip, anyway, and swallowed it down. In a panic, I jumped to my feet and rushed to

Grandma's side. I blurted out, "We have to do something! Grandpa swallowed coal oil."

"Gol doggies, Shirley, if I could yank a drink of somethin' away from yer grandpa, I'd already a done it."

Realizing how agitated I had become, Grandma tried to smooth it over. She promised, "I've seen others do it. Likely it'll be all right."

"But Grandma! Grandpa swallowed some." I couldn't let it go.

She turned up empty palms to show me, "Nuthin' I can do, no way."

I had watched Nancy dab coal oil on her poison ivy, and she told me, "If you get too much, it'll blister the skin." Lord knows what it could do to a person's insides.

Grandpa looked bad, sort of pale, and he was unusually quiet for days afterward. I had an eerie premonition that he was near death that fall. I believe he knew but didn't speak of it, how close my words—"It could make you die"—came to fulfillment.

On that difficult morning, God let an angel whisper in my ear. Might Grandpa have swallowed even more of the poison, and died from it, if I hadn't continually harped at him? My first impulse was to reach over and whack his elbow, making the coal oil spill. But at this point, I still thought he was going to spit it back out. If I had taken action, Grandpa would have seen this as an act of war.

My only recourse would have meant staying out of reach until the old man cooled off. Anyway, I knew that he, stubbornly, would have poured himself another gulp.

Scary thoughts of Grandpa's "throat cure" faded, and my attention returned to questioning Grandma's past. I became curious about how her life as a young girl compared to mine.

"How many brothers and sisters do you have?" I asked.

"There are ten of us. I'm the oldest. There are three boys and seven girls."

Grandma described her family life to me as a stirring time of sacrifice and constant change, of a togetherness that made each of the ten siblings feel wanted, and of a needed closeness that gave me pause to wonder if I had missed out on a fuller, more exciting life by being born too late.

My long, uneventful days as a young girl that summer, generally paled in comparison to the bold unfolding of Grandma's storybook youth. She made her past seem so interesting; I memorized everything she told me.

I hitched a ride on Grandma's skirts, listening attentively, as she retraced her footsteps to a bygone century. Through her hindsight, I saw me—instead of her—for as long as the adventurous tale lasted.

Oh! How I wish I could have lived back then, too. Each time, I exchanged places with her, I loved every minute of it. "Tell me something," I begged. "Grandma, what was it like when you were big as me?"

"Oh, let me think, Shirley," Grandma reflected. She grew silent for a moment, bridging the years and gathering her thoughts. "Well, I reckon it ... uh, umm ... was work."

Grandma coughed, attempting to clear her throat. I heard the familiar scraping noises rake across her vocal cords. "Harrumph!" The lingering effects of a chest cold had not gone completely away, despite a nightly Vicks salve rubdown.

Once she got her voice back, Grandma proceeded to recount a way of life that must have seemed quite commonplace to her. I found her storytelling to be an entertaining and mystifying walk through time.

She began, "It was my task to bake fresh bread every day. Couldn't run down to the store for a loaf nor a quart of milk, either. We kept a cow. Everybody did their share of the farm chores. Little ones did their bit, too—you know, gatherin' up the eggs and such as they could do themselves."

"What did you do for fun?" I asked.

"Well, we did play some when the chores was done up," Grandma admitted, "played a little bit. Fly sheepy fly—is about like the tag game you young'ns play of an evening."

"Did you used to go swimming?"

Grandma shook her head. "Not s'much. I guess the boys did more'n the girls. Oh, sometimes, when it was smothering hot we'd dabble our feet in the creek after we filled our water bucket."

"We had to traipse down below the house to get to the water, and it had snakes in it. Ever' drop of water we used a scrubbin', bathin', and cookin', we drew from the creek. We gener'ly took turns a spellin' one another while we carried the water up the hill and back to the house. Snakes lay in the weeds, so we stuck together and stayed on the path we'd tramped down."

"Did you skinny dip?" I had secretly wanted to swim naked—one time—just to experience the feeling, but my fear of being spied on prevented me.

I have to give my friend Shannon credit for her daring attitude. She had no such qualms when it came to swimming in the raw. Shannon could rise up out of the lake, minus her swimsuit, scramble atop a tree stump jutting out of the water, strike a pose and perform a fantastic dive.

I envied her all of that. My dive is a disappointing belly flop, and I bob to the surface with a stinging nose full of water.

Grandma was more natural than I. She had an attuned, almost earthy acceptance of herself. "We'd lay our things on the bramble bushes," she said, "and then, jump in and paddle around long enough to cool off."

"Snakes spoil my fun all the time," I complained bitterly. "Whenever I swim, I'm always scared I'll see one. I have to keep looking over my shoulder."

The sight of one of these ropelike uglies skimming across the surface of the water makes me shudder! I have scrambled up the mud-slick banks of the Old Lake more times than I care to recall. Usually my snake turns into a floating stick. I can't see very far away, so I won't know that, for sure, until after it bumps me, and I have already flinched.

I get lots of sage advice from Mary, Nancy, and Sonny: "Only blue racers will chase you: Snakes can't bite underwater: Water moccasin fangs are dripping with poison venom: You always hear a rattle warning before the rattlesnake strikes."

They thought I should know all of that.

If a wavy stick is going to stalk and scare the living daylights out of me, it will naturally occur when I am treading water over my head. It is a long, long way to dry land. I have discovered that snakes don't come from anywhere: They just materialize beside me.

I need glasses.

Water churned beneath my feet. "Look at her go!" I hear Nancy exclaim as my body blurs past her. I don't slow down or even look back at her.

The boys splashing at my left are laughing really hard. Something must be awfully funny. It's me, I suddenly realize, and that makes me mad! Once I am out of the water, I turn and look at them. Nancy is glancing warily, all around herself. "I'll bet Shirley saw a snake," she said.

"I'll bet she did, too!" I snapped back.

After my panic to escape the snake was over, I decided, more than a little sorrowfully, I'll never get back in that lake again. What a mess I looked! As I sat huddled on the grassy bank, I felt so homely, and I had been ridiculed besides. I wrapped my skinny arms around my knees to hide my discomfort. The droopy swimsuit I wore was several times my size; the big woman, built-in bra cups were empty and caved in, and the whole thing hung on me like a gunnysack. I was white faced, and I felt miserable.

Bending down to my level, Mary sought to comfort me. "It's gone now, Shirley. Come on, and get back in. Just don't go to the left." She pointed out the swampy area of the lake where the tall cattails grew. "Snakes hang out there close to the bank. Come out where we are."

I weighed what Mary said, and I believed her.

Boys can abide snakes better than girls can. Sonny has a pet green snake that is carried around in his trousers pocket. "Won't bite cha unwess you squeeze him," he assured me.

I knew better than to rely on Sonny's opinion; he was mistaken a lot, like the time with the bat.

With that thought in mind, I kept a respectable distance between myself and that supposedly harmless creature attached to the bark of the tree. If I'm not careful, I reasoned, that fuzzy, reddish brown bat could end up tangled in my hair or plastered to my face.

Sonny began to loosen its grip from the piece of bark by slowly rocking the bat. Its wings spread open unexpectedly, and I retreated another cautious backward step. I had never seen a bat close up. The webbed wings came as quite a surprise to me.

"You aggravatin' kids shoulda left it stay where it was at," Grandpa fussed at us. "It ain't natural for a bat to be out in the daylight. I'd say tis a good deal likely to be sick or have the rabies. Go on over and clean up yer hands." And he herded us to the outside washstand.

Bats are spooky. At least, Sonny's carrier pigeons are nice to look at. I followed him, in the dark of night, as he walked the rooftops of two-story buildings in search of more birds to add to the homemade coop. Though I cannot dive or handle snakes—for a timid child, I am quite the little climber.

Sonny hooked the flashlight to the belt that circled his waist. I stood back, waiting not so patiently in the dark, as he inched his way out onto a narrow ledge where the pigeons roosted.

Why does it take so long? Raw anxiety eats at me, and I hold my breath against the fear that the decayed wood will give way and hurl Sonny down to me, maimed or killed.

The last time I verbalized my concern about the danger, Sonny reacted in a loud whisper, "Shir'we, if you don't shut up, next time I'a weave you at home."

It's obvious that I worry all the time, and nobody ever listens to me. He needs me, I thought, and I felt empowered by that fact. Who else will hold a sack or hand the flashlight back and forth to him in the middle of the night?

I heard the clatter of a dozen or more bird feet shuffling nervously. A sound not unlike, I guessed, the fluttering of angel wings reached my hearing as Sonny shined his blinding light in their eyes. "I got one!" He exclaimed.

Finally, he shinnied back along the jutting precipice that overhangs the sidewalk. As soon as he climbed back onto the safety of the roof-top, I calmed down.

Sonny gently covered the pigeon's eyes with his hand and began to stroke its head. "They wike this." He showed me the effect. "Coo ... Coo ..." I wasn't sure whether it is the bird or Sonny who was emitting these muffled throaty sounds. Maybe both. No two birds of the feathered lovelies are exactly alike. "Ain't this'n a beauty?"

"Yes"... and Shirley thinks Sonny is wonderful. He climbs like a comic book hero. Before the clock struck 12, Sonny had bagged a couple more choice birds. I followed my big brother back home and to his bird haven.

The Old Lake is approximately a mile from town, and its waters are backed by a woods and rugged strip mining terrain. At road's end and just before the water's edge, a sign warns, "Swim at Your Own Risk."

We didn't realize the danger lurking there. I froze when I heard Nancy wail in terror. It was the type of piercing scream that lets you know that something awful has happened. Bad luck follows Nancy.

This time, she had dashed her foot against a sliver of broken glass. She came limping out of the lake with a stream of blood gushing from the slash. Our immediate fear was that she had severed an artery.

Nancy was fortunate that a man who lived nearby was swimming at the lake. He sent one of his children home to fetch a medical kit containing disinfectant, tape and gauze.

Speaking ever so kindly to Nancy, this angel of mercy cleaned and bandaged her wound and kept her calm. Nancy didn't see a doctor afterwards, but her foot healed just fine.

Two local toughs were responsible for Nancy's foot injury. They were observed, earlier in the day, marching on a path through the woods and toward the lake. Both boys had rifles slung over their cocky shoulders. One of them was a sinister fellow who rained trouble down on me at every opportunity. For good reason, I will call this dangerous thug "Hunter."

The only witness to their carelessness backed away. When asked if he would report what he saw, he said, "No. Don't want no trouble!" He declined to confront them. But "yes," he did see the boys using glass bottles, tossed up over the lake, for target practice.

I avoided Hunter whenever I could, because he teased and picked on kids who were either younger than he or who were too weak to fight back. The bully gets a charge out of someone else's torment.

Memories from our swimming hole days are bittersweet ones; the muddy waters of the Old Lake are a reminder of good times and bad.

Grandma resumed her description of the1800s: she reiterated the importance of work to their survival. "I was too busy doing chores for Pap and helping my mama to commence a play'n' much."

"Mama"—what a calming effect that enduring term has on everybody. When it's spoken, soft and low, it lightens a heavy heart in just the way a letting go of a deep, bated breath does.

I'm pleased that favored title hasn't changed from Grandma's generation to mine. Mama and Pap—it's fitting.

"In 1883," Grandma explained, "I turned 13, bigger than you are now. Late that same year, I hired out in a boarding house."

Separation from family is always an ordeal for me. I don't know how to make endings or to say good-bye. When loved ones leave my side, a chunk of my heart goes with them.

"How could your mama and pappy let you go away from home when you were only 13?"

Grandma's lips screwed up into a tight pucker.

"Phooey!" she said. "Wasn't far from home, and everybody worked at something—or else they got their comeuppance. The proprietor of the boarding house was a woman named Hannah, and I was a hired girl there."

I wanted to know more. "How old a woman was she? Was she pretty? How much did Miss Hannah pay you? What did you do at Miss Hannah's? Did Miss Hannah own the boarding house?"

All the world suggests that beautiful people are most likely to be loved. Young romantics hear the message: Be pretty or you'll be left out. The Ivory Soap Girl confirms it.

"Hmmm. Pretty is as pretty does," Grandma reminded me for at least the "eleven-dee-leventh" time.

"Miss Hannah was chunky, I'd say. And she was middle aged, a mature looking woman, you know. Never got any real money wages at all, but we had a nice place to sleep. It was clean. And we had enough to eat; that's all anybody had. People would work just to get their keep."

I was very curious to learn about the role of women in the 1800s from someone who had been there, and I needed Grandma to explain a great deal about herself and about this woman who seemed to be in charge. I assumed that the woman that Grandma worked for is dead, by now, because my Grandma is so old. I already knew that women didn't sign important papers in those days.

Grandma said she worked with another girl at the boarding house, and she didn't know who owned the place. "But we took our marching orders from Miss Hannah. She was a single lady, though. The only-est men on the place were boarders."

My fascination with days long passed caused my imagination to soar, and I envisioned a wondrous place to begin Grandma's boarding house adventures. I couldn't wait to go there and explore.

Through the magic of daydreaming, yesteryear 1883 becomes my destination. While I am a wayfarer (at play in my thoughts), I discover that I can be here beside old Grandma and there, in the past, with young Mollie, as well. Storytelling is like that.

In the blink of an eye, Grandma is swept away. The old, old woman sitting next to me is whisked right off her tightly swelled feet and deposited gently in a humble setting—sixty years earlier.

Mollie stands amid meager belongings. She has become a time traveler who is forever young—stranded and frozen in a world unfamiliar to me. But I do recognize her want; she struggles to possess any little thing at all. Truly a pittance to some is a king's ransom to others. I know, well, how that feels. There are not many trinkets for my siblings and me, either. We are very, very poor.

An old expression says, "It's no disgrace to be poor, but it's awfully unhandy." As a poor child, I can attest that this saying is true. I had to make do with fewer material things than other kids.

But being dirt poor wasn't all bad. I did learn to adapt and to spread my wings and fly at an early age. What I lacked in things was more than made up for in freedom. And I felt loved, at least by my grandma.

When I stood only head and shoulders above our old cooking range, Grandma taught me how to cook. There, on my own, her kitchen was my kitchen. I feel her presence with me still.

There is a wide chasm between controlling and guiding. Even though Grandma never went beyond sixth grade, she was wise. And she was a wonderful role model. Ordinary people can, and very often do, become everyday heroes.

Unselfish love is Grandma's true legacy. And it makes me feel rich, even to this day.

Not a lot is known about the particular short time period just before Mollie met Alf. From the boarding house to their old-fashioned courtship is quite a jump. I have some ideas of how Grandma's days at the boarding house were filled. She hinted of a maturity beyond her young age. I believe her thirteenth year embraced the same down to earth joys and sorrows that transcend time.

To show an example of Mollie's day-to-day activities and to better describe that time and place, I've used a blanket of words and deeds that I had picked up on, over time, from Grandma Mollie. Her stories give depth to otherwise lost years.

Once upon a time, in the gap period that I mentioned, Mollie borrowed days from her youth and lent them to me for a spell.

It was only a small area off the kitchen with a straw mat tucked in one corner, but it was a space to call her own. All that was missing was something familiar to remind her of home. Mollie had brought a quilt with her, and she placed it on the sleeping mat. As she unrolled her cherished coverlet, she gathered up the few personal belongings that were wound up inside of it. Besides the miscellaneous cloths, which she washed and used again and again for her monthly personal needs, there were long, curved hairpins, a set of ivory combs, and a Sunday-go-to-meeting dress. These things Molly stored away in the small oak trunk that Miss Hannah had loaned to her.

A turbulent gust of tepid air churned the dirt road into a dark, gritty funnel, and it spread an even layer of grime where the crude pathway ended: at the worn-to-sagging stoop of Miss Hannah's wide front porch. There, Mollie hesitated long enough to shift the crunch of rugs to her hip and pull the door shut with her free hand.

With the scramble of rugs wedged once more in the vise of her arms, Mollie turned away from the house and faced the open countryside. I am struck by how very young she looks. Is my old Grandma Mollie really in there somewhere?

The age endowed bright white of her hair is gone. Magically, it has reverted to the warm sandy hue of her youth—the color it used to be when she stood in the sunlight, I am told. Mollie is 13 again.

Walking effortlessly to the end of the porch, my drastically altered grandma drops the clump of scatter rugs at her bare feet. She stretches her back to get the kinks out, slowly arching her spine until she feels the pull down the entire length of her body. In that ecstatic moment, her face takes on radiance; Mollie positively glows as she stiffens and relaxes the muscles of her back in quick succession.

Mollie took a deep, out of doors breath. The faint, unmistakable perfume of roses enveloped her, and she was reminded of the day she left home. Her mama's parting words came back to her. "This will always be your home to come back to. Keep safe and well. Don't overdo, Mollie. Remember," Margaret prompted, "to stop and take time to smell the roses. It makes no difference, you know, how much you do, there will always be tasks a plenty for tomorrow." Impulsively, Margaret's fingertips brush lightly against Mollie's shoulders. Her motherly touch expresses caring better than words can say.

"I'll remember, Mama," promised Mollie, as she took her leave. Mollie's face is wearing the look of dismay that gives away her vulnerability, when the parting is anguished. "Good-bye, Mama, until I see you at prayer meet of a Sundee."

Molly began her journey into an adult world. Her mama had mixed emotions, as she watched the young girl disappear down the arduous path to independence and turbulent womanhood.

Mother and daughter have in common a genuine fondness for flowers, especially the rose. They are not alone in this appreciation; my mother, Norma, is never far from me whenever I glimpse a November rose. Mom's birthday is November 20.

On a snowy day in 1990, our first Thanksgiving holiday without Mom, a solitary red rose flourished on an otherwise barren, climbing bush. It seemed as if the rose was meant for me alone—sent as a velvety reassurance that love blooms forever. If you believe in your heart that it's true, then it is real for you: the believer.

What I draw from this experience is that roses can and do, somehow, produce miracles. For centuries, lovers have used the crimson rose to express their undying love, while a single yellow blossom can heal the brokenhearted. There is no sweeter fragrance in all the world, and its gift to someone who is sad is not a small thing.

The scent of roses is all around Mollie. Her heartbeat quickens with a sudden feeling of exhilaration. She tilts her chin sharply toward the heavens, and the rising winds tangle wisps of her light auburn hair, fanning her burning cheeks. Specks of gritty dust particles, trapped and spinning in the air, harshly sting her face. She shades her eyes with the flat of her hand to shield her sight from the churning debris.

Standing at the foot of the dirt path that winds its way from the center of town and on down to the boarding house, young Mollie stares as far away as sight will allow, through the swirling dirt devils.

The distant object in front of her eyes has grown from an inanimate speck to a lively, tail-wagging creature, an indication that it is coming toward her.

The street, except for the slowly advancing, pitiful looking excuse for a dog, is otherwise deserted. The hungry mutt is hopeful that Mollie will give him something to gnaw on. Grandma would always take in the strays, whether of animal or human origin.

Mollie is preoccupied with thoughts of the grove. She anticipates the faces of her loved ones, who will be present at the prayer meeting circle.

The powerful winds that tore at Mollie's skirts, ceased just as suddenly as they had sprung up, reneging on their promise of moisture to the thirsty land.

Resuming her tasks, Mollie grasped a soiled rug from the top of the heap and shook it vigorously. One by one, she flung the day's accumulation of dirt off the dusty rugs and back to where it came from.

At this juncture, my fantasy ends, and I depart the imaginary fork along the trail of Grandma's youth and continue on with the phenomenon that is genuinely ours—from the best of her recollections and my own memories.

At long last, Grandma sees one small wish fulfilled. She saved her old dresses and odds and ends of colorful cloth, and then she paid a woman to weave these discarded strips into rugs.

In the instant Grandma saw the finished product, I watched her eyes light up, and I would not have missed that merry twinkle for the world. Together, she and I admired the handiwork. "Oh my," she tells the woman, "I want to thank you for doing such pretty work."

"A nice rug or a flower," Grandma explained to me, "can turn plain into pretty." She tried to open the eyes of a dreamer to the simple things that would have otherwise been missed.

How these rugs did brighten our quite plain rooms! The contrast of old faded wallpaper and linoleum made these bright rugs stand out. Sometimes, all it takes to strike a mood or change from dull to spirited is a dash of color. "Rugs change the look of a place and soak up the noisy clatter of dishes," she said. She was so bothered by tinnitus.

Neither of the old folks can afford to spend their small income on unnecessary things. But Grandma is drawn to the little extras. She saves her pennies for tomorrow's splurge.

I studied her expression. She looked as pleased as she could be when she laid the last newly woven masterpiece down across the threshold, between the front room and kitchen.

She and Grandpa are not picking up their feet as high as they once did, plus, Grandma's equilibrium is poor due to her blood pressure. Rugs would not be safe for either of them, a whole lot longer, I knew. Besides, I think that men, just naturally, don't like these stumble makers.

Every time Grandma left her easy chair and tottered into the kitchen, she crossed over the rug covering the threshold—until the day when she tripped on it.

The old man grumbled, "Mollie, you're gonna have t' get shut of them ol' rags, or mark my words, one of these days you're gonna stagger around here and take a fall. I'm satisfied," he warned, "you could break a hip and be down a cause of it. It'd be a heap better t' listen t' me."

As I uncover my childhood, I can see the days when Grandma wore those dresses, collected in the rugs. She traded in her less desirable items of dress to brighten our surroundings. A touch of her character was imparted there. It was intertwined with the colorful housedresses and woven into the rugs.

Revisiting Grandma Mollie within these pages and recalling the quaint little house that I grew up in, brings me a measure of happiness.

"In my father's house, there are many dwelling places," John 14:2. I like to think, for Grandma's sake, that each room therein is brightened beyond dazzling gemstones. I hope her heavenly home is blessed with beautiful rugs (woven by angels) in colors of the rainbow.

Blessing follows blessing. My heart tells me that this is so. The roaring sound that so grieved my Grandma, has been replaced with the voice of Jesus, calling softly to her. "Come now, Mollie, your ears are healed."

My thoughts race to the candy counter at Berg's store. A nickel to spend lends wings to my feet.

All the way there, I cling to the hope that the nice lady, Mrs. Berg, is minding the glass case of the sugary treats, instead of the grouchy old man. I savor these moments when I am looking over the whole selection of candies, and before I choose my Butterfinger bar—every time. I am tempted to try a new candy, yet I am torn because I don't want to risk wasting my only nickel on an unproven.

The seconds tick by as I stand contemplating my dilemma. My nose and both hands are welded against the candy display case. The old man hurried right over—darn the luck— and slid open the back of it.

He raps on the glass top. "Rat-a-tat-tat," his knuckles demand that I speak up.

"Take your hands off that, girlie," he scowls. "I just cleaned it. And hurry it up, I ain't got all day."

The moment of truth was crowding me. As time slips through the hourglass in my mind, I chew my bottom lip and clench my fingers until the nails dig into my palms.

Keeping a respectful distance between Mr. Berg's sparkling clean glass case and myself, I swiftly go over my options for the last time. The Baby Ruth is calling my name; the boys, I have noticed, always buy Snickers.

"I'll have a Butterfinger," I hear myself meekly say to Mr. Crabby.

Once in a while, poverty comes as a blessing in disguise. I had an intense craving for sugar. It is a good thing that I never had an endless supply of nickels. In my quest for candy utopia, I may have instead found diabetes at an early age.

Nature provided a different sort of dining experience. On a notable summer evening, Grandma's resourcefulness came to light. It was shortly before sundown when she took a large metal bowl out of her cupboard. She added a pair of sewing shears to the bowl and handed them to me. "I need you to come help Grandma cut some greens."

I followed her outside, where unbeknownst to me, our supper was in the planning stage. My arms locked around the bowl, hugging it to my chest, as I sidled along after Grandma.

Bending down, with much difficulty, Grandma pointed out some greens, which looked a lot like weeds. She commenced to snip and gather dandelion leaves.

Each time Grandma straightened back up, it took more out of her. Her spirit was willing, but as our hunt for supper fixings progressed, the stooping and clipping fell to me.

"Greens will shrink as they cook," Grandma advised, "and it takes a good bunch." Finally, our bowl is lipping full.

An hour later, the fixings were ready to eat. Flavored with bacon grease and mixed with some other kind of greens, these tasty leaves were the evening's main course. My grandma is a miracle worker.

After our tummies were filled, Grandma fed the scraps to the hungry neighborhood cats and dogs.

Hmmm, I wonder … whatever would my descendants say to the prospect of this inviting meal? Theirs is a different time.

CHAPTER 14

—— ❧ ——

Sparking

IN DUE TIME, Grandma has a mind to speak again of her duties at the boarding house. It is 1883. Young Mollie continues her chores. She takes the straw broom in her willing hands and begins to sweep the porch in hurried strokes, brushing away the gritty trail of unwelcome dust that followed on the boot heels of Miss Hannah's gentlemen boarders.

How challenging is her plight? Our Mollie may have been penniless, but she was wading knee deep in ruggedly handsome cowboys—the pinnacle of any young girl's hope—and I told her so.

An expression of amusement crossed that old angel's wrinkled face; the corners of her toothless mouth curved upward, and a playful smile sneaked past her guarded lips, betraying her intention: Grandma was poking fun at me. She knew what I wanted to know.

Her teasing giggle proved me right. "Didn't have time for sparking or any such shenanigans as that," Grandma insisted. Grown-ups will swear that their lot is work, work, work, and that they never have any fun. "And," she added, "we never called them cowboys. They were hired men or hired hands."

"The men folk would commence to gather in the parlor of an evening, near suppertime, and they always brought a hungry appetite with them."

Grandma placed her hands on her stomach and rounded it out into a little potbelly, to demonstrate the bulgy look of a full gut on a cowhand who had just consumed the last meal of the day. I wondered if their supper involved greens that were newly snipped from the boarding house lawn.

"I gener'ly helped out in the kitchen and carried the food to the dining room, too. We run our legs off, spreading our food over those long tables. The men would empty the bowls as quick as we filled 'em, you know. And law ... but the cleaning and the scrubbing!"

It happens to us so young. My soul begged for the beginning to the love that never ends. Surely, a long time ago, Grandma must have felt the way I do. I was dying to hear her and Grandpa's love story.

"Where did you meet Grandpa?" I asked.

"The first time I ever saw Alf, he came to the grove with some boyhood chums." Grandma is in a jovial mood when she takes up her story about the grove.

"We had a grand old time!" I surmised that the grandest fun of all for them was played out on the long walk together with chums, before they arrived at the open-air worship service. Because they met in olden times, I anticipate that Grandma will tell me of a very proper courtship.

In my heart of hearts, I yearn to discover romance in all its depth and breadth. How do you make love be a beautiful thing? From this hunger, the words were forming inside my head. Later, I would write them down.

Grandma began to reminisce about their outings. "I walked to prayer meeting with my brothers and sisters, and some of our pals joined up with us along the way. There was a good bunch of us that hung together—older ones a lookin' after the smaller children. We sported as we walked, laughing and joking. You know, telling riddles, holding hands, and skipping similar to what you children do."

(Grandma's expression of "you know" is a familiar one. Robin, our first-born, is blessed to have inherited this tendency to pause in mid-sentence and add to her conversations, Grandma's most used catch phrase. These two words resonate in my mind and take me back in time.)

The grove sounded like a fascinating place to go. It had an other-worldly aura surrounding it that appealed to me. I hugged the idea to myself, and I hoped that Grandma had not mentioned it to the others. If nobody else knew about the grove, then it would be our secret. Nancy and Mary had many secrets that they whispered between themselves. "You're too little to hear this," they said.

Where was this unheard of place? Maybe I could go there sometime. "Grandma, is the grove close to here?" I asked.

"No, honey. The grove was all cut down a long while ago." Grandma went on to describe the woodsy setting where she and Grandpa first met. "It was at the clearing, inside the thick grove of trees, and within walking distance from my girlhood home."

She explained that during mild summer evenings, as was the custom with old-time religious gatherings, friends and neighbors worshipped and socialized together out in the open air and under starlight. It must have been a truly marvelous, spiritual experience—the blending of nature with God, and one that is unequaled inside a church building.

Religious differences are thick and heavy. Somewhere, I read that God is all good, all loving, all forgiving, and nothing in between—a thought that is easily carried everywhere.

Grandma was ahead of her time. In 1948, when we were growing up, we sometimes couldn't think to do the right thing all by ourselves. Grandma drew from her early upbringing of camp meeting spirituality, and she used it to make us think twice—and I should add, to take all the fun right out of our mischief—by reminding us "what the Lord would do."

"Grandma," I asked, "where did everybody sit at, out there in the middle of the woods? It sounds more like a picnic than church."

"The only bench or two was some boards laid across tree stumps, and these were saved for the elderly," she said. "We didn't care to sit, no how. The young'ns all played with buddies, tramping through the woods and dangling from the trees—wild as banshees—until we allowed we heard the singing commence. Then we skedaddled back to the clearing and took a seat anywhere 'twas handy—a tree stump or fallen branch."

"Some of the young girls, you know," Grandma continued, "that had a sweetheart, would spread their wraps on the grass and share it with their beaus."

I drew a mental picture of this romantic spectacle of sweethearts together on the ground, and I grew so enchanted by Grandma's nostalgic remembrances of the grove that it made me homesick for this quaint time and place that I never knew.

I wished I could go to the grove. The coattails of tomorrow are easily caught, but yesterday is a monumental thing to overcome. I could only be an outside observer to the past. I could never go there except in my thoughts—and by that wistful means—I sped to the grove and found the clearing.

An untamed wind convulsed above me, and the slumbering woodland quickened. Drifting strains of nature's primordial music—almost too faint for mortal ears to hear—played softly through the billowing treetops of the grove. More with heart than hearing, I listened to the celestial rising and falling of the winds, or maybe it was the sound of God breathing life upon the Earth below.

Grandma's voice invaded my rambling musings and brought me back to the old, faded yellow house.

"Yer Grandpa lollygagged behind after the other lads went on. I seen him, out of the corner of my eye, a lookin' at me, laggin' back, and a waitin' on me."

It's rude; I know that, and I try not to use it: a kid's scariest word— fat! Being careful to leave out this unspeakable F word, I asked her. "Was Grandpa … er … um … well, kinda big around?"

"Well, Alf wasn't but about the same as the other boys when he was a young lad. Built like... well, 'bout like one of the more hefty fellows, you know. Oh …" her voice waned, implying doubt. "I don't know!" She went back and forth until she decided. "He was chunky, I guess you'd say."

Evidently, Grandma couldn't call somebody a "fatty," either.

"Did Grandpa ask you for a date that night?"

"Pffft!" Grandma scoffed at the very idea. "We never heard of such a thing as that. Why, that'd be right comical." She burst out laughing and said, "My chums would make a good spoofing of that. We called it sparking. You might get handed a piece of fruit if you asked for a date."

That tickled my funny bone. Grandma's right: Their electrifying word, sparking, is a livelier translation for hugs and kisses than a dull piece of foreign fruit.

"Some of us," Grandma said, "might have a beau or a sweetheart. Nobody ever said the like of a date, or a boyfriend, or a girlfriend."

The two generations that separated us vanished, and we were of one mind. In that instant, I would trade off some of these foul-mouthed braggarts of today for the gallant, almost knightly boys that I was sure Grandma had encountered. The grass always looks greener …

"After prayer meetin' was over with, Alf kept on hangin' around, a lookin' sheepish at me and actin' tomfool. He stood there a fidgetin', shiftin' from one foot to the other, takin' his hands out of his pants pockets and puttin' 'em back in." I've seen Grandpa perform this nervous gesture whenever the words don't come easily. "Directly, he said to me, 'Mollie, can I walk you home?'"

I can't imagine a more wonderful place than the natural surroundings of the grove to discover your own true love. I can picture the two of them: Grandpa is uncomfortable with courting, but the desire to make Grandma his sweetheart, quickly overcomes the awkwardness he feels about himself. Alf, thrust out of character, gruffly stammers for the right words to woo Mollie.

"At first I told him 'no. I don't want no such foolishness as that.'" Grandma confided in me how she had rebuffed him. "It went on like that for a spell. Yer Grandpa kept askin' me again, anyhow. Directly, I said 'I would.'"

"Law …" She shook her head confoundedly, catching me by surprise and pummeling me with the unwelcome truth that marriage vows are not a promise of perfect bliss. "I shoulda kept on a goin'!"

My little girl shoulders sagged under burdensome disbelief. Well, this is something I never asked to know. I'm only prepared for love stories to conclude with "and they lived happily ever after."

I am left with my mouth hanging open. Where is Grandpa? I worried silently, my eyes nervously darting across the front room. Hurt feelings really bother me. A storm of empathy drenches my heart.

Grandpa's whereabouts becomes apparent to me when the bed springs sound a squeaky "ping-twang." A wire coil, noisily adjusting itself underneath the old man, signals his location as he shifts his bulky weight on the mattress. Tucked away in his bedroom, Grandpa couldn't possibly overhear Grandma's easily misconstrued words. Could he?

Grandpa can hear a pin drop from across the room. It is not unusual for him to follow Grandma's stories as she resurrects their past for my ears only.

Occasionally, Grandpa takes umbrage with something she says and he will scold her, setting her straight if he thinks she is telling me too much. "Mollie," Grandpa grunts, "you shouldn't oughta be a tellin' that malarkey to Shirley. She'll be a feared of it from now on, I'm satisfied."

Grandma's revealing thoughts about courtship and marriage continued to bother me, and doubt followed. Is a never-ending love possible? I wanted my experience with someone to be as sweet and lasting as the prince and Cinderella storybook romance. If Grandma had "kept on a goin'" as she had suggested to me, I would be a nothing … never born.

Did she mean it? I disappoint so easily. Nothingness is scary to contemplate; I wanted rid of that uncomfortable thought—in a hurry!

Her words could be, I needed to believe, the ravings of a worn-out housewife having a bad day. What Grandma probably meant to say is that a man can complicate your life right good, for better and for worse.

There was more. Her dazed look spoke volumes. Grandma's eyes avowed to me that marriage is next to a train wreck in intensity. Her tone was adamant and her expression defiant. I took note, too, of Grandma's dogged, out-of-sorts mood. Why, I wracked my brain for a reason, would she hesitate to let Grandpa walk her home if she had it to do over again? And … how come, I asked myself, she said 'I shoulda kept on a goin'?

It is a dismal thought, to picture this beautiful earth without Mom and the rest of us in it. The world would not miss us. Emptiness filled my shoes as it sank in that, maybe, love isn't always there—all the time. My romantic illusions of a perfect marriage was shattered, but the dream closest to my heart was untouched. I was convinced that in my destiny there was going to come one great love.

A couple of years later, while I was daydreaming in the front room, Grandma called out to me from the kitchen. "Shirley, come in here by me. I've got something for you to look at, honey." There is a suspenseful timbre in her voice.

Still wrapped in never-never fantasy, as only a childhood imagination will allow, I sprang out of my chair. Then leaping astride my valiant steed, Black Beauty's double, I urged him onward with a serious, "giddy-up!" Atop the back of a daydream, I galloped off to the kitchen and reined up my pretend pony beside Grandma.

She is bending over an open trunk and fishing around for something inside it. The trunk looks out of place. Normally, it stays put in the farthest corner of her bedroom.

Grandma straightened up, holding a mysterious bundle in her hands. "I saved your mama's dress in my trunk. Your mama wore it to her eighth-grade graduation." I watched her carefully unfold it.

"Really?" I asked. "You saved it all these years?" I marveled at the care Grandma had taken to preserve the dress. A child's sense of time is far different from an adult's. Mama's graduation seemed like a million years ago.

Grandma spread out the wonderful dress across the trunk lid for me to examine more closely. "We'll take a look at it," she offered. Knowing the dress is old and delicate, I handled the gauzy material gingerly. It felt as though I was touching a treasured family heirloom. Then Grandma put it into my hands.

I hugged Mama's fancy white dress against me in a slow wistful embrace. Someday, I would try it on ... someday.

The musty odor from old wallpaper that lined the inside of Grandma's trunk, mixed with the scent of mothballs, and the strange smell clung to Mama's dress.

Near the bottom of the trunk and among other sentimental valuables, Grandma had stored a calendar. Its tattered pages were curled and aged to a dingy yellow-brown. If a wish could make it so, I would want to know the span of happiness and sorrows it masked.

Back when Mollie and Alf had become sweethearts, in the sparking generation, the trunk would have been fashionably new. The ancient calendar shut up inside it, made those days seem more real to me. Except for the few, candid glimpses that Grandma showed to me, on that day in 1948, the course of hers and Grandpa's courtship was a past century-old mystery known only to a battered trunk and a spent calendar.

But using what I do know, so well, about Grandma, I try to think and speak in a manner that I suppose she would have done—especially in matters of the heart.

The name given to the woman who Grandma chored for at the boarding house slips my mind, but I choose to call her Hannah because of its soft, breathless sound.

The outstanding facts that portray Grandma's youthful experiences are accurate. Near her fourteenth birthday, she did hire out and room, under these conditions, at a boarding house, and she spoke at length of her duties there.

Throughout many cold and gloomy winters, Grandma's stories were a ray of sunlight piercing the mundane. Her fascinating memoir shortened uneventful evenings for me.

The grove was an actual meeting place for worship. I was immersed in her recollections of it, dying to belong, when she described to me the grand times she and her chums had while frolicking along on their walk to the grove.

Everything about the sparking discussion I had with Grandma and her chance meeting with Alf, at the grove, is true; things of romance never leave my brain. Much of Grandma's conversations with me, amount to her exact words—out of an old woman's mouth and branded directly onto a young Shirley's thoughts.

We always had a home, not just a place to stay, with Grandma and Grandpa. I am close to them both but especially to my grandma. She tried to polish me up—some—with good manners. To keep me safe, she recited dire safety warnings: "I once knew a boy—poor, poor lad, whose eye got put out by a long stick, during sword play."

Because I became mindful of the danger, all the merriment drained out of our game, and I lay down my trusty stick sword, ever after.

"Walk, never run, carrying scissors," and "hand someone else the knife, handle first. Turn pot handles in on the cook stove. You might save some little child from a scalding." And the lesson I remember best: "Shirley, honey, now when you cut the cake, always give your playmate the largest slice."

Manners certainly didn't make any sense to me.

CHAPTER 15

— ❧ —

The Dance

STANDING IN THE shadows of twilight, I recognized the sound of our back screen door stretching open. The uncoiling steel spring made a high-pitched "twang," announcing her departure. Though my back is turned to the house, I know that it is Grandma by the sound of her footsteps.

Her tottering along bears watching. Grandma's wrinkled arms strain to lift the heavy skillet, and her lax muscles grow taut from the effort. When she reaches the end of the porch, she stops and cautiously braces the cast iron against her thigh to balance its weight.

Progressing on visibly shaking knees, her left hand still clutching a firm corner post, Grandma maneuvers the last step down and off the porch.

As she totters ahead, the crusted skillet bottom rubs back and forth across the front of her bib apron, and it leaves a blackened tattoo streak just below her bosom.

I fell in step beside her, and we finished the few short paces together, walking to the edge of the property where Grandma parceled out the day's table scraps between the dog and cats.

I will never forget these kind and striking things about her. I have been blessed—to remember and to visualize her as she was then. It is comforting to think of Grandma Mollie as a sort of little, old angelic ghost who always knows when my thoughts turn to her.

Grandma remains alive in my heart. At our usual haunts, in the place where I grew up, memories of what used to be, endure. The stray pets that she was kind to, linger in my mind. I remember we had a couple of regulars—mopey, long-eared town hounds that showed up every evening, and Grandma took a liking to them. She would talk to and feed them right alongside our pets. Besides these, there was Tom. He was all hers. Tom sidled right up to her, winding himself around Grandma's ballooning ankles, and making Grandpa declare, "That cat will be the death of you in a fall."

Recalling Grandma's lack of wages, when she worked as a hired girl, reminds me of an interesting monetary discussion that arose between some old-timers.

Days gone by were being resurrected on the occasion of Mollie and Alf's 50th wedding anniversary. Aunts, uncles, and shirttail cousins had gathered at the home place. Our house figuratively bulged at its seams with well-wishing friends and relatives. Everyone had a story to share.

The convergence of dozens of voices, all speaking at once, created an incoherent buzz that sounded not unlike passing beneath a bee's nest.

Intermittently, Aunt Alvera's jolly chuckle rises above the ceaseless drone of humming confusion. I can't untangle any one person's words from the host of muddled voices in the background. I suspect these relatives have learned a foreign language. My spinning head sought refuge in the great outdoors.

I waded through the maze of chatterers until I reached the kitchen. There a large helping of unclaimed dessert caught my notice, and I proceeded to scrape the last bit of Grandma's bread pudding out of the baking pan and onto a saucer. Grandma's manner rules did not seem to apply here.

A sudden urge to dance sent a surge of uncontainable energy coursing through me, racing to the very tips of my clueless toes. My feet began moving spontaneously, to a silent rhythm playing inside my head. I opened the screen door and danced out onto the back porch—still balancing my dessert on one confident palm.

The dream of a great theatrical ability whipped my skinny legs through their best paces. I leaped high in the air, clicking my heels together. A split second later, my feet came back down to "tap-tap-tap" the wood of the porch. For my breath-taking finale, I gave the screen door a wild fling, twirled my talented self around, bent over and let the door spring back and whack me on my fanny. "Not bad," I congratulated myself as I shuffled off.

I segregated myself to a spot along the concrete well curb where I could savor Grandma's specialty, without any distractions. The spicy aroma of warm cinnamon wafted off the bread pudding, hinting at its goodness. A hungry Eve, I decided, would likely have passed over the notorious Garden of Eden apples in favor of Grandma's bread pudding.

Across the years, she reaches out to me. I associate this classic dessert with Grandma. A vision of her timeless face comes to mind with every dish of bread pudding set before me.

Among the titters of feminine laughter spilling out from inside the kitchen, Aunt Alvera's chuckling is easily distinguished from the others'. Their words, though, are barely audible through the clatter of dishwashing.

The white-haired gentlemen left the drudgery of clean up to the ladies, and they began to file outside. On a rustic porch bench, set below our kitchen window, this wizened group congregated to socialize.

They rested in the shade, leaning against the house and forming a row of slumping, old men backs. The crowded bench, which ran the full length of the porch, was across from the well curb where I sat finishing the last crumbs of bread pudding.

The old-timers began to refresh one another's memory with this and that from their early days.

Pushing my empty plate aside, I turned to Grandpa. "Can I borrow your pocketknife?"

Grandpa wavered, and finally grunted at me, "I'll allow you can."

His hand dug into his side pocket and withdrew the knife. After opening out the blade, he offered it to me, handle first, and with the usual stipulations: "Don't move from off the well curb, and don't cha forget where you got it from. I want cha to put it right back in my hand when you're done a use'n' it."

Being considered trustworthy enough to handle Grandpa's own knife was important to me. Had I seen anyone else fooling around with it, I would have felt let down. Maybe none of the others wanted to whittle. Besides, Grandpa realized how badly I wanted to learn carving. I was still searching for a talent. (I would take anything.) In any event, he watched over me, to avoid a bloodletting. I still had a beginner's natural inclination to hack away at the wood and toward my hand, when Grandpa's attention wavered.

In my mind, I could do it; I could carve a whistle just like the one Grandpa once made. But my untrained hands only sloughed off some shavings. The end result was a smaller version of the same stick I began with. As the wood chips flew, I listened to the spark of rivalry flare up between these old guys. Each one tried to outdo the last fellow's hardship account.

My attention was drawn to one of the gentlemen: a short, stocky fellow wearing prominent round eyeglasses that rode the end of his nose. He strongly resembles Grandpa's obnoxious impression of a hoot owl.

The 9 p.m. town whistle never failed to set Grandpa off in that direction. The old man lived to tease. He used to make circles using the tips of his finger and thumbs. Then he would squint out at us through the finger holes, chiming in with the wailing sound of the whistle and laughing like a buffoon. "You hear the hoot owl?" he would bellow, "Hoot! Hoot!"

The man with the eyeglasses remarked on the poverty-stricken circumstances of old: "My kinfolk was up again' it," he declared. "They slaved for pennies—an intolerable fifteen cents a day. Can you imagine that … by today's standards? and they was damned glad to get it."

"Yessiree Bob!" A new voice added weight to the owlish characters' opinion. "These Johnny-come-lately, the boys coming on nowadays, are used to soft living. Why, they're a bunch of sissies."

Grandpa chuckled at that. The indignant man continued dressing down spoiled youths. "They don't know what a hard day's work is about, and they'll never amount to nothin' because they've had everything handed to 'em."

Grandpa clacked his tongue against the roof of his mouth. He looked for the worst to happen, and he told his peers, "I got an idea we could sack up and go to the poor farm, yet."

Grandpa's threat loomed over my head. Where is the poor farm? I wondered. Later, I put the question to Grandma.

"Why, Shirley!" She declared, "Where in the land of Goshen did you hear that from?"

"Grandpa talked about it."

Grandma explained what could happen to people who were caught up in the tentacles of poverty: "What was called the poor farm really was a government place that took in pitiable folks—old people and desperate other ones—all forsaken, penniless and hungry. The country couldn't leave poor souls without a place to lay their heads or nobody to turn to—starving, you know. And the Great Depression wiped out farms that had been worked by families for generations."

That was not a pretty picture. I said, "I wouldn't want to go to the poor farm."

Grandma assured me, "There's not such a place, anymore. The government replaced it with WPA and old age assistant programs."

WPA ... where had I heard those initials? My friend Bobby had once gloated, "Our outhouse is tons better than you guys' because our outhouse is WPA built."

WPA, of course, stands for the Works Progress Administration. Sonny filled in the blanks for me—how they are bolted to concrete. "They can't be tipped over on Ha'wo'ween night."

CHAPTER 16

Loves Me—Loves Me Not

GRANDMA MOLLIE DOES not waste much of her dwindling energy taking sides in family disputes or sorting through each one's faults. I was attempting to rake Grandma Pella over the coals because her stinginess hurt my feelings and left me thinking that she didn't want us there.

"It's not like your Grandma Pella boxed your ears," Grandma Mollie pointed out. She brushed my grievances aside with an understanding nod and a dismissing piece of useless advice: "Don't take any of it to heart."

Well, the heart of the matter is that I was more bruised on the inside, where is doesn't show, by the toast, jelly, and toilet paper episode.

Out of the blue, Dad had invited Nancy, Carol, and me to a sleepover at the farm. I'm not sure that Grandma Pella was expecting us. Time had put a gulf between us.

The hour was late when we arrived, and Grandma Pella was already in bed. As we prepared to turn in, Dad cautioned us, "Be quiet as little mice."

He switched off the overhead bulb, and the room was bathed in moonlight. Immediately after their heads hit the pillow, Nancy and Carol began to breathe deeply and regularly. I have to unwind before sleep will come. I winced and complained to my drowsy sisters, "By morning, my eyes will look like two burned out holes in the sheet."

Sometime later, Grandma Pella appeared in the doorway and looked in on us. She knew I could see her, too. I couldn't tell, by her just standing there, if she was glad to see us. Nervously, I made the first overture.

I guess people don't smile or wave back, either, in the middle of the night. Grandma moved away, as silently as she had appeared, without acknowledging my presence.

The rest of the night passed quickly. In the morning, Dad was in good humor, and everything was all right while he remained nearby. He left the three of us in the kitchen with the makings of breakfast: bread, butter, jelly, and the toaster. Then, the nitpicking began.

Grandma Pella and Dad would have passed each other. The sound of house shoes dragging across the floor from the next room, preceded her. Grandma approached us and stood beside the table. We weren't prepared when she issued her rules for making toast. "Take one or the other. Don't use my butter—and—the jelly. You don't need both. That's wasting."

Her face was straight; she wasn't kidding. That knocked my socks off. I was too "got" to think of a reply.

Nancy humored her. "Oh, well, all right Grandma, okay." Grandma turned and left us then. I whispered to Nancy, "What happened to hello, and I'm glad to see you? You know where I wish she had that jelly stuck?"

At that moment, Dad entered the kitchen again. He was still acting pretty chipper. "Hey Snookums, put some jelly on that toast!" He urged Nancy, pushing the jar toward our slices of bread.

It cuts to the quick to admit it, but I wanted to get back at Grandma for hurting my feelings. I was ticked off because I thought that Grandma cared more for the jar of jelly, than for us. I repeated her instructions to Dad, "Grandma said we could not have the jelly. She told us, 'Use one or the other. Don't take both butter and jelly. That's wasting.'"

"Put some jelly on that toast!" Dad scowled in the general direction that Grandma house-slippered off in. I saw her stiffen, but Dad's angry look rolled right off her back.

I stayed out of Grandma's way by an emotional arm's length. Just the same, when Dad set out to do some outside chores, she struck again.

This time she confronted us, clutching a roll of toilet tissue. "Don't waste the paper," Grandma instructed as she unrolled a strip of it just a few inches long. "Don't use any more than this much. You fold it over," she demonstrated by doubling it once in half. "Use it and then fold again and use it again."

"Yes, all right," Nancy said. And she promised we would be careful not to take too much toilet paper. I was so mad I saw stars!

After Grandma Pella was duly satisfied that there wasn't any wasting going on, in so far as it was practical without following us around, she left us and went back to whatever it is that stingy old women do.

I said some rather bratty things about her to Nancy. "Oh, Shirley, she's old," Nancy said, offering excuses for Grandma and taking the winds of vengeance out of my sails. "Don't pay any attention to her ol' malarkey."

"She hasn't seen us in years," I said and let out a slow, defeated breath. "And toilet paper is more important to her than we are."

Grandma had put us in our place, whether she meant to or not. She picked at us, and our opportunity to bond with her for that day, at least, was wasted because of it.

Carol seemed unaware of the tension in the room. What's behind a 7-year-old's silent gaze is anybody's guess. Inquisitive blue eyes question me as if to say her usual, "What's-a-wrong?" Then her interest wanes, and with a jaunty skip, our carefree little sister resumes circling the kitchen table and humming to herself.

By now, I am less mad, and I begin to feel guilty about what I said. It bothers me that Nancy is taking Grandma's peculiarities a lot better than I am, and thinking about the jelly-saving and tissue-folding ordeal leaves me conscience-stricken and sorry about the words my "evil twin" has spoken. I should feel bad, I admonished myself, because I was wrong to not use patience with Grandma.

Patience is not easy to keep when disappointment comes knocking. God's answer to my dilemma is not usually instantaneous, and very often not even one I would expect. I ask anyway.

In my early teens, Dad came back into our lives. It was always my hope to insert him back into our mother's life, as well. Her current marriage was certainly a stumbling block to it.

Dad tried his best to make up for the unity that we had missed while we were growing up, and I began to see my father in a different light. After he found himself alone, the weight of the world came crashing down on his shoulders. Although I continued to hope that Mom and Dad would reunite, I could not make it happen; that door closed a long time ago. I happened to be in the kitchen on the day when it slammed shut.

Further down the road, a change had come over this lonely man, this stranger who is my father, a change built from the sorrow of a lost love. Dad carried a timeworn picture of our mom inside his wallet until the day he died.

I don't know the answers; I just have the questions and a photo. When these two meet again, in Heaven, God surely has his work cut out for Him.

Self-assurance is just beyond my reach. I must admit that I crash under duress. When trouble confronts me, my first impulse is to back away. An urgent sense of—I have to get out of here—is a familiar one that ends in a cloud of dust. Shyness is a trait I was born with; it is not one that I would choose.

My lack of confidence is balanced by an abundance of greater blessings. There is love all around us. I can share my every uncensored thought with the man I love and our children. I could not ask for friends that are more loyal.

My daughter/friend Dawn once found my cloud-of-dust response to social anxiety amusing. In a lighthearted manner, she asked, "Get out of where? your body?"

"Yes, exactly," I admitted, feeling free to laugh with her at my insecurities. Laughter makes any burden feel lighter. If I have a hidden thought, though I bury it deep, Dawn will uncover it. Sometimes I think that this one can read my mind, and that makes me smile.

The next do-over of my childhood takes me to the late 1940s again. Nothing compares to the soul searching that accompanies a family divided. I had assumed the discord between my parents could be laid at Dad's feet. He was very authoritative in his prime.

Hard to please, comes to mind. This is one of the reasons that I never considered choosing (as Mary had for a short stay) to live out on the farm with Dad. I could not fathom being shuttled to Grandma Pella's doorstep. I would have wilted there.

"Loves me—loves me not?" When we were youngsters, we played this simple guessing game. The answer to the question at hand, comes when the last daisy petal falls to the ground. It is all about belonging. You know when you are someone's favorite person. You know even better when you are not.

Places in the heart of loved ones are ever changing. Some hearts can switch loves as carelessly as they change socks.

I have been among those loved best, too, and I savored it. Either I was a favorite or someone very wise made each of her grandchildren feel that way.

Conversely, our paternal grandmother's ways had seemed rigid to me. All this happened before I discovered that perfection is a myth. Flawless families are not just around the corner, nor are they found in the house next door.

After my small world expanded, I learned that Grandma Pella was really not so unusual. What her manner actually showed is an example of how ordinary people generally relate on any given day.

The closer we are to someone, the more we look at them through eyes of love, glossing over their faults and personality quirks. It is worth remembering that we may be judged by the same touchstone that we use to measure others.

That which we think to be true becomes our reality. Look on every day as a gift, wrapped in happiness. And expect to open it.

Today is the day when I awaken to a new dawn. Before me is a time and tide to fill with trust and love. Let nothing less than these ideals spill over on my tomorrow.

I begin with the story of Pella, as Dad related it to me. First, he explained her background.

"Mom was treated badly in her formative years. Her own family worked her like a servant girl, from sunup to sundown. As soon as she could, Mom fled her home."

"How did you know all of this?" I asked, wary of his motives and wondering if Dad was making excuses for her aloofness toward us. "Did she run away from home?"

"No. She was of age," he admitted, "Otherwise they would have made her stay. Mom was free help. Anyway, she struck out on her own. I had opportunity to get acquainted with cousins of hers from St. Louis. Shortly after leaving home, Mom went to work in a dime-a-dance place where men, mostly service men could purchase tokens to dance with her."

I found the description of Grandma's past very intriguing.

"It was there, in the dance hall, that Mom met Dad." I visualized my grandfather: the handsome 6-foot-plus blond stranger, longingly awaiting his turn to waltz with Pella. My Grandpa August paid for the chance to woo her. By the time he had used up all of his tokens, August was in love.

In those days, Pella was a beautiful young girl who might have stolen any man's heart. I've seen the proof of this in photos. So small and delicate was she that you could almost have mistaken her for a princess doll. What an odd mismatch this couple seemed to be. Pella looked more childlike, than bride, beside her lanky groom. Small wonder then, that August is seated in their wedding photo, while Pella stands at the side of his chair.

August passed away in 1948, and a few years later their only daughter, Helen, succumbed to breast cancer. Dad and Uncle Bud continued to live on the farm with Grandma Pella for the rest of her days. Dad never remarried.

The last time I saw Grandma Pella, she was a bare wisp of a woman. She constantly wore a pair of men's brown cotton work gloves to warm her arthritic hands.

In my sixteenth year, Grandma Pella seemed more tolerant of me than when I was a scrawny kid who used to get underfoot. I wish I had known her better, and I wish we had been closer.

From beginning to end, our heavenly Father sees through us. Guided by his invisible hand, certain emphatic days of my past are there for a purpose. I am not sure that I would want to change or swap these lessons learned the hard way, for a childhood lived on easy street.

CHAPTER 17

— ✆ —

Hair Trigger Temper

FLORENCE (ONE OF Mom's older sisters) was born a twin. The second child, a brother named Charles, had not survived.

We often called her "good ol' Aunt Florence" because she had a heart of gold. Jesus was her constant companion, and every decision Florence made was dependent on "the Lord willing."

She and Uncle Rudolph lived in an apartment in Canton, Ohio. They made frequent bus trips back home to visit Grandma and Grandpa, and between visits, Aunt Florence mailed clothing for whomever they happened to fit. These new clothes were a lifesaver to Nancy, who was down to near rags before these arrived. Everything that Aunt Florence sent us swallowed me; I was a scrawny kid.

Apart from the spiritual, Florence the woman, was a puzzling contradiction; she had a thorny side to her disposition. "Good ol' Florence" possessed a hair trigger temper. The sweetness could turn to vinegar without warning, and then there was hell to pay. It was like she had two heads. The head with the halo would send us to the restaurant for a pint of ice cream, but the other one made us keep out of her way.

Uncle Rudolph was a retired watchmaker. He was twenty-nine years older than Aunt Florence and much smaller in stature. She would easily have made two of him. He was a kind and quiet man with a gentleness about him that made it easy for me to like him.

They were complete opposites. When Aunt Florence was unhappy, the house knew it. Linens popped and cracked in her hands as she shook and folded them, dishes clinked and pots rattled.

War clouds were gathering on the horizon, inside the kitchen. Carol and I made ourselves scarce, and we huddled next to Grandma who was already in the front room.

"Law! I wish that woman would quit her banging and clanging in there," Grandma said. "All that racket is giving me a headache."

"What's-a-wrong with her?" The words were classic Carol, but her face held a solemn expression.

"Your Aunt Florence has got her hind end up about something," Grandma said. "It's hard t' tell what she's mad at. Stay out of the kitchen. She'll settle down directly and go to her room. You and Shirley stay quiet here by me."

I was uneasy around a riled-up Aunt Florence because I thought she might get after us, and so I gave her a wide berth, just in case.

Six months later, she and Uncle Rudolph came for another visit. Well, I had never in my life heard someone raise such a ruckus. She sure was carrying on. It sounded as though her tongue was loose on both ends.

I didn't see it coming.

The little guy, Uncle Rudolph, got the heck out of there, and Grandpa lunged toward Aunt Florence. He rushed to intervene while I just stood there, big eyed and open mouthed. It happened so quickly that I was stunned.

I figured out that Grandpa was the only person who could stand up to one of Florence's tantrums, but even he couldn't always stop her. She didn't give you any warning.

"Now, Florence, you cut that out and behave yourself! Leave well enough alone now, ya hear? You set that down. Right now! Do ya hear me?"

She was poised to begin throwing dishes.

"Listen to me now!" Grandpa's voice boomed. "You ain't a throwin' things here. You ain't a gonna do it!"

Aunt Florence was unyielding in her rage. She was rattling off incoherently, a mile a minute, at the same instant that Grandpa was trying to calm her.

Grandpa had moved around the kitchen table to confront his daughter, directly. "I'm a telling' ya t' stop that! And go on. You go on now! Go in your room! Go on now, I'm done with it. You'd a heap better listen t' me."

I was frozen, as I watched the whole confrontation. Aunt Florence had wedged herself between the table and the back kitchen wall. Heedless to Grandpa's words, she began to wail there, uncontrollably. He shouted in her face, "Shut up! Shut up! I ain't a listenin' to it n'more."

Disregarding Grandpa's pleadings, Aunt Florence flung the dish she had been clutching in her hand. She sobbed, inconsolably, like her heart was broken. Her hands went flailing up, and she began tugging at her hair: her beautiful, long, wavy hair.

She wouldn't stop herself because she couldn't. I had panic clawing at my throat, and I couldn't bear to see anymore. Poor Grandpa: he was stuck with a hysterical woman on his hands. As I left the kitchen, I heard the stinging slap behind me.

"There now," Grandpa groaned. "You wuddn't gonna be satisfied till I smacked ya." Disappointment filled the old man's haggard voice.

It was over, as quickly as it had begun. The reluctant slap had brought Aunt Florence to her senses, and she stormed off to her and Rudolph's bedroom.

From that day forward, I had a greater appreciation of Grandpa's difficult role in the family. To be a man is not as easy a thing as I had thought. It is even more phenomenal when I consider that Grandpa was nearly 80 years old on the evening when Aunt Florence went to pieces. She was in her late 50s. I never knew what it was that had set her off on a tirade. I was in the room when she exploded without any apparent reason.

Aunt Florence dearly loved Uncle Rudolph. She meant well by him; I am sure of it. They never had children, but to my dismay, she treated him more like a young son, than a husband.

She was bossy. "Come on Rudolph; it's our bedtime." He followed her like an obedient puppy. Promptly at 8 p.m., Aunt Florence would tell him, "Wash your face and hands, now." It irked me to see him defer to her commands. I hoped he would revolt and get a life of his own. It might have been too late for that, though. He was older than Grandpa.

Grandma didn't approve of the high-handed way her daughter controlled Rudolph, either, and she said so as gently as possible. "Now, Florence," Grandma suggested, "maybe Rudolph isn't sleepy yet."

Florence was not persuaded. She knew very well "thank you," what was best for Rudolph. Subject closed. I heard the water pour from the pitcher and splash against the tin wash pan. Soon afterwards, he followed her straight into their room, and they sat together on the edge of the bed. Rudolph opened his Bible and read, in silence, for the exact interval that Florence read hers.

We had to pass by their bedroom to get to the kitchen, and the door was left wide open until they retired for the night.

After they finished the Bible verses, they laid the Bibles back on the nightstand and knelt beside the bed in prayer.

Every time Florence prayed, so did Rudolph pray. I never understood whether he was talking to God or pleasing his wife, or both. Throughout the day, it was not uncommon to enter the kitchen and interrupt the both of them kneeling on the floor, in front of a chair, in quiet prayer. At these times, I made a quick exit.

Prayer seemed such a personal thing that I could not have shared mine easily, and I felt somewhat like an intruder in theirs.

Uncle Rudolph truly was a gentle soul, who it seemed to me, was drowning in a sea of religion. I thought he needed saved from that fate. He was being swept along by a current not of his choosing. He just never said.

Their lives together ended on a sad note. Aunt Florence flew into a rage at their landlord when he attempted to raise the rent. A piece of china, she lobbed at his head, met its mark. He beat a hasty retreat and called authorities.

They came and took Aunt Florence away. She was admitted to a hospital. Suddenly, Uncle Rudolph was his own boss. A few weeks later, the hospital was set to release Aunt Florence to Uncle Rudolph. After all, she wasn't a mental case; she was just doggone mad at the landlord! By this time, however, Uncle Rudolph had a changed life.

"I'm sorry about it," he apologized, "but I can't handle Florence, anymore. I'm not well, either."

Rudolph, the watchmaker, died from heart failure before the year was out. He passed alone, in the apartment that he and Florence had shared.

Florence finished out her days at an assisted living home. She loved Rudolph to the very end of her life. Often times, she expressed a wish to visit his grave. I doubt that she was able to do that.

I soon figured out that disobedience, or disrespect, can include almost anything that the more fortunate person who wields the power decides. Consequently, both concepts sometimes lose their true meaning, altogether.

Abuse of power surpasses even the "green eyed monster" in relationship failures. To obey is not big on my list of how man and woman best relate to one another.

CHAPTER 18

꩜

Measured Footsteps
Among the Sleeping

THE SUMMER SUN hung directly overhead. It was a day meant for an empty-handed kid to embrace. I lay with my back to the soft earth, marveling at the openness above me. Otherworldly beings, formed of transparent clouds, roamed the heavens before my eyes.

After a while, the changing skies became old hat to me. My attention strayed from the wonders of the universe, and my bare feet itched to get moving once more through fresh territory.

It had been a productive morning for this little mover and shaker. This land was mine—from the heat softened tar road just outside our door, to the back alley that separated our domain from public school property.

Every tree with a low hanging branch had been scaled; each flowering shrub and tall clump of scraggly weeds had been sifted through or trampled underfoot.

Only once during my backyard exploration, did I court danger; after venturing out on a slender limb that couldn't include me, I became momentarily stranded there. The drooping branch popped and cracked under my weight, threatening bodily harm. Hurriedly, I calculated the risk of turning back, shook off caution, inched forward, and rode the bough down to the ground.

Next, I became mesmerized by the action of a black and yellow garden spider. Because of its color, we mistakenly called these "banana spiders." I watched it from as close-up as I dared. It watched me, too, as it spun a web to incorporate another bush into its sinister trap. The inch-long neon monster had already wound up and killed several other bulgy eyed victims. The sight of their gristly remains left me questioning the motives of nature.

Mother Earth can be so casual and conscienceless toward her inhabitants. I would not want to be a fly.

The remainder of my roving is spent trailing after delicate butterflies as they flutter about in Grandma's garden, tasting her flowers. With outstretched arms, I mimicked their erratic flight. We waltzed together, dipping and rising, through towering stalks of golden rod—until an uninvited dance partner interrupted us by buzzing around my head.

Dodging and twisting in fear and dread of the kamikaze bumblebee getting tangled in my hair, my arm wings dropped to my sides.

Leaving the pest behind me, in the garden plot, I romped nearer to the house and came to a standstill in ankle deep clover. There, something soft and fluffy began to tickle me. A dainty butterfly (I later learned these are called Aaron's Skippers.) had mistaken my toes for a flower. Its light-as-a-feather kisses to my ankles made me giggle.

Time was wasting, and I was pressed to move on—the bumblebee had taken over my play land, and fear of bees prevented my fighting for it.

Naively, I began to squander my childhood days. If only I were older, I mused. In these young and restless days, I am convinced that the sixteenth birthday is the one when everything changes for the better. Freedom meant turning 16. I was sure of it.

Midst the sweet scent of blossoming clover and the kisses of a ground hugging skipper butterfly, I sprawled out on the ground, dreaming of the future and plotting the next move.

In the meantime, turning up the hem of my skirt to fashion a pouch, I set about gathering up the long stemmed purple clover. Tying the ends together and forming a simple lei was something I often did. One slender stem at a time, the garland lengthened.

Before I could try it on and test it for size, I heard Grandma call. "Shirley ... aw, Shirley."

Intent on tying love knots for an undeserving Bobby, I hadn't heard her approach.

Another loop joined my string of blossoms and I answered her. "I'm over here, Grandma." Squinting through rays of dazzling sunlight, I saw her coming.

My head was filled with lofty expectations of a gallant knight who would rescue this fair-haired maiden from obscurity. Somewhere, out there, is my soul mate: the one who will light a fire inside this blue-eyed child, and make love burn forever.

Grandma made her way to the patch of ground where I sat day-dreaming. Lowering my gaze against the bright sun, I found myself conversing with swollen ankles that are stuffed into a pair of dowdy, black lace-up shoes.

"Come take a walk with Grandma, will you, Shirley honey?" the gentle voice above the antique shoes inquired.

"Are you going right now?" I asked.

Grandma nodded. "I'm ready to go, honey."

"I'll go with you, Grandma," I assured her. The purposeful neck-lace, looped with romance in mind, dropped carelessly from my fingers. Showing little regard for my handiwork, I scrambled to my feet, abandoning the clover chain on the ground. All thought of romance vanished. The unfinished lei no longer mattered. My itch to roam was about to be scratched.

Leaving behind the phantom clouds, I bid farewell to butterflies, spiders, bees, blossoming clover, and one imagined gallant knight.

About that time, Grandma's pampered escort, old Tom, sidled up to her, twining himself underfoot as usual. The alley cat wove back and forth between Grandma's feet to coax some affection from her.

Tom crisscrossed the front of her legs, rubbing both sides of his silken coat against Grandma's shins. Grandma pays Tom no mind. Her hands don't budge, to appease him, from the handle of the utility wagon that trails at her heels.

It is not a plaything, and I am puzzled to find the seldom-used wagon out of its place inside the shed. The red paint is scratched and chipped, and the rustic wagon has a few dents. All in all, Grandma's old work horse has seen better days, yet it keeps on rolling when she needs it for a chore.

Grandma wheeled the creaking and groaning wagon in front of me, while I traveled in its tracks to safeguard its contents. The wagon bed is loaded to the rim with stacks of clean laundry.

"We can commence back to home on the short cut through the woods," Grandma promised, "after we leave off the wash." She indicated the things in the wagon. "We'll be back, directly—before your grandpa can worry his ol' head off about us." "Directly" is an old woman's measure of time that could last ten minutes or all afternoon.

My happy feet began to prance at the prospect of an adventure. Without any doubt, my most enchanting hours have been spent while tramping in the woods. These hungry eyes are expecting to devour the most peculiar of sights.

I fantasize a march of creatures, already in progress there. Beneath the rustling leaves, where field mice play, a timid rabbit is betrayed. In the blink of an eye, bushy tailed squirrels race from trunk to tree top.

Colorful birds chirp to themselves, and I hear the flutter of wings overhead. It is fascinating to watch a centipede, with only two eyes, gadding about on one hundred legs.

There is an air of excitement in the woods, as well as an element of danger. Step carefully, now, on the forest floor; a snake slithering off the beaten path is easily camouflaged.

Taking on a more serious manner, Grandma said, "I want to go by the cemetery, before dusk. It's in the woods, too, you know," she added. "Shirley, I need you to help me down the hill to visit my mama's grave. My old legs won't let me, anymore. I've already raked up my arm on the edge of the cook stove, a staggerin' around." Indeed, her skin is as thin as tissue wrap.

"Shirley, honey, you'll help Grandma, won't you?"

To be needed motivates me. But I was unprepared when she asked me the scary thing. "Ummm ... yeah. I will, Grandma." Nobody ever says no to Grandma. I don't exactly know why. Maybe it's the gentle way she asks. There's just one problem with my promise to help: I'm afraid to go to the cemetery because I won't know where to step.

Nancy talked about treading lightly there. "Never walk on some-one's grave. It shows disrespect for the dead," she cautioned, and then she whispered, "something ... bad could happen."

"Aren't the people buried where their names are?" I asked.

"No, Shirley," Nancy said. "It's not that easy. Some of the grave stones are old. The names get worn off. And besides, the dead could be on either side. It's real hard to tell the front from the back."

I could not fathom what awful consequence would follow any mis-steps, however I surely wanted to avoid it. I carried that resolve with me, as we bid farewell to old Tom. Grandma, I, and one enduring wagon set forth.

I had doubts that I would do the right thing. If past mistakes meant anything, I was in trouble. Suppose, I was testing myself, I can't tell which way the graves are?

Behind us, the town shrank until it resembled a miniature village. An old woman pulling a wagon with a half grown worrying child at her side, turned down the country road.

Our wagon bumped and skidded in several furrowed places. And every so often, the rear wheels slipped into a deep rut, hit bottom, and jostled the load inside the wagon. A small, well placed hand kept everything stable.

While I am not overly superstitious, this graveyard affair sounded riskier than the goofy sidewalk challenge. Even though you know there is no truth to it: "step on a crack—you break your mother's back"—once that silly rhyme got stuck in our heads, we walked carefully, anyway, to avoid sidewalk seams. It was a dumb dare that demanded we take risks.

Nancy's words came back to me. "Never walk on someone's grave." Her warning sounded more sinister than the cracks-in-the-sidewalk concern.

After I had skipped along beside Grandma's slow paced footsteps for about an hour, (My own wanderlust feet did the Zip-a-Dee-Doo-Dah dance step in place every few yards, to stay even with her halting movements.) I began to have some qualms about our impromptu hike. What will I do if Grandma's tired legs give out on her? I could just kick myself for agreeing to tag along and letting this happen.

At the beginning of our trek, the day had not seemed this warm. Then gradually, the traitorous afternoon sun turned on us, and the road became a gray powdery inferno. The dust soaked up the sweltering heat and reflected it back in wave after wave to our faces.

Grandma's hypertension occasionally causes a dizzy spell that she refers to as the "whoosies." But oh Lord, not today! I pleaded fearfully. I watched her move ahead of me in a straight line. Old people overestimate their abilities and endurance. She looked about done-in to me. Underneath the wide brim of her sunbonnet, Grandma's increasingly weary looking face glowed suspiciously crimson. Her breaths were coming with a ragged gasp.

"We can take turns," I suggested to her. "Grandma, let me pull the wagon now. I won't dump it over."

Would she consent? She did, and we switched places.

My all-consuming plan for a wilderness adventure had been ruined by constant worry. Right now, I just wanted to get this fragile old woman home in one piece. Again, I reminded myself, I can't carry

Grandma—at least one of us knows her own limitations—and I won't leave her side.

I was desperate to see another human face. Once we had turned off on the remote road, we had not met another soul.

A decaying barn, with its roof caved in, is the only building we had passed since we left the streets of town. Although my eyes were searching for any sign of life, I hid all that from Grandma. The quiet out here in the middle of nowhere is deafening.

Though the vision beyond my nose is limited, I finally recognized the wavy outline of a chimney, jutting out against the blue horizon. As we drew nearer to the fuzzy image, a house took shape. Over and over, I mouthed, "Please don't let it be an empty shack with all the windows knocked out."

Other houses appeared, slipping by us, one by one, as we continued walking, and I started to unwind. Grandma finally gave in to her tired body. Awkwardly, she eased down beside the road, in the shade of a thicket.

Secretly, I had come close to dissolving in a panic. I'm conscience stricken, too, because I want to go play in the woods—so-so-bad! An inner, accusing voice reminds me: "You should have kept her from doing this. You know she is old. If something happens to her, it will be your fault."

The clouds grew merciful and shut out the sun for the remainder of our walk. Grandma seemed all right, so I began to enjoy the outing. Unhurriedly, she and I basked in nature's ever changing landscape. With every further step, my enlightened Grandma showed something different to me. She pointed out a poison ivy plant and identified several varieties of wild flowers.

It was only after we arrived at our first destination that I had any inkling of how our stroll might look to an outsider. Like a stranger's gloved hand around my throat, shyness softly squeezes. I stayed close to Grandma. As quickly as her old-fashioned shoes lifted, my bare feet filled in her footsteps. I pulled the delivery wagon across the freshly manicured lawn and toward the large frame house.

As we approached the house, a middle-aged woman rushed outside to meet us. She was dressed in trendy attire, and there was an air of sureness about her. The way she hurried toward us, dressed so fine, caused me to think: She must be going somewhere really grand. I'm afraid that Grandma was detaining or even making her late.

I felt every speck of road dust that was clinging to me. The immaculate person, standing in front of Grandma and me, looked as though she had just bobbed-up out of a Saturday night wash tub—squeaky clean, all over. Her sparkling white blouse was tucked, just so, into the full, blue and white pinstripe skirt. And here we were, dusty and sweat streaked—especially me. It's amazing! Scant seconds ago, I looked fine to me.

She was very pretty, this stranger. She seemed disturbed that Grandma had walked this long way, (She must surely have disliked me because of it.) and her voice didn't at all match her pretty face. In fact, she sounded rather irritated. "Mollie!" The woman exclaimed, "Mamma would just be so upset if she knew you'd walked here!" Then just as abruptly, her expression softened, revealing another side and a true concern for Grandma's wellbeing. "My gracious, dear, I told you we would come by for these things. Are you all right?"

Suddenly, I felt wearier than Grandma looked, more tired than I had ever been. My legs went numb and useless. They were two wooden stumps.

I wish we hadn't come here, I thought, I'm awkward as a fish out of water. I was flustered because we came here unexpectedly and because I look like this—all straggly and barefoot. I compared the stranger to me, and I came up short: she was flawless, and I was a ragamuffin. Worse yet, she had misunderstood the true reason for our long walk on this lovely, although deceivingly hot afternoon. Why, Grandma didn't mention the woods or the graveyard to her at all!

Until this second, it never dawned on me that Grandma, when she was younger and more able, had been a washwoman. At the same time, I made another uncomfortable discovery: This perfect woman, who was so anxious over Grandma's welfare, is Grandma's niece.

These days, Grandma's hiring out has trickled down to a smattering of favors between family.

"Come in," the niece invited. "Oh, Aunt Mollie, do come in and visit Mama. Just don't mention that you walked here," she cautioned. "Mama hasn't been well, and I don't want to upset her or worry her in the least. She'll fret about you so, if we tell her that."

I fidgeted, while Grandma and her niece chatted. Silken strands, as soft as baby doll hair, slipped through timid little fingers. I brushed the blond straggles away from my face and out of two extremely naive, blue eyes.

Childish hands pulled and tugged on my outgrown dress. I tried, unsuccessfully, to make it longer than it was. It still—barely—covered the small round bottom beneath. I must have resembled a rather forlorn little clown.

Looking down, my eyes focused on my grimy big toe. As uncomfortable as I already am, the possibility of dragging my dusty shoeless feet across a stranger's clean floor, distressed me more.

Grandma declined to enter the house, to my profound relief, saying, "Shirley and I commenced our stroll after Alf took up his tote sack and went to town. He's apt to set out a seein' about us if we're too tardy. He'll likely worry his old head off if he comes back to the place and finds me gone. We better go along."

I wish Grandma would mention our intention to tramp through the woods or the cemetery. That's our excuse for being way out here. But she doesn't say, and the cat's got my tongue.

"All right, Aunt Mollie, if you're sure you won't come in. Let me get you something to drink. I can make some lemonade," the niece offered.

My gaze locked on the woman's face. I needed to feel reassured that we were welcome here. I watched her every move to that end. I would have liked some lemonade, about now. Why didn't I say so? My lips moved, and I heard myself say "water" just because Grandma had asked for water.

I intimidate myself by assuming that Grandma's niece is an example of perfect womanhood. I watched in awe, the grand lady gather up the clean laundry from our wagon. Moving gingerly and with such feminine grace as I hoped to someday imitate, her flowing skirts retraced their previous course and disappeared inside the house.

When she reappeared, her pretty hands carried tall glasses of chilled water. My mouth still watered for the taste of lemonade.

Grandma handed back our empty glasses, and I saw the white handkerchief, knotted at one corner, pass between them. The subtle exchange is a woman thing and a common practice for us. Unless I have a pocket to tuck her errand money in, Grandma always ties it up—just so.

This knotted hankie marks the end of an era for Grandma. She will never again take in family laundry, nor do our household's wash. Grandpa takes over that weekly chore, and now it is not as much fun.

Oh, occasionally, Grandma comes out onto the back porch to lend a hand. I think she misses the routine. Grandpa is quick to fuss at her, in a show of authority, and he tries to shoo her out of his way and back inside the house.

"I'm a doin' this," Grandpa insists. "Mollie ... now, the doctor done advised you: You're not to be a bendin' over and reachin' n'more. 'Tain't doin' no good to go see a doctor if'n you ain't a gonna listen to him."

Grandma sasses him right back: "I'm not stirrin' around that much. This little dab I'm doin' is not a hurtin' anything."

The slightest discord makes me tense up. I wear my heart on my sleeve.

"You go on now," Grandpa ordered, "and let me take keer uh the wash." Losing patience, he snapped, "I'm a doin' this—old lady. You'd be a good deal better off t' listen t' me."

The aged machine grinds out a dull vibration, as it churns the whopping load of soiled clothes inside the tub. Above the knocking racket of the agitator, Grandpa's grumbling continues, "I work my fingers to the bone … to the bone … pffft! To the bone."

I enjoy washday. It is a weekly break from the usual. And even though my efforts are not appreciated by everyone—"No, Shirley, you're too little: you'll catch your fingers in the rollers." I protest when Nancy says, "Get out of the way!" Mary will often let me run the soggy clothes through the rollers when it comes her turn to wring.

One memory often leads to another. Remembering our washday calls to mind the many sentimental references that Grandma made to her "wash-buddy."

There was nobody like Grandma's friend, Mary Curdy. "Mary had ways of doing things better than anyone else," Grandma said. "It was lively when she was here. Mary had a shortcut for almost anything there was. Her pockets were like an extra pair of hands."

Grandma spoke wistfully about her friend, "I wish I knew whatever happened to her. I've asked around, but nobody seems to know nothing about Mary Curdy. It's been so long now. I'd dearly love to hear from her. I don't even know if she is still living."

Grandma's face revealed a longing to recapture the chumminess they once shared. A faraway look clouded her eyes as she reminisced: "Mary was such a joy to be around. She was always pleasant, always laughing. Mary and I did our wash together. It made the chore more enjoyable, you know."

"I had someone once advise me that I might find her if I had a way to check at the nursing homes. Mary Curdy was a few years older than me," Grandma acknowledged.

Someone else's loss makes you want to cling to what you have—all the more.

Calculating the years, I reasoned to myself, Mary Curdy is dead. But I asked it anyway, "How long ago was all that?"

Grandpa has been paying attention to our conversation, all along. When he answers for Grandma, it is clear to me that he does not like sharing Grandma's mindfulness with any outsiders. I detect a note of envy in his gruff response. "Mary Curdy had a good deal of time to waste a runnin' all over town. Mary had a bad reputation. Tis just as well she left town quick as she did. There was rumors goin' around that Mary Curdy was a fallen woman. There could have been stories spread about you, too, Mollie, because you befriended her."

"Mary was my friend!" Grandma lashed back. "And you can't believe ever' no account thing you hear. Mary was a good soul." Grandma's eyes flashed angrily.

"I'm just a tellin' you what 'twas said ... now, Mollie." Grandpa wanted no part of an argument he could not win.

Mary Curdy and Mollie shared hopes and dreams as much as washday chores. Grandma looked for the best in people. I decided that even a fallen woman deserves a friend. Besides, I secretly admired Mary's somewhat reckless, devil-may-care attitude. (I couldn't even ask for lemonade!)

It is one of those things that confound. Why did her friend leave town, practically overnight, and Mollie never hear from her again?

Some people considered Mary Curdy a loose woman, and they expected her to cause trouble. Affairs happened in the 1800s the same as they do today.

I learned about affairs from a modern-day entanglement that ended badly, and it left me blurring the line between right and wrong.

As far as I knew, the storekeeper husband of the short, chubby woman was good-natured and kindhearted. The man knew darn well that I did not have a nickel to my name. Still, he smiled down at the little barefoot girl who stood next to his magazine rack, and he let her read his comic books—for free.

It happened one day that the man's wife stopped by, unexpectedly, during a lunch break. Chance would have it that she interrupted a romantic interlude between her mate and a willowy acquaintance of theirs.

"Walked in on them!" These stunning words of betrayal spread across town like wildfire.

"Poor, poor woman," Grandma pitied the unfaithful "other woman." "We need to feel sorry for her, Shirley." Then she whispered low, "It's the change of life she's going through, you know."

It is her doing, but it's not her fault. Incredible! The change of life can cause a wed Sunday school teacher to turn to the arms of another man.

I was not convinced. Why does Grandma always think the best of everyone? "Oh … honey," she persuaded me, "I've even knowed it to make a woman lose her mind."

I stored all this change-of-life and affairs information in the back of my mind. In these times, that sort of relationship (love affairs) was pretty well unforgivable. Both families that were involved relocated.

Grandma, her workhorse red wagon, and I were on the roll again. We said goodbye to Grandma's niece and resumed our trek to the cemetery. It nestled, just as Grandma had promised me, in a fine thick woods.

Before we headed to the more distant burial sites of Grandma's family, we visited the grave of her father-in-law, Albert. "Your grandpa's daddy is put away here." She directed me to a grave marker. "He was a horse soldier … belonged to Arkansas Cavalry."

Grandma had a tale to tell. "Albert and his brother, John, found themselves in a sorrowful fix. It was during the Civil War. Lordy, Lord, they came nigh on to being laid out over it. The Union accused the both of them of desertion."

Grandma was watching for my reaction, and she found my shocked expression comical. A broad grin spread across her face when I exclaimed, "Oh, no! Grandma, how did it happen? Did they run away?"

"Both of them were put on trial, and they were convicted of that. I don't know as the Union would have shot or hanged them poor boys, but it came *that* close to happening then and there," she confided. Sentences were carried out quickly in time of war.

Although it is not generally spoken about, I think most everyone worries that they will be afraid to die. I worried about it too ... the crack of gunfire sounded loudly in my mind. The taunting shadow of the gallows darkened my thoughts. How afraid they must have been.

Self-preservation dictated that I didn't want the stain of Albert's cowardice to reflect on me.

"It came by word of mouth," Grandma explained. "The folks told Alf, you know, that Albert and John were like as scared to death. Law... Albert looked so bad. They said his skin sagged in great folds from all the weight he'd lost—his face all drawn. Albert and John, but especially Albert—he suffered the worst... wasted to nothing. He had been a big strappin' boy, and now his clothes were so big on him that they hung off his body. Albert was little more than a skeleton. Him, locked up, pitifully, he almost died there."

"By golly's ... down at the last minute," Grandma revealed, "and just before their executions were to take place, General Sanborn arrived at the post, and directly, he set the boys free. The general believed their story—that they became separated and were cut off by Confederate raiders, as they said all along. And that's what caused the boys to be tardy in getting back to their lines. The year was 1864."

"Prior to the day when he volunteered, Albert had celebrated his fifteenth birthday. He was too young to enlist, but he commenced to fib about his age." Grandma smiled her knowing smile. "The boys will 'story,' you know, Shirley."

Yes, I learned the hard way from Bobby, on the day when he swore to me, "I promise, I won't look."

Great-grandfather Albert's stretching of the truth about his age is not unusual for a boy intent on signing up for the military.

A century later, my brother, Sonny, will follow in Albert's risky footsteps; he, too, will "story" and end up fighting in the bloody battlefields of Korea (1950-1953) when he turns an unsettling 15 years old.

For the love of a rough and tumble fight, headstrong young boys stage backyard war. They play with weapons not meant to be lethal. Our brave little warrior brother digs holes throughout the day. Come sundown, Grandpa Alf, takes his shovel and fills in the danger of collapsing tunnels and leg-breaking trenches.

True to form, Mom had done exactly as Sonny asked; she added her signature to his enlistment papers. By the time the Army learned his true age, Sonny had already turned the legal age of 16.

All of the boyhood days that he spent hovering around a circle drawn in the dirt and taking aim at someone else's marbles, paid off with an exceptional hand to eye coordination. Sonny proved to be a crack shot with his rifle, and his keen eyes earned him an impressive collection of sharp shooting medals.

"After Albert and John were cleared of wrong doing," Grandma said, "they were given their full back pay. Their good name, Shirley, was more valuable than the soldier pay."

The cemetery proved to be a place of great fascination, but the grounds were not well kept. I stayed near to Grandma because there were piles of rubbish that she might have tripped over, strewn where we walked.

Grandma knew exactly where to step, and I followed her attentively to avoid the perils of walking on somebody's grave.

"Lookie yonder. Shirley, do you know what that is?" Grandma asked. I stared down at the curious looking hunk of marble that lay flat against the ground. It was polished to a smooth lustrous surface.

It's too little to be a tombstone, I reasoned. The strange rock looked out of place next to the taller, upright standing pillars. I didn't have a notion of what Grandma meant for me to guess it was, and I gave up easily. "What is it?" I asked.

"This slab of marble used to be a part of my dresser," she told me. Suddenly it came to me, and I realized what Grandma was hinting about. I was remembering that something was missing on her dresser—something about the size of a small oblong food platter or oddly enough… this chunk of marble at our feet.

This makeshift monument marks the gravesites of Mollie and Alf's littlest angels. "We called her Lillian," Grandma murmured softly. "She was stillborn. Our baby, Eulas Mofata, passed on before Lillian came."

How much love can a broken heart still hold? That Grandma can continue to give love, so freely, after losing so much of it is beyond my understanding.

They are buried side by side. The cold marble from the dresser top is all that identifies this hallowed spot as their last resting place.

"Your grandpa carried the stone piece out here and left it so we wouldn't lose the place where we buried them. As time goes by, Shirley, things change: a large oak used to stand nearby the graves, but it came down in a windstorm."

I knew what it was like to search high and low for a dropped coin and be unable to find it. How much worse was this for Grandma? The bitter reality that these two children died when they had barely tasted life, cannot adequately be explained away by what I knew, thus far, about God's workings.

I hadn't thought that something as sacred as a loved one's grave could be lost as easily as a coin that rolls on its edge and out of sight. If looters or ruffians ever vandalized or carried off the dresser stone, these babies' whereabouts would be forgotten. I wished that someday they would have a real gravestone. But I believed that would never happen. There was never any money. We move on ….

Grandma and I waded deeper into the overgrown, more ancient part of the cemetery. There, she cautiously stepped to the brink of a steep ravine. Shoulder to shoulder, we viewed a winding brook that flowed peacefully at the bottom of the hill.

"The graves are washing away," Grandma groaned. "Soon the water will take them. I want to move my mama before it's too late. Do you see, Shirley? Lookie here how the graves are all sunken in. Oh, shame for it. Shame, shame."

"N-no," I stammered. "Grandma, I can't tell where they are."

My thoughts took over. A nightmarish scenario unfolded, and in it, the ruthless waters unearthed caskets. I pictured long wooden crates bobbing and weaving on a swifter current than was actually there below us.

The warm air shifted, abruptly, to the damp coolness of an evening breeze. My hand instinctively encircled Grandma's arm. Although the wind was gentle enough, even a weak, passing gust could topple an old woman who relies on spindly legs to support her.

"Look yonder, over that away!" Grandma pointed to a brushy area along an incline (one that she could never maneuver herself down, I knew).

At this distance, my poor eyesight kept me from detecting the graves that she was so intent on showing to me. I didn't realize it yet, but Grandma's aged, blue eyes could see better than mine. I didn't want to disappoint her, further, so I just pretended to see the graves.

"The graves are washing away," Grandma repeated. "I want to move my mama."

Later on, when we returned home, she spoke about all these things to Grandpa. He scoffed at the very idea.

"They ain't nuthin' left there, Mollie. Your people was all of 'em buried in pine boxes. You'd best leave well enough alone and not be a disturbin' the dead. That creek has been out of its banks a dozen times as I know of. If'n they was anything left in them graves after all these years, I'm satisfied it's gone now."

"Ain't no such thing!" Grandma snapped.

Leaning on sketchy belief in an afterlife brings a measure of solace to me. How else would brief lives make any sense?

Candles in the wind—a time to be born and a time to die that overlaps, is confusing. If it's true that God had the very hairs on their heads counted, then surely, the cemetery was not the end of that wonderful old woman's people … there's more.

Alas. Believing in forever should come easier. In the absence of a better idea, I take heart from the faith that someday everything will even out.

Back at the cemetery, I had felt a closeness to our grandparents' angelic babies. We share likenesses in spirit and in physical traits—sometimes large, sometimes small—that will go on … and on … and on.

The radiant sparkle and bright blue eyes is a hand-me-down from Mollie. Time and again, her family's distinctive nose reappears on a brand new face. Arms that soothe and cradle are somehow familiar … and unfortunately, Alf's fondness for whiskey has been passed to another.

As a child, I looked at myself with a critical eye. To make matters worse, my siblings all agreed, "Shirley takes after Daddy's side. She is going to be tall and thin. Just look at them arms on her."

These hands are his, I sadly decided. They are not the womanly, delicate ones that I wanted. Gangly and sorry handed—that was me.

And eventually, the bony hands that I despised were replaced with my mother's gentle hands, which were someone else's before her. Hands stretch across eternity. Nature charts her own course without regard to time.

CHAPTER 19

Albert

AN OIL PAINTING of Great-Grandfather Albert, dominates the far east wall of the largest bedroom in our grandparents' house. It hangs beside a window that separates two full-size beds on opposite sides of the room. It is a life-size portrait.

After hearing Albert's Civil War "desertion" story, I was fascinated by his image in the portrait. Albert is impeccably groomed. His thick black hair is combed in a center part, forming a wide swoop at each side of his forehead and ending on his temples. Albert has well-proportioned facial features. The nose is good, I decide. Whose honker the middle of your face inherits seems to be a big deal.

I carefully studied the imposing gentleman's face, again. He could have been a "ladies' man," or worse yet—a "dandy!"

My eyes followed the outline of what I considered Albert's one great flaw: his ridiculous looking handlebar mustache. It fanned out from under his nearly perfect nostrils and vined separately upward on either side of his nose, where it coiled in loops and ended in waxed curls that graced his cheek bones.

Grandma joined me in my study of Albert. "Sissy or Romeo?" I good-naturedly kidded. She snickered at that. Furthering the joke, I added, "I'll bet he'd be a handsome devil—without that gosh awful mustache."

"Pffft!" she scoffed. Grandma always made sure I understood that good looks don't really matter. "Pretty is as pretty does," was a familiar refrain.

"Was he stuck on himself?" I was curious about this because the portrait was quite large. How did Grandma feel about a huge, dominating picture of her father-in-law hanging where she saw it every day of her life?

"Albert was a bit vain, I guess you'd say." I could tell she remembered him fondly. I didn't detect even a hint of resentment in her answer. "He was a right fine looking man," she offered, with a mischievous twinkle in her eye. Grandma was enjoying my interest. "He cut quite a figure, Albert did. The women all seemed to gravitate towards him and butter themselves up when he was around, but I never knowed Albert to be a carouser. He was a family man."

Grandma hadn't any harsh words for Albert. I swear that woman hadn't a vindictive or jealous bone in her body. I admired her for that.

CHAPTER 20

Backyard Play

LIFE IMITATES FICTION. We read the book and watched the movie, and Tarzan set the stage for our newest diversion in Bobby's backyard.

After the role of Tarzan went to Bobby, his younger brother, Teddy, was an obvious choice to be Bobby's sidekick, Boy.

A twinge of conscience reminds me that I always used to claim the part of Tarzan's mate, Jane, the only human cast opening left in our jungle play-acting. Long after our days of swinging through tree tops were over, I came to terms with our inequitable casting decisions when Carol said, "You know, I always hated being that darned monkey."

"I didn't know that, Carol. I thought you liked playing the part of Cheetah."

"Well … I liked it a little bit," she explained. "But I wanted to be Jane, too."

Carol could do a convincing portrayal of Tarzan's pet chimp, Cheetah. She could mimic its high-pitched squeal and chatter—and she did the chimpanzee walk in unison with all that racket.

Loping forward, her shoulders hunched "Cheetah Carol" dragged her knuckles across the ground. Intermittently, she'd stop to scratch her armpits, and then resume screeching and howling fluently in ape talk.

Doing monkeyshines is only part of Carol's unique abilities. Her best impression is of the unpredictable fighting rooster that ruled our home ground. Billy, our pet rooster, had two wicked spurs that jutted out threateningly behind his claws. Often in self-defense, we had to swing a broom to get off the back porch.

Did Billy want to sit on my lap and be petted? Or was he going to hold those colorful wings tightly against his "mad self" and charge lickety-split right for me? I never knew which mood that chicken would be in. But when I saw Billy's outstretched neck and wide open beak, it was a clue that he intended to do me harm, and I nervously backtracked.

My little sister sure did a take on Billy. She began throwing herself totally into crowing mode by ratcheting up her neck and gliding it forward and back. Blond wisps of Carol's baby fine hair pursued her darting head. Once she had the head movement going, Carol added the chicken strut: folding her skinny arms under and pumping her sharp elbows. She confounded her audience of skeptics.

In the spur of the moment, or by popular demand, Carol would revel in her comedy act. Anytime one of us would brag of her talents and request, "Do the rooster," she loved it. Our little chick imposter would ruffle up her imaginary feathers, puff out her chest, and begin to strut. Carol would loose a "cock-a-doodle-do" that sounded phenomenal.

During a tumultuous childhood, my grandparent's home was a refuge. All I know about motherhood, I learned from Grandma. She taught me well. A more innocent time, finds the little girl of my youth at play in the outdoors. I imagine myself an acrobat in the world's greatest circus. My doll lies just out of harm's way.

Nancy comes to join me. She has gained a new wealth of information that she wants to share with somebody, and I am there. While I push the limits of bodily endurance, performing acts not meant to be watched by the weak hearted, Nancy is giving me an explanation of abortion. "They say, they aren't babies until they're born," she said.

It didn't seem right to me; the picture that filled my mind was real enough. When I called abortion "mean," Nancy responded, "I know, but that's what I heard."

Her words sent shock waves through the heart of a little mommy who was just now learning the role. I kept my baby doll wrapped in a blanket because she hadn't any arms. I don't know what happened to her before she came to me. Her face was still beautiful, and I carried her, anyway. She was a symbol of helplessness then, showing a glimpse of who I was within. "They" believe that everything is not black or white, but in the eyes of a child, everything is.

Questions that a child shouldn't have to ask, needed answers. I felt burdened with abortion knowledge. Somehow it seemed threatening, and I took that emotion directly to Grandma. We did not have a long talk about the subject of women's rights. She only told me what I already believed. "They are babies," she said.

Grandma had been present when children were born prematurely, and sadly, sometimes stillborn. In the past, she had assisted a midwife. "I was there and saw them." She promised, "They are babies."

Her carefully chosen words forever shaped the way I think of abortion. Life is fragile. I don't take anyone or anything for granted—not the friendship with Earl that blossomed into real love, and not the four beautiful faces of our babies. Our sons and daughters grew to be more kind and unselfish than I had ever wished for.

CHAPTER 21

— ✢ —

Digging to China

BOBBY IMPATIENTLY RAPPED the collection of tablespoons against his pant leg, clinking them together and making a ringing sound that resembled wind chimes caught in a breeze. "I've been waiting for you to show up," he said. "Today me and you are gonna dig to China!"

Ours was never a handholding, romantic type of relationship. When his buddies came around, he completely ignored me. Hanging with a younger girl would damage his "top gun" image. But I guessed I was good enough to help him dig a hole.

Together, Bobby and I cased his yard. He scoped out an area behind the house, and we finally settled on a site where his granny couldn't poke her head out and see what mischief we were up to.

"Grandma don't come around to this side of the house that often," he said. "Chances are, Shirley, we can pull the wool over her eyes for all summer."

He passed me a regular size tablespoon, kept the largest one for himself and tossed the others to the ground.

"Hey, Shirley, did you know that if you and me started digging and kept going through to the other side of the world, we'd end up in China?" Bobby was just trying to show off how smart he was. He knew, good and well, we couldn't dig a hole that deep.

But we set to work anyway, building our "castles in the air," one spoonful of dirt after another and swapping ideas about the foreign lands below us, on the opposite side of our world.

Much later, I had read about discrimination against women in China. I was really touched by the sadness of their fate, and I wondered why the unfairness lasted so long—why they continued to follow at the heels of men, for a thousand years.

There was a time in this distant land, half a world away, when its people were guided by some outrageous customs. In this land called China, God made boys and girls, and He gave to them lovely dark, almond shaped eyes. God also designed the rest of their bodies. From head to toe, the Creator intended these children of His to be born equally blessed.

Unfortunately, the girl child was singled out by ritual and deemed secondary to the boy.

What, you may ask, has all of these facts to do with Bobby and me? Knowing the unholy pitfalls of yesterday, could spare some poor child the misery of landing inside one today, and there, but for the grace…

For the sake (love) of small feet, the girls were severely deformed by something called tradition. Why the practice of binding feet (only the girls') gained popularity, is hard to grasp.

After the little girl had grown to her predestined size, except for her feet, the petite woman was allowed to hobble obediently on tiny crippled feet, walking two steps behind the more valued man.

Change comes about gradually. The worship of feminine tiny feet has rightly fallen from fashion, and they walk in step with their men.

I am a fortunate girl (I can wiggle my unbound toes.) to have been born in the land of freedom and to grow up in kinder times.

Burying this piece of China's bitter past, I return to digging, side by side with Bobby. I knew that he and I were equals. I was happy about that, even though it meant that I would take half the blame for it if our excavation project went awry.

"Bobby," I asked, "What will we do if your grandma decides to wander around here in the dark?"

"She won't," he replied casually.

"But what if she does?" I worried

Bobby let out an impatient breath. "I told you she won't."

Still I had doubts. "She might fall in the hole." I dreaded the thought of it. "Grandpa says that old people's bones break real easy."

"For cryin' out loud, Shirley! If she starts out the door after dark, I'll stop her before that happens. Cross my heart and hope to die. Jeesh!"

I was satisfied with that. It is amazing how much earth can be moved by two motivated youngsters with a couple of spoons. The dirt was really flying! We finished the day's work and decided to dig more the next morning.

The digging continued unabated, and within a few days, Bobby and I could fit comfortably inside the crater with nothing of us showing above the ground, except for our heads and shoulders. Our new goal (China is much too deep.) is to dig a swimming hole and then wait for a pouring rain to fill it.

The silver spoon glistened in my hand as the sunlight struck it. Up and over my shoulder, I tossed one heaping spoonful of dirt after another, unaware of the trouble brewing above us.

It was the startled look on Bobby's face that drew my attention. All of a sudden, he dropped his spoon and froze, staring up at something behind me.

My eyes followed his. The toes of her shoes extended past the edge of the hole where Bobby and I were crouched, and pointed directly under my nose. Bobby's grandma was big as life and twice as intimidating. She cast a wide shadow.

"Hmmm." Chunky old woman shoes, poised at my eye level... whatever can this mean?

We dug ourselves a hole, and we were stuck in it. Bobby's grandma hovered, looking sternly down at us.

The large boned woman planted both hands firmly on chunky hips, fortelling her attitude.

A long, stony silence followed. Then, without mincing words, she ordered, "Cover. It. Up!"

From my perspective (languishing in a hole in the ground), Bobby's grandma seemed to tower over me, looming as tall as the Statue of Liberty. He and I, immediately, began to shovel dirt back inside the hole. Satisfied with our compliance, she turned about and left us as stealthily as she had appeared.

Bobby started laughing his butt off. "Ahh ... ha ha ha ... Ahh ... ha ha ha! It hurts ... it hurts. Oh my stomach hurts," he roared. In between side splitting howls of glee, gasps for breath, and crude jabs of his finger at me, he sputtered, "You shoulda seen your face!" Bobby convulsed again, and a string of "hee-haws" exploded in my ears. "You looked *so* funny!"

"Dang you Bobby!" I squalled.

If that jackass was not so all consumed with getting the best of me, he would see that inside this dirt-caked playmate, beat the heart of a little girl who secretly adored him.

Our day would not come. Shortly after the swimming hole plan was thwarted, Bobby's mother remarried and the family moved away. Our paths crossed never more.

CHAPTER 22

— ✂ —

Prelude to Love Songs

THE CROOKED PATHS dividing the jungle-like location from the rest of the world were the result of nomadic tiny bare feet. A dozen or so rambunctious lads and lasses had claimed this rugged space as their own, and they have turned it into a novel play land. The woods reverberated with the sounds of Tarzan calls, whistles, howls, and the high-pitched ring of childish laughter.

What a great escape this place really was! I hadn't an inkling of where we were, and other than Nancy, I didn't know anybody who was playing here. Seeing those new faces, all at once, and exploring unfamiliar ground was an exciting prospect.

Earlier that morning, before we left Grandma's house, Mom had cheerfully fixed a lunch to bring with us. A date with a certain admirer and a picnic basket filled with her favorite foods put a spring in her step and a sparkle in her eyes. Plainly, she was anticipating a good time. Mom was happy as a lark to have a beau again.

Her good mood translated into a general bustling around and a sing-along with the radio. When she was content, nobody else sang or hummed as readily as our mother. In a voice that rang high and clear, recalling the days she sang in a church choir, Mom became our morning songbird. These silver toned, early risings were long before the darkest days of her mental illness.

I sat quietly, perched on the tall kitchen stool while Mom put the finishing touches on me. She carefully slipped the last curled lock of my hair off her finger—just the way Grandma used to do it for her, I imagined. Making finger-wound ringlets is as much a way of showing affection between mothers and young daughters, as it is a ritualistic part of grooming.

By the time "Mr. Wonderful" arrived, Mom had readied the four of us (herself included). Nancy's bangs were slicked back and secured in place with crossed bobby pins. Carol's normally straight hair was jellied stiff with wave-set lotion and hung in rows of rigid banana curls.

We looked downright presentable as we left home. Nancy and Carol quickly settled into the rear seat of the fellow's car. I was next to climb aboard. At the last second, Mom produced the large picnic basket and set it where my feet should go—whereupon I stood my ground. With my body blocking open the car door, I discretely protested this unfairness, "Can't you move it somewhere else?"

"No," Mom abruptly responded to my whining. "Now get in there and shut up."

I thought that the big, floor-hogging basket should have been transferred from beneath my feet to the front seat and between Mom and the driver. She and her suitor had more wiggle room than I did, and gosh darn it, so did Nancy and Carol. I eyed my sisters' seats, hungrily, but they stared me down.

I tucked my unlucky feet up under me, and after a long cramped ride, we turned off the pavement and rumbled along another mile or so on a country road. It ended at an out-of-the-way, big old barn of a house. The folksy people who belonged to it came out to greet us. After our welcome, they took the driver and our mother back inside with them, leaving Nancy, Carol, and I to fend for ourselves and to become acquainted with the large brood of children who were openly gawking at us.

Their eager young faces had swelled around us the instant we got out of their uncle's car. Like human stair-steps, their ages varied. My eyes were drawn to the youngest of the group, a simply adorable cherub who had nothing on except a baggy pair of cotton trainers that drooped to his chubby knees. A strip of worn elastic, trapped in the babe's one fisted grip, was the only thing postponing a "mooning" incident.

One of the toddler's shoes was missing. The other, a white lace-up high-top, was cradled, most protectively, inside the crook of his baby-ish arm. He hugged it tenderly against his chest. Little boys do so love to play with shoes.

The oldest of the bunch was a youth about Nancy's age, and he wanted to recruit additional mischief makers into their midst. Nancy, being the social one of us, warmed up to the leader immediately, and she urged me to fall in with her and the others.

Carol and the droopy-drawers cherub were too little in the britch-es to run with the older, wild pack, and they were led inside to play. The rest of us swarmed to the woods. One of the boys, whose age was close to mine—I was 11 years old at this time—was especially atten-tive to me. His name was Ray.

As much as I wanted to join in the fun, I drew back from Ray. Because of a past, bad experience, I had learned to be wary of new-comers. The last boy I became isolated with was a pudgy bully who thrived on intimidation, and I recalled that incident all too well.

It happened on the school playground adjacent to our house.

I had the swings and slides to myself, or so I thought. He was in my face, before I knew it. In little to no time after Jake confronted me in the schoolyard, his mood changed from aggression to stark anger. Jake's face burned red and contorted with ugly rage. It was just him and me—school was not in session.

My eyes scanned the vicinity, finding the playground otherwise deserted. There was no one to come to my rescue.

Jake kept repeating, "You're scared, ain't you? Yeah, you're scared all right. I can tell." I could feel his hot breath on my face as he repeat-ed, "I know you're scared." The bully doubled up his fist, sneering at my feeble attempts to be brave. Had he been any surer of our seclu-sion, Jake would have knocked my brains out.

I hoped that my wide-eyed appearance did not betray my fear. Denying the terror within while speaking calmly to him, I asked, "What do you think the other boys will say about you when they find out you picked on someone smaller than you are … and a girl, at that? I'll just bet they will make fun of you." I added, trying to touch a nerve.

I asserted that his manly reputation would be ruined by this encounter, but Jake seemed unmoved by my thinly veiled threat. Thinking it wiser to still my trembling insides than to provoke him further, I endured more of Jake's chest thumping antics. Instead of adding fuel to his flame of madness, my racing thoughts searched for the words to appeal to his sense of pride.

"Only bullies beat up on girls," I said. "Real men defend them." Would Jake let go of me? Maybe he was just toying with me. As I was allowed to back away from him, I thought: For this performance, I should get an Academy Award.

Later, I was shocked by the obvious connection when I learned that his father was an abuser who regularly beat up on Jake's mother. After the family moved away, I hoped some other girl didn't suffer Jake's wrath.

This boy was different. Ray's boyish grin and friendly manner took away from the unsettling fact that he was a stranger. I convinced myself that he was not after anything, nothing up his sleeve. He liked me—for me, and that's all there was to it.

Ray's actions matched the sincerity of his words, weakening my aloofness to join in the fun. I couldn't see any strings attached to his friendliness. This winsome kid was different from the raw mannered toughs that I had encountered.

Why the "Maker of Boundaries" came to set my personal space wider than most others, leaving me possibly the world's most insecure child, was a mystery.

From the moment Ray singled me out, I felt an affinity to him, and my usual standoffishness gave way to trust. When Ray's hand closed, unrepentantly over mine, I wavered, but I didn't shrug it off. The sensation of his hand covering mine was a new experience and unlike anything I had ever felt. The sense of being physically connected to someone was striking.

Linked together, we set out to explore this wonderland. Ray led the way through the dense wilderness, which made up his own unique backyard. He knew the best places to explore, and I was drawn to this engaging boy. Ray was going to be a gallant exception to the rogues in my budding life.

There was a magical discovery around every bend. Come follow in our abandoned footsteps, and enter a more demure and less hurried age when innocent romance flowers before passions grow hot...

Here and there, shards of broken sunlight falling from the daystar knife through trees cloaked in summer green. As the landscape switches rapidly from sun to shade, a mosaic scroll of light and shadow rolls chameleon-like across our smitten faces. It was as if each had always known the other—always had been friends.

Blazing his own trail, Ray zigzags around natural barriers until we reach his secret hideaway: the place he runs to, he confides, when he needs solitude or to dream impossible dreams.

Ray's Shangri-La is everything he told me it would be. His piece of earth even has a brook—an added charm that he calls a wishing pool. We walk the plank to the opposite shore, daringly crossing over a log that lay suspended above the water.

A rock hunt along the bank turns up some unusual pebbles, and we collect the best ones. All the while, we talk about ourselves—exchanging aspirations. Looking through a window to the future makes time seem irrelevant.

Deep in the heart and near to the soul, there is a haven for secret wishes, and these longings are the stuff our dreams are made of.

Ray's pebble drops before mine—as if to show me how to dream.

A love that is deeper than the haven inside my heart, wider than the swirling ripples that form when my wish plunges into supernatural waters—this is my desire. Who has walked in the shoes of a dreamer and not begged God for one step more?

"Shirley ... oh Shirley! Hey you ... Shir... ley!"

How in the heck did she find me? My wish interrupted, I swallowed the urge to pretend that I did not hear Nancy drawling out my name. Darn it!

"What do you want?"

I will say one thing for Nancy: she is persistent. Her voice rides the winds, echoing from afar, and it is hollow as though she's calling in a canyon.

"We have to go now ... now ... now. Come on... on ... on..."

Grudgingly, I give up my place on the crossing log and beside Ray. As I work my way back across the water—away from the wishing pool and my new friend, I feel his eyes on my back. Ray is sorry to see me go.

Once my feet are anchored on dry land, Ray stands up, looming straight and tall on the crossing log. Using his outstretched arms as a balance beam, he quickly steps right over left, left over right until he touches shore.

Oh, no. It's over. I sigh a sad note of resignation. My very first romance is left unfinished. I stare behind me, like a kid who is being dragged from the circus grounds without a bag of peanuts or a tube of cotton candy.

A parting kiss, as sweet as a circus treat, would have provided an ecstatic memento to take back with me (only in my impossible dreams). Anyway, the thought of a first kiss is better than an actual smack on the lips. A bitter or less than perfect kiss could have spoiled the whole day. The most intriguing part of romance exists in the anticipation of it.

"Have you ever been here before?" Ray asks. We are grasping at straws to meet again.

"No, it's the first time." I want to say more. I want to add: I really do like you. But I could not be that brazen. This was a time when girls waited to be asked. They were never the pursuers.

"Do you think you could come back sometime?" He wanted us to get to know each other better as much as I wanted it.

"I don't think so." This is all there is.

It is written on our faces: We know this is goodbye forever, and both of us are sorry.

I had never been so close to a boy, and now to lose our fast friendship felt confusing. I used dragging my feet as a delaying tactic. To go home without a finality of some kind—a meaningful ending, something salvaged, is a sorry affair. Ray had not even kissed me.

It seemed fitting that we part exactly where we found each other. He watching me... softly.

At the edge of the deep woods, where the ground rises sharply, I caught up with Nancy. Turning around to face the wilderness, I looked back to the spot where I had left Ray. He was still standing there, watching after me. I waved a last contemplative farewell, and he returned it.

Is there such a thing as love at last sight?

How can a day have passed so quickly? Clouds of gray, lazily draped themselves across the blush rose skyline, creating a spectacular backdrop for the golden sunset. The glaring white center of the brilliant globe put spots in front of my eyes as I watched it sink beneath the western horizon. I dreaded the last gasps of daylight. Time was relevant, after all.

In autumn days that followed, after Ray, I was more certain than ever that true love would find me. If there is one prince, then others must be out there. I could not begin to explain away the contrast between Bully Jake and Prince Ray—between storms of anger and stillness of harmony.

I recast that extraordinary afternoon, over and over in my thoughts—step by thrilling step through the woods, moment by fateful moment at the wishing pool. I considered how our meeting might have ended differently, had we been older, or progressed to the dramatically charged first kiss.

Much later, after I had forgotten his face, I continued to recall that friend's sensitivity and chivalry. I watched for these traits to show up in later beaus, and I used these qualities as a touchstone. And I mostly came up empty.

Memories have a way of their own with our hearts. A simple wooded setting became, for me, larger than life: a sort of Eden. All I truly had to draw from was a single fleeting encounter, which was far too short to fall in love. Ray, a boy who played fair, happened along just when I had begun lumping all males into one predatory category. In the balance of things, even though I never saw Ray again, his sincerity mattered.

The fledgling romance, born too soon, on this accidental afternoon and nurtured by the lure of a pristine setting, never had a chance to grow. It was only a prelude of what was to come.

Sometimes I follow the words "love you" with "always" to make the term of endearment stronger. It means, among other things, that I will keep my promises. I have stored up lots of "always," holding back this ultimate expression of love for those nearest to my heart.

"Always" promises: I will never go away—never leave you alone.

CHAPTER 23

Always

SOMETIMES VERY YOUNG girls let their emotions out with exceptional intensity. Mine ran away with me like that. I was a starry-eyed romanticist.

The idea to put my thoughts down on paper came about as we neared the end of an otherwise long, uneventful summer. When I kicked back the covers to another empty morning, I knew I had the freedom to use that day however I desired. I filled it with more passion than a lonely, young girl can keep bottled up inside: I wrote love songs.

This uncommon page of my childhood might well have been lost, if not for fate. It is almost as though the songs that I made up when I was a naïve little girl have a will or a life and voice of their own.

The remarkable set of events that spiraled out of control began in a simple enough way—coming from a morning of daydreaming spent slouching in Grandma Mollie's rocking chair.

My creative ability didn't kick in until my indulgent little bones meshed with the wood of the inspirational rocker.

"Why don't you quit a wallerin' and set up straight?" Grandpa Alf demanded. "You're a ridin' that chair like a pony."

As soon as the scolding was finished and the harmless old guy left the front room, I went back to my antics. I had turned myself around and faced the tall back of the chair. I slid my feet between the wooden spindles and rode that pony "high, wide, and handsome!"

As the words came to me, I sang out: "Rockin' chair, rockin' babies, rock-a-bye, rock of ages. Side by side, we'll be together always."

After I had the guts of my song down pat, I knew it needed more, and I wracked my brain until I came up with another verse. In typical, little lovesick fashion, I wrote more lines: "I'll be your friend. I'll be your lover. There will never be another."

I sang best to an empty room. My voice carried throughout the house, but I could handle an audience of two elderly folks or one of my siblings in a separate room.

Although I had heard the term in church, the meaning of "rock of ages" was not perfectly clear to me. But the words seemed to fit in my song. All of it sounded good to this child's ears. I worried some about it, though: whether "rock of ages" would make sense used in this way. Did it belong with babies, rocking chair, or cradle?

Everything changed after I noticed advertisements seeking original poems to set to music. Now I was hooked. I read all the small-print promotions in the classifieds and on the back pages of comic books. Tucked in between "can you draw this" and "send for these super X-ray glasses," I found several other promising offers to choose from.

A plan to send my song poems to a recording company began to form. I slaved ever more diligently on the words, trying to make them sound just right. I kept my intention secret while I deliberated on where to send my work. The back pages of comic books plus the classified section of the Sunday newspaper were my sources for addresses. After considerable thought and indecision, I finally narrowed my search to a couple of music companies whose names I'd seen on a record.

I never told a living soul what I was about to do. Making consequential decisions is difficult for me. Although I was ready to mail my first scary attempt at fame, I kept pondering the refrain to my song. Worriedly, I erased "rockin' babies" and exchanged the words "rockin' cradle" in place of them, and that sounded okay to me, as well.

In my uncertainty, I wondered whether using the word "cradle" might sound more reasonable to an adult, because cradle and rocking chair name two things that rock. Feeling conflicted, I sang the song over both ways. It needed the "babies" in there, and so I struck the word "cradle" and penned "rockin' babies" right back into my song. Before I could change my mind again, I sealed the envelope, borrowed a three-cent stamp from Grandma, and skipped off to the post office.

By the time I arrived, my heart was beating in my ears. Skipping to the post office had nothing to do with the fast beats. I was wrought up with anxiety. Perhaps the thumping I was hearing was a sixth sense warning, trying to tell me that this event would follow me. When premonition makes a heart do cartwheels, it is a sure sign that Somebody up there is urging that its owner reconsider what she is doing.

It is true that for every action, there is an equal and opposite reaction. Because I mailed those songs, much confusion came to me. (I can still feel a twinge of empathy for the impulsive little girl I once was.)

I wavered, nearly breathless while pausing in front of the outgoing mail drop. This felt risky! Would I get into trouble for pretending that I am an adult? Could the music people tell from the lyrics that I was just a kid? They never asked my age. The arguments I presented to myself were done away with. Quickly, and before I could change my mind, I shut my eyes and let the ominous envelope drop into destiny.

I did not expect to hear from them—not really. Just the same, I prayed it would happen. Then I forgot about it. Until the record company answered.

Inside the impressive business envelope was a glowing report on my writing ability. The sender claimed that I had talent and that my song showed excellent potential. How I wanted those promising words of praise to be sincere!

The record company was interested in recording my song poem, I just needed to sign the enclosed form and mail it back. I affixed my underage signature on it and skipped back to the post office on the very next day.

Time is a paradox: When I wanted the few hours I had with the gallant Ray to last, they flew by. Now, while I was on pins and needles and waiting for earth-shaking news, time crawled.

Then one day, which began the same as any other, my young life was changed. Immediately after the rickety screen door whipped shut behind me, I spied the unopened piece of mail lying on the kitchen table.

When Grandpa picked up the official looking sleeve of mail and handed it to me, I didn't accept it right off. Not fully understanding that the mail was mine, I just stood there staring at it.

I rather expected another letter in reply to the form I had signed and returned, but I never ever considered that a package would come, and the sight of it left me dumbfounded. My name and address seemed to leap out at me.

The household gathered around while clumsy fingers—I hardly recognized them as my own—nervously loosened the end flap. Carefully, I slid out the contents. In my astonished hands was a shiny golden record. It stood out as brilliantly as a perfect sunset.

"Ahhh!" I gasped.

Right away, Nancy was glad for me. "Gosh, I wish we had a record player, Shirley, so we could listen to your song."

If I read the letter that came with my golden treasure once, I must have read it a dozen times. Here was a request for money to continue with my song. It would cost fifty dollars to cut Rockin' Years onto the shiny gold record. I was instructed to mail back the blank record along with the sum of money.

Everything I wanted was something I couldn't have. In the entire pinched, young years of my existence, I never jingled over fifty cents in my pocket, at any given time.

Grandpa read the letter after I did, and I could tell he felt sorry about it. "'Tis nothin' but a 'come on,' Shirley. More'n likely if'n they can get enough folks to send them the fifty dollars, I'll allow, they can rake in a good deal of cash." He spoke gruffly, "I'm a heap satisfied that's how they make a livin'. They can make them records for a dime."

Since scraping up fifty dollars was a hopeless task, I did the next best thing: I gave everything to Grandma. Into her safekeeping, I placed the golden colored record and all the related correspondence.

I trailed at her heels to her exclusive piece of furniture. Grandma's chiffonier gobbled up one whole corner of her tiny bedroom. It was off limits to everyone in the house except herself. Her best clothes along with a few sentimental trinkets were stored in the deepest interior of it.

She pulled open the door to the left side of the spacious chiffonier, parted back her good coat and dresses, made a small cubbyhole on the bottom of it … and there, stashed away my dreams.

I did not completely give up the crusade. I was still desperate to discover a way to satisfy the music label without sending them money. At this point, I responded to their requests for the impossible by sending in more song poems. If the songs were good enough, I hoped they would overlook the matter of money. I was singing and scribbling up a storm, and Grandma's rocking chair witnessed every word. I was a driven child!

Another of my songs was accepted, and I grew optimistic once more. These words rose from my heart like a wellspring: a profession of undying love that I called "Always."

I chose "Always" as the title because I thought that "I Will Always Love You" was too long a name. There were so many issues that I was unsure about. A second blank record arrived in the mail. Everything was exactly as before, except in this instance the color of the record was black.

When this second record came in the mail, Grandpa just shook his head. "I've had my say," he declared.

Besides the two songs that were accepted: "Rockin' Years" and "Always," I mailed off two more that were rejected. The names of these were "Top of the World" and "Happy Years." Since these last works were returned to me with the word "reject" stamped boldly across them, I guessed they were not very good. It hurt my feelings.

Before the end came crashing down, the whole experience had been enlightening. Success does not come to little girls this easily. While it lasted, it seemed that I had uncovered my true talent, and I had been anxious to share my brush with destiny. I especially wanted my father to know of it.

It was usually in the evening when Daddy came by and picked us up for a short visitation, mostly spent inside his car. On this particular occasion, it was nearing dusk when Grandma told us, "I see your Daddy is out there." It was Nancy, Carol, and I that hurried out to meet him. Mary was still living with Dad during this time, Sonny was at odds with him, and Dee was newly married.

Now, Daddy's divorce tantrums are put behind us, and he seldom mentions our mom, anymore. Whenever he does, in passing, he asks almost politely, "How is the ol' gal?"

Notice me, Daddy, my heart pleaded. (Poor Daddy, he only took notice of how unhappy he was.) I needed to feel that I was worthy in his eyes, and I wanted him to know that I had written songs and that a record company wanted to use them. I couldn't blurt it out because I thought if I told him my story, it would sound like bragging.

I could kick myself. Why was I born so incredibly bashful? A stern glance or a cross word was devastating. God knows, I could never take the pressure of being in the limelight.

Nancy came to my rescue.

"Shirley wrote some songs," she told Dad, and then she recited all that had happened—even that I get mail because of it. Getting mail was a big deal!

Daddy smiled broadly, and he said, "Kiddo, if it's a hit, you could get rich."

Even as I played along, I knew Daddy was only kidding. I saw his wink. Yet for those few seconds, I had Daddy's full attention and I did feel worthwhile in his eyes.

At the end of our hour together, Daddy said it was getting late. "Poozie," he crooned softly to Carol, "Daddy has to leave." He stroked her hair down and flat against her head. Daddy is picky about groomed hair for someone who is almost bald himself. The few strands at the top of his head are always in place, and before he takes us out in public, he whips out his fine-tooth comb, making us presentable.

"I'll see you later," Daddy promised. "I gotta shove off." After we said our quiet goodbyes, Nancy, Carol, and I got out of the car.

A couple more coaxing letters were sent to me from the record company, and that was it. They never contacted me further. I was charred by the whole worrisome affair, and I didn't want to think about it, anymore. I quit writing and went on with my little girl life.

The things Grandma stored away for me, in the bottom of her chiffonier were purposely neglected. I left the two blank records buried and forgotten, and I felt it was good riddance. As time went by, the songs I wrote represented a disappointment in myself, and I did not want anyone to know of it. They represented dreams, not reality.

My heart's desire was always to become a mother —rocking chair, rocking babies. And "I will always love you" is a promise that came true when my gallant knight finally appeared.

Looking back on childhood acts of daring, I understand how fortunate I am to have had fame pass me by. Over the years, I have noticed others who were not so lucky. They felt the pressure and fell apart. Fame worked them like dogs. God had something else planned for me, if only I, the kid who had no patience, would wait for it to happen. I would, in time, be most blessed with the husband and the children of my dreams.

Years of destiny accumulate behind me. Over a quarter of a century had elapsed since I willingly put aside pen and paper. Then, on an unsuspecting summer day, the past came calling.

Our second child, Dawn, and I were sharing the front porch swing and a box of raisins. Country music was blaring from the radio inside the house. The volume was turned all the way to max so that we can hear the music on the porch.

The words of the song drifting out to us, struck a chord of recognition. It wasn't possible, I told myself. My eyes widened in disbelief as the knowing washed over me. "Oh, no!" My thoughts erupted aloud.

"What's wrong, Mom?"

My thoughts stumbled backwards. I struggled to answer Dawn's question without dredging up an emotional past. It was exactly like me to push out of my thoughts any reminder of unhappiness. Although I hesitated to stir old emotions, the door to the past was now opened, and I let this child of ours look inside.

"I wrote a song that I called 'Always' when I was a young girl," I told her. Dawn fell silent, thinking about what I had said.

Then she asked, "Can't you do something about it?"

"No," I affirmed with a certainty that I admitted must be fact. "I can't. Record companies are big, and I am small." She seemed to understand that this was unfixable.

The beautiful love words that I had rocked up from the bottom of my heart, so long ago, were mulled over in my thoughts and then promptly let go of once more. I determined that my writing simply went from my hands to theirs.

I had not thought about the two blank records in a very long time. Because I felt so vulnerable, I just wanted the whole darn thing to go away. We can't turn back the hands of time.

I never talked about the songs again; it was just too complicated to explain how it all happened. A little girl made up what she thought could turn into a string of nonsense rhyming. But instead, at least parts of two songs she wrote, sold in the millions. The awakening of "Rockin' Years" and "Always," is not necessarily a good or a bad thing. It was a reminder to me of a little girl's feelings that I had long ignored.

Yet some things refuse to disappear.

On a common day in the year 2000, three of my sisters met for a luncheon get-together at my place. A cloud of cigarette smoke hovered above my kitchen table. The four of us—Mary, Nancy, Carol, and I—were well into dredging up one another's peculiarities and rattling old family skeletons. Reminiscences that began "Do you remember when …" brought forth groans as well as giggles.

Cherished moments meant to be shared again before it's too late, keep the conversation lively. Then Nancy turned to me and said, "Shirley, what did you ever do with your gold record?"

Once more, the past overtook me. Nancy went on, "You know, I remember you singing that 'rockin' chair, rockin' babies' song when you were little."

I had put the records out of my mind until Nancy spoke them back into existence. The memory was fully unwrapped, and there was no putting it back. When I least expect it, something lost just seems to find me. Memories of the past magically reappear.

Simply listening to the words of "Rockin' Years," especially once you know the words were written by a child, shows exactly what this song is: a little girl's romantic yearnings turned into a simple poem. But it sounds catchy—I was right about that.

The same thing holds true about the main line in the song "I Will Always Love You." Turn that line over in your head and hear the thoughts of a starry-eyed and love-starved young girl.

If you have ever read a music company's advertisements seeking original songs or poems—and then have wondered what happened to all the material that folks sent in—well, now you have one possible answer.

The romantic spirit behind "Always" still lives in my heart. Nearly a lifetime has passed since the words to "Always" almost wrote themselves. I bared my soul on paper when I wrote that one, and the words left me misty-eyed and wanting.

"Always" does not have the unique and easily recognizable refrain that "Rockin' Years" has. Although "I will always love you" is a beautiful thought, others have written down or sung the thought as well. No one can claim ownership to a sentiment. Although the song on the radio wasn't exactly the same as I wrote, it had a similar title and some of the same lyrics. I'm not accusing anyone of plagiarizing the work of a little girl, but it does strike me as odd. I don't know how these things work. Perhaps a song writer will read something, somewhere, and he'll store it in his memory and forget where he got it. Over time, he takes ownership of it. That's possible. But to me, that song will always be mine.

My "Always" was a song about staying, about never abandoning the one you love. A similar song that came along afterwards is more about leaving, more about saying goodbye. I wrote with passion and meaning. The last line to my song: "I will always love you," I spoke in a soft whisper instead of singing out the words.

I am just describing what happened to me. Whenever I hear the words, "I will always love you" in song, my heart remembers, and I am a part of it. Mine is the better part; I lived out the message of my songs.

Once more, metaphorically speaking, I stand at destiny's outgoing mail slot. Not too surprisingly, the unveiling of my story—the one you hold in your hands—feels as risky as the song writing that came before it.

CHAPTER 24

The Heart Never Lies

MY LIFE'S JOURNEY continues. By chance or by kismet, memories collect and need a place to call home. A written account of my thoughts, in the form of a book, is meant to find rest in the embrace of my family.

There is a familiar little girl who—still—lives in my heart, and I search for a means to be faithful to her childhood endeavors.

The desire to transfer my imagination onto a blank sheet of paper is something that I thought I had used up and let go of—all in a single disappointing year of song writing.

Then one day, my early passion returned as a driving force that filled long winter evenings. With fresh determination, I set about composing another poem. The words honor a 17-year-old boy who waited through a friendship to become the one, great love of my life.

For Earl, when love was new…

The Heart Never Lies

You waited for a long time,
Hoping I would change my mind.
I was content to be your friend.
It was love that happened in the end

Chorus:
You are the only, only one
The heart never lies.

I will always want you close to me.
You never make my cry.
I will be your love,
And you will be mine until the day I die.

Chorus:
You are the only, only one
The heart never lies.

I knew you would never walk away,
You loved me from the start.
When I felt how much you cared for me,
It lit a fire inside my heart.

Chorus:
You are the only, only one.
The heart never lies.

You are everything I'll ever need.
I love you more than words can say
When you hold me close and call me Babe,
It takes my breath away.

Chorus:
You are the only, only one
The heart never lies.

(Repeat)
I will always want you close to me
You never make me cry.
I will be your love
And you will be mine until the day I die.

CHAPTER 25

❧

Macabre Games

"Lizzie Borden took an axe
And gave her mother forty whacks
When she saw what she had done
She gave her father forty-one ... two ... three ..."

THE JUMP ROPE chant rolls off my playmates' tongues. With each suc-
ceeding revolution, the rope whines ever louder. Faster and faster it
twirls as the impatient rope turners switch from "Lizzie" to the frenzied
beat of "red-hot pepper." The jumping frenzy continues, increasing
their odds to make me miss.

The sinewy length of braided rope whistles sharply above my head,
before it falls, skimming my airborne feet and whacking the ground
just a hair's breadth beneath my toes.

It was over in one more breathless count. Indeed: Lizzie had axed
her last blow in step with my final skip of the rope.

I dragged my limp limbs to the porch stoop where I collapsed next
to Grandma.

The freshly picked garden green beans sounded a crisp "snip-
snap" as their tender ends dropped quickly through her apt fingers.
She kept her eyes on the task at hand and addressed me without looking up. "I'll declare," Grandma remarked, "do any of you young'ns
know who Lizzie Borden was?"

Grandma's question held the promise of an interesting yarn. "Is Lizzie Borden a real person?" I asked. More intrigued by the axe-wielding mystery, I pressed on. "Who is she?"

I had just assumed that the words we skipped rope to were nothing more than a meaningless rhyme that somebody made up.

"The newspapers ran with the story for weeks, 'twas gussied about in big bold type," Grandma reflected.

"I never read such an awful, awful account in all my born days." She clacked her tongue against the roof of her mouth, to indicate her testy emotions over the shamefulness of the sordid details.

Grandma didn't believe Lizzie was guilty of hacking to death her own people. "Law, how could a young girl murder her mama and papa in cold blood that-a-way? It must have been a tramp a hightailed it off one of the trains: a stranger, most assuredly. Criminals have been known to frequent the tracks and hide out in boxcars."

Grandma's theory deserved consideration. I had good reason to be suspicious of guys who walk the tracks.

When Hunter and I happened to share the same set of railroad tracks, I hurried to get away from him. Because I lived on the edge of town at this time, I sometimes took the shortcut home. If he came within shouting distance of me, I could expect the worst—especially when there was another boy for whom he was showing off.

Hunter called out obscene suggestions. Sometimes he replaced English slang with some foreign-language vulgarity. "Suck a blankety-blank!" I didn't know what it meant, but the intent was obvious.

My anger supersedes my fear of Hunter, and I lash right back at him."Suck your own blankety-blank!" I flung his dirty words right back in his face. Hunter threw back his head and laughed. He was getting something out of my reaction.

Grandma had weighed the evidence against Lizzie and thought it pointed elsewhere. "Some of these beggars and wanderers," she whispered, pitying the homeless also, "are not in their right minds, you know. Likely, a bum could have come and gone and nobody alerted."

My eyes took in her serious expression. "Honey," Grandma explained, "I don't believe that poor young thing had the physical strength to do such a heinous deed. Why, she'd of had to overpower her daddy. No," she determined. "It was a big strappin' man that commenced to kill the mama and papa."

Grandma was far too naïve and compassionate to impartially judge someone's character; everybody got the benefit of doubt. Would that Cain never slew Abel, and that the world turned to please God and Grandma.

It is curious how evil worms its way into children's play. I was more attuned to that strange practice—after I learned of the bloody history behind our counting Lizzie Borden's axe swings, to keep the jump rope score.

Love is not a balm meant to heal every hurt. This sad revelation takes me back to an unforgettable winter when the Christmas Spirit had a real damper put on it.

It begins early one morning as I woke to an unsettling quiet. There was a macabre chill hovering inside the house—a hush that was more pronounced than the winter cold outside.

Leaving a pair of still sleeping sisters in our shared bed, I wandered into the front room, rubbing my sleepy eyes and anticipating the warmth of the stove.

Grandpa and Sonny were already there. Grandpa's expression was decidedly somber, and I could tell by the slack fall of his stubbly jowls that something very disturbing had occurred.

In low but confrontational voices, Grandpa and Sonny were discussing the previous night's event.

"He didn't have no other choice," Sonny contended. "He had to do something. What woke him up was he heard his mom cryin'. And when he got out of bed, he saw his dad on top of his mom. His ode man was crazy drunk. There wasn't no other way to stop him."

Sonny's voice sounded grave as he explained. "That's when he took the gun off the hook and shot him."

"He didn't mean to murder his dad. He had to do it to save his mom. His dad had her pinned down, and he was choking her. She was dying there."

At odds with Sonny's reckoning, Grandpa waded right in. "Tain't right!" He persisted, "That boy could a picked up a club or a chair, same as a rifle, and hit his daddy in the head with it and knocked him unconscious."

"No he couldn't," Sonny argued, "because it happened so fast, and besides, there wasn't no cwub wayin' around the house. Why, his daddy would have turned on him, too, and murdered them both."

"'Tain't right, is all I'm pointin' out to you," Grandpa insisted. "That was his daddy."

Watching those two discussing a killing while the sleepy sand was barely out of my eyes, made the whole thing seem nightmarish. I told myself it was a dream. This couldn't be happening! Pretty soon, I would wake up, feeling all cozy and warm on the edge of the crowded bed, lying next to Nancy and Carol.

I located my voice. "What happened?" Grandpa and Sonny looked at me. All they saw was a dumbfounded, scraggly looking kid standing there in her nightie. I asked again.

Silence...Grandpa just acknowledged my presence and then looked away. Clearly, he was disturbed, and he seemed unwilling to deal out this sort of drama to a spongy young one's psyche.

Sonny's voice lacked the kind of emotion that I would expect to hear when the subject is an untimely death. Evenly, without holding anything back, he said to me, "Hunter shot his daddy in the head. Ki'wud him deader than a door naywoe."

"Oh"... I said, in stark acceptance. There was nothing left to say.

Hunter was never charged in his father's demise, because of the circumstances: a panic-stricken boy's finger on the trigger. His mother's devotion to him, thereafter, was not enough to make a gentle man of Hunter. I know he continued to be a thorn in my side. He pursued me, crudely, with ruthless determination. I did my best to evade his advances.

I was the one who got away. How many others were not so fortunate?

CHAPTER 26

❦

One of a Kind

AGE SPEAKS TO the heart of us all, and the passing of years had sufficiently mellowed this worn out carouser. As his days shortened, sobriety was forced upon Grandpa; he was just too darned tired to stay on a "toot" for long.

Grandpa had a rather brooding personality. With misgivings, I listened to his intermittent ranting about tedious things or the general shortcomings of "the lot of them!" On this occasion he was concerned with the boys that Sonny was running with. I drew my own conclusions.

Grandpa's ways may have seemed odd to some who didn't know him well, and even to others who did, but this character was the sole male authority presence in our household and the only constant masculine figure that Sonny could model. Our dad was out of the picture.

Grandpa agonized over Sonny. The boy seemed not altogether unlike a stray lamb, and Grandpa would have moved heaven and earth to rescue the wayward one. At the same time, our exhausted shepherd predicted that all sorts of dire consequences would befall his grandson unless he changed his errant ways.

Grandpa reproved the spoiled young tough with a lecture. It usually began with a disapproving "tsk-tsk" and ended with a declaration. "You'll nary hold a job of work. I'm obliged of it."

But destiny rides the winds, and Sonny remained quite the same smart-alecky and thoroughly confusing little brave who led four of his scaredy-cat sisters across the long ago and far away bull pasture and on to the mysterious Indian Cave.

Sonny turned a deaf ear to Grandpa's warnings and to everyone else's as well. Grandpa was not in a good position to correct Sonny, anyway. Advancing age, plus the fondness he had for the boy, let Sonny walk all over him. Poor old fellow, he didn't have the proverbial "snow ball's chance in hell" of getting through to Sonny.

My brother certainly had a mouth on him. "Kiss my bony ass" was his standard reply to anything and everything.

To have the last word, anyway, Grandpa would snap right back at him, saying, "Bare it!"

Although it never did come to blows, careless words hurt just as much, and their cutting remarks gave me pause for concern. I felt just awful for that eccentric old man, goofy mannerisms and all. My mouthy brother has way too much power. Someone needed to take that bad boy out back and knock the chip right off his shoulder! If I were not such a scrawny kid, I would have done it. (Realistically, I knew better. Sonny could have beat the tar out of me.)

How in the world could that grumpy boy not know that Grandpa is the truest friend he will ever have? Sometimes love makes no sense at all.

One day, as I rounded the corner of the house, I unexpectedly met up with Hunter. I stopped in my tracks. He saw me first. Otherwise, I would have turned around and sneaked back out of my own yard.

While he stood and waited for Sonny to come back outside, Hunter took advantage of an opportunity to aggravate me. "I saw what you and Bobby were doing. Shamey ... shame." My tormentor poked out an accusing finger toward my chest and proceeded to slide it slowly down the length of another finger to insinuate what he had just charged. "Shamey ... shame," he said it again.

"Oh no you didn't!" I struck back at him, "Because we weren't doing anything wrong."

"Yes I did." Hunter smiled. He was fishing and enjoying the moment. "I was watching you. I was looking through a knot hole in one of the boards of you guys' play shed."

Hunter was bent on humiliating me. Even his wink came across as an obscene gesture.

"I wouldn't put it past you to spy on me, Hunter," I fumed. "But I know you couldn't have seen anything. There was nothing to see."

I remembered Grandma's warning: "The world is full of villains." Hunter threw back his head, laughing at me in an obnoxious glee that, coming from him, was eerily familiar. The sinking feeling in the pit of my stomach can identify his cackle even in a packed movie theater.

When Sonny came out of the house, Hunter hadn't any more to say. He breezed by me with a smirk of contempt on his lips, and in his eyes I saw a promise of the continuing cat and mouse game.

Always the bully, Hunter was not to be trusted. Another terrifying day flashed through my mind. I was not any older than 7 or 8 when Hunter first struck fear in my heart.

After wading out until the muddy waters of the infamous Old Lake lapped at my navel, my attention fell on an area where a small group of boys was splashing one another. Rendered motionless from shock, I witnessed the distress of a boy in danger.

From a distance of several yards away, I saw that Hunter was holding a young boy under water, much too long. Fearfully, I stared at the churning waters, until I heard someone calling out, "Let him up! Let him up!" Other voices took up the chant. The scene was so traumatizing that it still plays out in my head.

When Hunter yielded to the frantic calls and brought the boy to the surface, he was almost drowned. The boy fought for breath, coughing and gagging.

Of course, Hunter began to apologize. "Sorry, sorry, so sorry," he begged. Was he sincerely repentant? I really can't say—but I did wonder whether Hunter's true concern was more for himself, than for that poor young boy. I think it's safe to say that Hunter was afraid of bringing trouble down on himself. Cowards are like that.

I never saw the near drowning as a case of horseplay among boys. Hunter went just short of murder—and he knew it.

Trouble is his middle name. Sonny is his first. I feel a tug at my heart over my brother's sad fate. In the whole world, he is the only one who will ever call me Shir'we. Nobody else on earth is quite the same as he. Nobody walks with that spirited half skip in every other step. Sonny is definitely one of a kind.

"Well, lordy, lordy, lordy … tsk-tsk," Grandpa declared to himself and to an otherwise vacant back porch. "I can't hep it. I'm 75 years old. I'm an old man … an old man … an old man."

My willful brother makes all of us want to pull our hair out. For a good part of the day, Grandpa had been brooding and muttering to himself as he warmed the porch bench and waited for Sonny to grace us with his presence.

He was running out of patience. His gnarled hand curved over the edge of the rough-cut bench, hewn before my time, and he began tapping out his frustration. Calloused fingers drummed a steady "rap-a-tap-tap" against the scarred wood.

I thought to myself: As soon as that snotty nosed kid sets foot on the place, he is gonna get it! A few more "rap and a-taps" later, Grandpa is primed to give that arrogant young pup the tongue-lashing he well deserves.

Sonny comes and goes as he pleases—no pesky rules for his royal self to obey. Being the only son out of six offspring has unmerited advantages.

As he paces down the narrow cinder path that ends at our back porch, I zero in on his familiar gait. I've tried to mimic his cocky lift and twist of the hip, but Sonny's walk defies imitation.

Grandpa lit right into Sonny. "Well, it's nigh time yer a showin' yerself. You've been a runnin' with that pack of ingrates, I'm satisfied."

"Kiss my bony ass," Sonny answered.

Grandpa ignored the insult, and he plowed on, "That Jamison boy ain't no account a'tall. He'll nary be anything but a hoodlum. I'm a heap satisfied that whole rabble is incorrigible. We'll see the whole kit and caboodle peekin' out from behind prison bars a fore 'tis done with. Mark my words—you'll rue the day you throwed in with that bunch of misfits. And I'm a declare'n to you now— if'n you don't get shut of them ne'er-do-wells, they'll take you down with 'em."

Grandpa gulped a fresh breath and continued to bark at a defiant Sonny. "I'll abide—when that outfit is caught a thievin', Laddie, and you're hangin' with 'em, you'll nigh go to the reformatory, same as the guilty. Nary one of that sorry lot is a friend of your'n."

Grandpa tried to scare Sonny straight. "Across the ocean, mind you," he threatened, "they have a sure cure for sticky fingers: the first time it commences, the thief's hand is chopped off."

Horrors! "What if it happens again?" I shuddered to think of it.

"I don't oblige there's any cause for a second loppin' off," Grandpa answered me.

"But what if someone is taking food because they're starving?" I was having a real hard time with unheard of and brutal punishment.

"Stealin' is a stealin'," Grandpa advised me. "It's the law over there. And the jailer will cut off a hand just as quick 'ery it's for a loaf of bread or a poke full of money."

"Boo'a shit," Sonny sneered. "That's boo'a shit!"

Grandpa cautioned, "You'd heap better listen to me now. Ol' man Roberts was on my back about you boys. He commenced to raisin' Cain over some gear that was took outta his boat yesterdee."

Sonny shrugged his shoulders as Grandpa continued, "The man declared to me that it was one of you'ns boys what stole his tackle box. Somebody out at the lake, see'd you and recognized all three of ya— Jamison and that thievin' Hunter. And you too, Laddie, you was one of 'em out yonder by the water and a foolin' around Roberts' boat."

Grandpa tried to shame Sonny. "You're nuthin' but a flunky to them. You foller them thugs around like a little yeller puppy dog."

"Shit fire and save the matches! I ain't got none of his crap," Sonny vowed. "Hunter swiped that ode man's tacka box."

Grandpa brushed aside Sonny's denials. "You was with 'em and that makes you as guilty as the rest." He let his anger rip. "The authorities have already been a peckin' on their door and made one of 'em fetch the tackle box out and hand it over."

Grandpa said, "Ol' man Roberts got his property gave back to him, and he allowed he'd not press charges. He's willing to let it go if'n each of you boys make restitution by pickin' him five gallon of dewberries. You boys have got to earn your pardon. 'Tis only fair, now you take a learn'n. He made work a condition."

Grandpa urged Sonny to do right. "You'd best pay a little heed to what I'm a tellin' you. You have to hep yourself."

Sonny turned a deaf ear to the sage advice, and Grandpa grew impatient.

"You ain't growed up yet, Laddie," Grandpa warned. "Don't abide what I'm saying to you, and you'll be a heap sorry of it. After the authorities take you off, I'm obliged you'll do a good deal of cryin' and sobbin', and they'll pay it no heed. Once you're incarcerated in a reformatory, you're theirs—body and soul. Cain't nobody help ya. Won't do 'ery good a'tall to cry for your mama."

Getting his point across, Grandpa rubbed the area below his right eye to simulate a line of flowing crocodile tears.

Although Sonny was tuning Grandpa out, I was listening with all my might. His harsh words stung my ears when I heard him preparing Sonny for the worst. "You're apt to sing a different tune 'ery they strip you naked and hang you by your thumbs. They got the cure for them what won't obey the rules there: big, burly guards will whip you with cane poles. Sure as you're a tootin', they'll beat you till you're bloody. You'll be a believer 'ery it's too late."

Grandpa's final words worked on me, but Sonny wasn't having any of it.

"Heywoe's beywoes! (hell's bells) "I ain't a pickin' no damn berries," he said. "That ode man can't do nuthin' to me. He got his stuff back."

The graphic description of reform school chilled me to the bone. Could this cruelty ever happen? Something told me that it could. How sad that there is evil in the world, and even worse, that it masquerades as a good remedy for unruly children.

Realizing that Grandpa loves every contrary bone in Sonny's body, bony ass and all, I know very well who will actually pick those berries. As the sun rose, a weary but vigilant old grandfather sets out, toting an empty five-gallon bucket. I feel sorry that Grandpa is the one who will pay.

He labored several days—returning, each time, before the noon heat of the day until he had picked, in Sonny's stead, the prescribed quota of dewberries. None of the smug and guilty plucked a single berry.

I counted on the perfect woman to magically appear and right all of Sonny's wrongs. That bad boy would straighten up and fly right when he met that special person—a sweetheart who would really care for him. Ahhh! Romance ... romance ... romance.

By and by, a pretty girl did come along that took a shine to Sonny. Because he didn't keep his faults under wraps for mere sisters, it was hard to tell if my brother was as obnoxious as he seemed to me. I hoped Grandpa was mistaken when he fumed, "She's a gold digger. Pay attention, now, to what I'm a sayin'. That floozy didn't want nuthin' to do with you until you got a little bit of money in your pockets. That cash you made huntin' rabbits will go in a hurry. I declare, I can see it a comin'. I'll allow that aft'en you've blowed it all on her, she'll drop you like a hot potater. 'Ery long as you'll buy her candy and sodie pop, she'll hang around and be your sweetie."

Sonny gave Grandpa a stony look that said—I'll show you. Still, Grandpa predicted, "Mark my words, Sonny boy, they ain't nuthin' to that hussy! 'Ery you're back to a 'goose egg' in your pocket and flat of your can, that hussy won't care a lick about you, n'more—nary come around. A fool and his money are soon parted."

Grandpa's long john clad arm pumped up and down as he spoke, making a tight fist of his right hand. "Mark my words, no money—no honey."

Sonny went out of his way to stop at home before he and Emma went to the movies. It was his first date and a moment to savor. He looked pleased as punch as he escorted his young lovely into our front room. If he were not my brother, he would have been handsome—I'll give him that.

This was Sonny's big chance to shine with a girl and to insinuate "na-na-n'-na-na" to Grandpa.

Nevertheless, I was impressed when my brother waltzed his date by me. I gawked at the pretty, blond girl who clutched Sonny's arm, and I hoped she would be a permanent attachment there.

My yearning, blue eyes fell on Emma's bright red dress. Yards and yards of white cancan slip beneath it, rolled and dipped with her every motion. Shimmering cloth rustled softly about her knees, and the whisper of crisp circling taffeta followed her. It would be pure heaven to wear a dress as beautiful as this one—the likes of which was far out of my reach.

Brought face to face with Emma, the cantankerous old man was a pussycat. Donning a poker face, Grandpa lounged back in his easy chair. Even though he'd had his say, the words—I told you so—were already forming on the old man's lips.

Emma was not going to be the solution to Sonny's problems. Their romance, as Grandpa had presumed, was brief. Although there were not any apparent hard feelings between them, when Nancy quizzed Emma, she replied, "It just didn't work out." Whether it hinged on the jingle in Sonny's pockets—I can't say.

CHAPTER 27

— ✂ —

Something of My Own

"YOU YOUN'NS QUIT yer caterwaulin'. Lay down there and go t' sleep now," Grandpa threatens, "or I'm a comin' in there to ya ... you aggravate and aggravate. I'll not hear n'more of it."

His bark is worse than his bite. After Grandpa has thundered from across the other side of the house, Carol and I lower our voices to a whisper.

Boys are pampered. Our brother has the cushy featherbed under the window, all to his lonesome—except for Spotty, the small spotted beagle that Dad gave to him for a birthday gift. Spotty sleeps at Sonny's feet. Like everyone else in our household, that dog adores him, also... usually.

Spotty could get grouchy and territorial when he settled in for the night. This is one of those nights. Sonny has to rouse Mom, because Spotty will not surrender the center of his and Sonny's bed. The naughty dog defends his right to sleep where he pleases with snarls and baring his sharp white teeth.

"Spotty won't wet me get in bed," Sonny complains. "He won't scoot down, and every time I try to make him move he snaps at me!"

Mom crawls out of bed intending to read Spotty the riot act. She begins to scold, "Get over there and let Sonny in bed." Spotty raises his head and responds with a menacing growl, showing fangs that mean business. "You go on now," she demands. "You go on!"

"Mom," I said, "I don't think Spotty knows what you're saying." I am positive that he can't understand the meaning of words, "Dogs are not that smart."

"Oh ... ho ... yes—he—does!"

Mom glares at the obstinate hound. But the spoiled dog will not budge from his curled up position until she threatens to undo him with the fly swatter. Begrudgingly, Spotty retreats to the foot of the featherbed.

I always wanted a room of my own. The best I can get, these days, was two to a bed—three whenever Mom paid us a visit. She occasionally spent the night with us when she had a day off from her barmaid job.

On just such a night, we ended up one pillow shy. The youngest, Carol and I, always drew the short straw.

"It's not fair! Why do we always have to be the ones to share?" Mary and Nancy never have to."

I jammed my head down on the bottom corner of our pillow. I felt Carol's breath on my face. Carol liked to grab on to somebody's ear as she fell asleep, sucking on her thumb. "Let my ear alone," was a constant nighttime message that Carol received from Mom. I thought Carol was after my ear, too. "She better not," I said out loud.

"Shirley Ann!" Using the no-nonsense addition of my middle name, Mom demanded, "Will you shut your mouth and go to sleep? You have the big pillow."

I would gladly have swapped it for a smaller one of my own. Did that make me selfish? I curled up and turned my back to Carol, still feeling shortchanged. "This is not fair," I complained under my breath. "I need my own stuff."

Aided by the stream of light filtering in through a window, I resentfully left the inhospitable bed and fumbled my way around in the shadows to reach the miraculous wall of shelves. These were the same shelves that had once provided my windfall school clothes. On the morning of my distress, when I had nothing else to wear, Sonny's out-grown cowboy outfit saved the day.

Rummaging through whatever my fingers blindly felt, I came up with a pillow substitute. The flannel of a long nightgown felt soft and snuggly, to my touch. I crept back into bed with the lucky find in my hands. After I folded the thing, it made a better headrest than the stiff corner of the shared pillow. Besides it is all mine.

Where does that missing pillow traipse off to? Normally there were enough pillows to go around, and I had a whole one to myself. Yet sometimes, due to unknown reasons—somebody secretly hoarding an extra one, or having an overnight houseguest—our pillow shortage became acute, and the last kid in bed would spirit away (not exactly steal) any pillow left untended.

When two older sisters were arriving home at a later hour, it was a good idea to trap one's pillow in a bear hug. That way, if somebody (who shall remain nameless) was short theirs in the night, I would feel mine move when it went "slippy-slide" out of my arms. And I'd raise a ruckus. Nobody wanted a long john clad grandfather on the warpath and "a comin' in there to ya."

When Dee still lived with us, she used her ingenuity to construct a sort of makeshift personal space for herself. Like me, she wanted a room of her very own.

In a corner of our front room, Dee organized a number of milk crates, stacking them nearly five feet high on two sides and thereby enclosing her single bed.

After Dee was finished building her room, she fastened curtains on the inside, hanging them over the milk crates. Nothing showed above these walls except for Dee's neck and head. The room within a room was a novel idea. Inside this unusual place, Dee appeared to possess magical powers. Gradually, I became accustomed to seeing her bodi-less head floating back and forth above the milk crate walls as she walked around in there.

Soon afterwards, Dee and Delbert were married, and while we were happy for her new life, our world was less bright without her in it. The milk crate walls listened for her voice to join ours. The house was sad because she left it. There was an emptiness. The makeshift room seemed to whisper, where is she?

How reluctant I was to see these treasured walls come down! I wished we could save Dee's room exactly as it was, forever, but Grandpa declared the space was only meant to be a temporary harbor to give Dee some privacy.

Change does not come easily. After he and Mom divorced, Dad traveled to Wisconsin where he reconnected with an Army buddy. I guess he found a certain peace there, roaming in this wilderness that he referred to as the north woods. His life, without us in it, was as lonely as those empty walls that Dee left behind.

Meanwhile, the rest of us made our home where our hearts were. Except for the few well-placed stones, our grandparents' house sat directly on the ground. During winter months, the bare floors turned into slabs of ice.

In the wee hours of these frigid mornings, Grandpa would leave his warm bed and lumber on into the front room where he would coax into flames the previous evening's banked coals. Scooting his comfy chair up closer to the stove, he would wait for the fire to catch hold.

As the warm air seeped through the open doorway into the bedroom, the frozen breaths hanging above our noses melted to nothing. The hard chill was broken.

Once the belly of the iron stove had turned cherry red and began to glow, the fire had to cool before it could be left safely unattended. As Grandpa waited for the cool down to happen, his calloused hands rubbed back and forth across the grizzled stubble of white whiskers. It would sound like gritty sandpaper gnawing against a block of wood, and it gives me goose bumps today to think of it.

"O-dee ... o-dee ... me," Grandpa bemoaned his hard lot. "Well ... I'm an old man ... old man ... old man." His tongue lightly clacked against the roof of his mouth. "Tsk-tsk-tsk."

When the dancing flames would begin to ebb, the self-declared old man would rock back in his chair and on its return motion, he'd rear up out of it and shuffle back to bed.

He'd rise again at daybreak with the house still warm from his own work, and he'd soon fill the kitchen with the aroma of fresh perked coffee.

Then he'd shatter our dreams.

"Shirley ... Carol!"

"Oh, no!" I groan and roll over onto my back. My body refuses to exit the snug place it has hollowed out in the mattress. Carol, I self-ishly reason, should have to get out of bed first and buy me a few extra minutes to lie here, steeling myself against the cold.

Unfortunately, Carol is nobody's fool "Nuh uh, Shirley. You go first."

Exasperated and murmuring, "Grandpa, go away," I pull the covers over my head. The next trip he makes in here, Grandpa will mean business.

"Dang it, Carol!" Slipping grudgingly out from under the warm comforter, my bare feet react in shock to the icy floor. I bound toward the front room, touching down only once or twice before landing on the warmer surface.

My feet prance up and down, in front of the stove, to stop my teeth from chattering. Making silly noises because I am so cold, I grunt and hum under my breath, "Nuh-nuh-nuh-nuh-nuh"—march, march, march.

I scoot closer to the potbelly stove, warming my backside until my thighs burn red hot, and I catch a whiff of scorching panties. In a wave of panic, I turn to look; the searing heat has singed the seat of my un-dies to a toasty brown. I shrink away from the stove just in time—my bottom looks sunburned.

Grandpa is dependable, particularly in the mornings. I hear him rattling around in the kitchen, and the dilapidated house creaks and groans as Grandpa wears a path between the icebox, cook stove, and cupboard. The old man could use a pair of sea legs; it only takes a bubble in the linoleum to start his arthritic knees to rocking.

Grandma slumbers to a later hour. Lord knows she's earned it. Meanwhile, the clatter of dishes tells me that Grandpa is standing at the cupboard. He resembles a tubby, aged elf. Even though he is positive that none appreciates his worth, Grandpa is pleased with himself for all his goodness.

One after another, tousled heads—Sonny, Mary, Nancy, Carol, and I—appear at the breakfast table. I take note of the white stubble on Grandpa's jowls. He hasn't done his weekly shave yet.

Grandma eats sparingly, her breakfast consists of a large Nabisco Shredded Wheat biscuit and half a peach. Canned peaches probably are an extravagance, but the elf of goodness adds them to his burlap sack, anyway, and he totes them home. He makes sure Grandma never runs out.

Never-ending cans of peaches are one way I know, for sure, he truly loves her.

Beside each of our cereal bowls, Grandpa places a cellophane wrapped Twinkie for a before-school treat. I think that gruff talking old man likes us, too, but he doesn't know how to express affection. He uses sweet cakes instead of words. These are a gift of love unspoken.

CHAPTER 28

Things of Old

Undreamed of possibilities abound for Carol and me on both sides of the room where Grandpa's shelves are full of wonders of the past, and the family wardrobe is packed with old clothing and secrets. On those shelves and behind the wardrobe's long doors are stored the most unique, discarded dress-up fashions a child can lay hands on.

Grandma's and Grandpa's keepsakes make up a strange conglomeration from a long-ago era. Hanging on the garment side of the wardrobe were some outdated, fancy dresses made of lush velvet and crisp lace. These were special things, collected and saved over a lifetime from sixteen children's best formal wear. Two full-length fur coats, one black and the other a reddish brown, were crushed against the back of the wardrobe.

Rainy days found Carol and me alternating between fashion shows and circus acts. She and I pulled the bulky coats up over our heads. Our blue eyes peeked out from the neck holes of the buttoned coats. The hems of our furry second skins dragged the floor when we walked.

After tiring of playing wild bear, we took turns wearing the black coat to perform the seal show. Our short arms, dangling inside the long satiny fur sleeves, make a perfect set of flippers. Sprawled on the floor, with our backs arched high and clapping our hands inside the long coat sleeves, we barked "Ark! Ark!"

I can't hold a candle to Carol's talent for mimicking animal calls, especially barking like a seal or crowing like a rooster.

Behind the second wardrobe door was a section of drawers. Tucked away inside here were several frilly hats. In Grandma's prime, these fashionable bonnets adorned with flocked veils, stunning pearl-tipped hatpins, and eye-catching feathers, turned many a young man's head.

Another of the drawers contained mismatched pieces of gaudy jewelry and other accessories left over from the flapper craze. Grandma's collection of mature garb looked quite hodgepodge when Carol and I were all decked out in it.

The bottom most drawer slid open to reveal a genuine fox stole. Slipped over my narrow shoulders, the stole drooped somewhat lop-sided, fitting me more like a cape. The fox's long, pointed nose was positioned just so, with the animal's face staring up at me through shiny, cold marble eyes.

Carol drew my attention to the sad look it wore. Suddenly, I felt so guilty. A twinge of uncertainty settled over me. Wearing something on my back that has a face attached to it was no longer comfortable, and the magical dress-up moment, for me, was dampened. I can't quite throw off a nagging feeling that something had gone wrong. Up until now, there had been so many previous entertaining dress-up, play days when I wore the fox stole and thought I looked just grand in it.

As the fox stole slid from my shoulders, I knew I would never put it there again. From now on, I would feel too guilty to have those cold, lifeless eyes looking up accusingly at me, that way. I regard that moment as a sudden understanding: an epiphany of sorts.

A conglomeration of Grandma's girlhood pastimes sat high on Grandpa's shelves. Stored out of reach of small hands was an old-fashioned metal stereoscope with a flip-down handle grip at the bottom of it. But Grandma didn't mind my climbing up and standing on the foot rail of the bed to reach the highest shelves. On the heels of her generosity, the stereoscope became the vehicle that took me to visit distant lands in another time: archaic places that were locked inside the contraption's picture cards. As I guided the cards into the viewer and lifted it to my eyes, each card took on an amazing depth.

The top shelf also was home to an interesting library of old books, two of which are ingrained in my memory. The first was a collection of wonderful poems, complete with antiquated pictures unlike any of the modern versions of prose that I was used to reading. Now, the second book was a real eye-opener!

It was written long before my time, and its yellowed pages were meant to shock the senses of the reader by exposing the "other" slave trade: the forced prostitution of young women. In the book, the author searches for his dear little sister who had been kidnapped and sold. Often, I read, he had to flee in fear for his life as he canvassed brothels in quest of her. I felt his heartbreak as he haunted the streets for her in vain.

Here to before, I was unaware that such things existed or that these hellish circumstances could befall someone who was just like me. If mistrust has a beginning—this could be mine. I never forgot that true story.

Other than handed down accounts that echo warnings of roving bands of gypsies who would steal babies and small children—as every generation has its own folklore—my world seemed safe. I never thought about kidnapping or knew of sexual addictions until I read that book. I guess the world has not changed from that day to this.

On one of the lower shelves, Grandma kept her collection of assorted greeting cards. Across from the boxes of cards, and wedged into the corner of that same shelf was one of Grandma's sentimental treasures. The beautiful red silken pillow, edged with gold fringe, was a gift from Roy, her youngest son, who was stationed overseas. It was embossed with a touching tribute. The following verse, from memory, is a close facsimile.

Ere I roam
Whether near or far
There is none other's
Love more true
Nor fair...
Than my own dear mother's

Oh, what a big tease my Uncle Roy was! He would either have me in stitches or bring me close to tears from embarrassment. "Well, hi there Shirley Ann peed 'n a pan," was his jovial greeting to me.

But that was so long ago.

After an absence of many years, Roy moved back to our area. He was trying to put his life together again on old stomping grounds. Roy's lengthy marriage had ended, but the hurt from its failure lingered on. And then a major heart attack nearly finished him off.

The details of his broken marriage were private. He never spoke of his ex, and I never brought up the subject. Roy was Sonny's mentor, and those two were almost like father and son. Just the same, when Sonny expressed an interest, Roy told him, "Mind your own business." This, too, was a distant memory.

It's Christmas time, and I am making plans for our family celebration, which includes about forty or so dinner guests. My family will pretty much include anybody, and around our table, there is always room for one more.

For some reason, Roy crossed my mind, and I thought perhaps I should reach out to him. He had recently moved back to the area, and we hadn't seen him in so long. I worried that he could be alone on Christmas. Still I hesitated.

Would he think I was inviting him because I felt sorry for him? Would he feel like last-minute company?

I can't explain it, but it was a clear voice that told me to call him now.

I rehearsed my invitation before I dialed his number. It rang and rang; I was about to hang up when he answered.

His voice is distant and edgy—strange. I tell him we would very much enjoy his company. I can't be sure if he appreciates the invitation. But he says, "I've already made some other plans."

Oh well, I tried. I felt uncomfortable and wished I hadn't called.

A few days later, I heard a knock at my door. It was Uncle Roy.

"Got a cup of coffee?" he asked. We sat down at the kitchen table and started talking.

"Shirley," he said, "I have been very depressed—for a while. You may know that my ticker is not good; I lay in bed at night, wondering if I will see daylight again."

He shared more of his troubles: his pain, and depression.

Then he said, "I was gonna do it. The gun was in my hand; it was against my temple."

I am shocked. I'm at a loss for words.

And he looks me in the eye and says, "Shirley, I had my finger on the trigger when the phone rang."

CHAPTER 29

— ❧ —

Home

LACKING BENEFIT OF time travel—without an enchanted looking glass or a magic carpet—my only road back home lies within my thoughts.

In the reflection from a long ago world, where a grandmother's stories of triumph over adversities inspired a small wallflower to join in the dance of life, ghosts of my past still visit. These friendly spirits remain close to my heart and live in my dreams.

Empowered by a cache of vivid memories, the past revolves around me. In childlike marvel, another soulful fragment from my less than ordinary youth, rises to meet me.

The banging and clanging of our lively household, reassuring somehow, reaches out to draw me closer. The familiar din of confusion from my rambunctious brother and sisters wraps around me like a pair of comforting arms.

Outside of my grandmother's room, I detect the telltale sounds of her movements. The noise alerts me that she is on a mission. Again, Grandma has misplaced one of her valuables.

A rickety wooden footstool is Grandma's handy extension to the out-of-reach places where a tottering old woman should not go. It screeches and groans as she shuttles and drags it across her bedroom floor. In its rumbling and squalling, Grandma's trusty step stool grinds out its whereabouts.

There is silence as Grandma investigates the nooks and crannies that her pocketbook might have carried itself off to. A final slam of wardrobe doors announces that she has given up her quest. Rumbling back to its home at the foot of the bed, Grandma's wooden helper churns out a last, sharp "knock-knock-thump."

She calls on me to retrace her steps, rummaging for the things she misplaces. Because it makes Grandma dizzy to bend down, I stoop and fetch the difficult-to-reach pots and pans that are stored on the lower shelves of the cupboard.

Once the knocking and bumping ceases, I know what to expect next. At any moment now, Grandma will appear in her doorway looking disheveled and thoroughly flustered.

When she wants me to step in, she will call. How frustrating her forgetfulness must be to her! Sifting through a maze of hanging garments, tightly squashed together inside the wardrobe, has left her exhausted. Wisps of white hair frame her search weary face. I am accustomed to seeing Grandma emerge this way.

It is Grandma's heavy breathing that captures my attention. The bodice of her cotton housedress visibly rises and falls. From across the room, I hear the rattle of each gasp and I begin to worry.

Soon her spell of breathlessness passes, and Grandma, admitting defeat, summons me. "Shirley ... aw, Shirley! Come here to me, honey. Grandma's gone woozy. You'll commence to help Grandma find her pocketbook, now won't you, please?"

My heart goes out to her. How easily I can scramble to my feet. It occurs to me that on some future, dismal day, I will be old and gray— or possibly as snow white as Grandma—and this depressing helplessness could also be mine. Will I be this forgetful? Will someone care enough to come to my rescue?

When the time comes, that another old woman (who greatly resembles me) cannot keep track of her pocketbook—to whom will she turn?

Grandma frets over her absent-mindedness. I am used to these circumstances, though, because she often misplaces things. She possesses a number of other purses. Of late, I had persuaded her to use only one pocketbook at a time. Otherwise, the task of locating the money whenever I had to run an errand for her was time consuming. And she did her best to plan ahead, entreating me to help her keep on track.

From her bedroom, she beckons. "Shirley, (always adding a term of endearment to my name) honey, you come now and commence to watch me and see about where Grandma puts away her pocketbook."

Later, she might putter around in there and change the location of the pocketbook, and then we'd both be in the dark. But that was all right, too. I never minded coming to her aid—nor could I turn her down when she asked, "Will you carry my pot out to the back?" Now and then, I saw Nancy walking down the path to the outhouse, doing that chore for Grandma.

If I could turn back time, have a do-over of everything, I would not change the days that I spent with Grandma Mollie. Nothing else can compare with the state of being wanted and needed. Grandma had a way about her that made us feel that we mattered.

Usually, if the errant purse was not found at the bottom of Grandma's wardrobe or in one of her dresser drawers, it was underneath the mattress and wedged just out of reach of her frail arms.

Why didn't Grandma simply place her pocketbook on the dresser top, leaving it within easy reach? Ours was a household of alcoholics. In a tryst with "John Barleycorn," honesty was suspect.

Besides that fact, there are friends and acquaintances of my brother and sisters—some new faces and some old ones of questionable character—who come and go. In any case, nothing was ever pilfered from our house that I recall. Old people just naturally squirrel away their belongings in unhandy places.

When my thoughts turn to Grandma, I can still hear her calling out my name, beckoning me close. "Come help Grandma, will you, honey? Lo and behold," she declares, "Grandma's gone woozy again."

My memories of home would not be complete without a piece of my history that includes Grandpa Alf.

Weather permitting, the back porch was Grandpa's afternoon resting spot. With his back to the kitchen window, he'd sometimes sit on a long white bench. There, he did his thinking out loud and named off the downfalls of the younger generation.

On a lighter note, he was also quite the prankster.

"Come on over here b'me," quipped my rascally grandfather as I rounded the corner of the house. "I've got my knife out so's I kin cut your ears off." He chuckled, jolly well pleased with himself over the least bit of aggravation he can stir up.

"Grandpa, that ain't funny!" I scoffed. His futile attempt at old guy humor was embarrassing. Approaching the steps at the base of the porch, I surveyed my surroundings, making certain that nobody else was witness to my blush, over Grandpa's silliness.

He slid his pocketknife back to its home inside his pocket. "I got me a whole trunk full of pretty baby dolls," he bragged.

"You have not!" I shot back, letting him know that I was wise to his windy tales.

"Yes, I do," Grandpa answered, matter-of-factly, and I caught the mischievous twinkle in his eyes. "I got 'em alrighty. I just ain't a showin' 'em t' you." Slapping his knee, Grandpa reared back, hooting with laughter. The old man, finished with me, declared a victory.

Well, I skipped to the right, stepped to the left, dancing past the great spinner of yarns, and in singsong tone, I murmured, "Liar, liar, pants on fire."

Although he is in charge of every one of us, except Grandma, Grandpa is an amiable caretaker. I left the "paper dragon" in his lair, (the back porch) to amuse himself with the next unsuspecting lair trespasser.

The time and tide to argue with an old man's peculiar sense of humor has come and gone. All I have left of Grandpa Alf is memories, and I think kindly of him.

CHAPTER 30

—— ✃ ——

Bed Time Story

THERE COMES TO mind a late night episode when Carol experienced a sleeping malady that was quite baffling.

"Shirley!" Grandpa's hand was on my shoulder, nudging me awake. "Set up now, and open yer eyes. I need you to hep me: Carol's gone."

Grandpa sounds breathless, as though he has just finished a hard run.

Instinctively, my hand went to Carol's empty sleeping place beside me, and it felt cool. She must have left our bed some time ago.

I tumbled out of our bed and into a foggy wakefulness. Even though my brains were rattled by the urgency in Grandpa's voice, my body still responded when my feet hit the floor.

"You'll have t' run and fetch Carol," Grandpa prompted, lamenting his sluggish hobble and admitting, "I'll not be apt to."

"What? Grandpa, tell me again. What's the matter?" As my eyes fastened to the grim expression on his face, an uneasy twinge of apprehension settled between my shoulder blades. "Where is she? Where did Carol go?"

"Aw," he grumbled, "the dang young'n's gone and left out the house! When I got up t' go out t' 'the back,' I looked out the wind'a and I saw Carol out yonder, a runnin' and a hootin'. I'm too old for such a nonsense as this is. You young'ns are apt to be the death of me."

I didn't know what to expect next, but I followed along, in a daze, behind Grandpa—out into the night. He mumbled repeatedly, "Aggravate n' aggravate."

I squelched an urge to rub my eyes and make the unbelievable scene explode. My little sister bathed in moonglow and looking so bewildering to me, darted between light and shadow in our front yard.

In my rush to catch her, my feet suddenly went wild, slipping out from under me on the dew-drenched grass. The hard ground rose up to meet me, and I felt a shock of impact in my ankle. The burning pain from the twist was intense. It was all I could do to swallow back tears.

I lay sprawled there, thanking my lucky stars, as the pain began to ebb, that nothing was broken. Only my pride was shattered. I thought to myself, "No wonder that old man gave up the chase! Bigger and faster just wasn't getting it. That skinny brat was greased lightning!"

Weaving and bobbing like an athlete, Carol zipped past me, time and again. Whenever I attempted to nab her, she changed directions and left me empty handed. Several times I had her in my grasp, but she wriggled and squirmed free. Finally I managed to wrestle that elusive shadow onto the wet grass.

"Carol! Carol! Carol!" I shouted. "Listen to me!" My struggle is against her state of mind—something I do not exactly understand.

"What's the matter with you? Why are you acting like this?"

She squirmed to free herself, and I tightened my hold.

Hoping to initiate a stir of her conscience and make her feel concern for me, I feigned an injury. "Carol," I moaned, "my ankle is hurt real bad, and you are scaring me." I left no stone unturned.

The transition from a warm bed to the chill of night left me without my wits. I can hardly believe it is me rolling on the damp ground. The whole thing has a dream-like quality about it. Had I truly left behind my own small world and wandered into someone else's weird, nightmare? Because everything seems so out of focus, I am drawn to test the very night, itself.

Carol's reply, in the face of my demands, is a string of denials. Things seldom are the way she perceives them. I tell myself, that if I can reason with her, then possibly, I will find a solution that I can deal with.

"Let go of me!" Carol demanded. "You let me go! I can't breathe." Her frantic cries weakened my resolve, but I could not back off while she was out of control.

"Carol! Stop! Stop! Stop! You don't understand. Listen to me for a minute. I can't let go of you. Not until you tell me what you're doing out here. I have to help you."

"Lordy. Oh lordy me." Grandpa's voice sounds full of misery. Although he is weary, he backs me up, lending me credence as I wrestle with Carol on the wet grass. "Carol, now Carol! You cut out yer shenanigans and behave yerself. I've had all I kin take."

Carol flailed around, squirming every which way, trying to slip free of my securely locked arms. At last, Carol gave up. Pinned down with arms stronger than hers, she blurted out a response, "I don't know! I told you already, I don't know why."

"Give me the reason, and I'll turn you loose," I bargained.

"It's the frosting," she sputtered. "I ate the frosting. It makes me not be able to breathe. I have to run out here."

"Hmmm," I reflected on what Carol said. "She runs in the cool night air to catch her breath." At last, Carol says something credible. Even though I am skeptical of her interpretation, I was less anxious when she didn't bolt and run after I released her.

Grandpa was standing over us and he began scolding Carol. "You march yer hind end on back to the house!" She returned to bed, and I vowed to find a way to fix this—tomorrow.

And so, early next morning, I am ready to pounce at the instant when Carol climbs out of bed. Determined to hammer out a plan before night falls again, I cornered Carol. Face to face, eye to eye, I confronted her. "Tell me why—in the light of day—you want to get out of bed and run in the dark of night? You run like a crazed banshee! Are you out of your mind? And how could you wander around out there all by yourself? You are afraid of the dark! Even when you have to go out to 'the back' at night, you wake me up first and drag me along with you!"

Carol grew thoughtful. "I don't know, Shirley. I think it really is the frosting. Every time I eat it, I feel real bad. I ate some last night before I went to sleep."

It didn't make sense to me, but I warned her, "You had better not do that anymore."

Carol turned my words over in her mind before she said, "I can't help it. You know, I always think I won't eat it, but then I want it—so I do it anyhow."

At that disclosure, my heart went out to her, and my resolve weakened. I spoke more softly, almost pleading with her. "If frosting does this to you, Carol, you have got to stop yourself."

Carol shook her head, revealing her helplessness against her compulsion. I threw up my hands in dismay! Could the dusty particles from powdered sugar, somehow, have coated Carol's lungs or glued itself to the roof of her mouth? As I went back over what she'd said—"Shirley, I can't help it"—it sounded vaguely familiar.

There it was: an image of her and the trouble-making powdered sugar slowly coming into focus. Now I can remember seeing Carol standing at the kitchen table, clasping a tablespoon with one hand and the guilty box of powdered sugar with the other, her face beaming happily.

How much of it did she consume? Was she accidentally breathing the stuff into her lungs? These questions I asked myself, and then I wondered—was it possible for Carol to be addicted to powdered sugar in the way Mom and Dad needed nicotine?

Not every worry that preys on the mind of a kid, leads to action. Thoughts are fleeting, and as children often do, I quickly forgot all about Carol's sleeping problems—until another late night chase ensued.

When it happened again, Carol offered me the same answers. She adamantly claimed, "When I eat frosting, I can't breathe, so I have to run outside."

Before it could slip my mind again, I retrieved the ominous box of powdered sugar and secretly stored it in an out-of-the-way place. (Yes, I hid it from her.) Although that put an end to one particular problem for me, for Carol, it was only just beginning. She, ever after, struggles to overcome. An endless dependence on psychiatric medication, with serious side-effects, dominates her life.

Throughout the years, from playmate to cherished friend, perhaps I have needed Carol as much as she needed me. Truly, life is not fair. My little sister deserves better. The why of it all still eludes me.

CHAPTER 31

The River of Tears

THEIR EMPTY ARMS symbolized what might have been. Neither of my parents must have stopped and truly looked into the other's eyes. This is not the way things are supposed to be.

Long before their flame of love died out, Mom was exhibiting signs of a mental disorder, while Dad was bossy and temperamental.

In his prime, Dad could be stubborn, and his social affair with the bottle strained the family. On either side of my kindred, there were men who, come payday, drank their cares away. Some made merry and turned into good fellows. Others grew sullen and mean. Grandpa Alf was one of the former; Dad belonged to the latter.

Mom was struggling, day to day, with her emotional health. Nothing on earth could change the course of events that was already set in motion. There was growing discontent. As clearly as the gathering of dark clouds foreshadows a thunderstorm, the start of depression was, for Mom, the harbinger of worse yet to come.

One day, in a rage that can only be described as coming out of nowhere, Mom turned on Dad and ordered him out of her parents' home. We were all living in one house then. By chance, I was caught up in the midst of all this craziness, and I became a captive witness to a marriage burning to ashes.

In stunned disbelief, I was drawn into a sequence of events of grave consequences for our family. In my memory, it plays out like the opening scene of a tense movie. The leading man is hit by an unexpected torrent of words from the leading lady, and the viewing audience—one young child—takes the harsh brunt of their encounter.

A little girl is the sole spectator in this kitchen theater. Only the three of us share the stage in Grandma Mollie's kitchen, where the drama unfolds.

The dish towel, still casually draped across Daddy's shoulder, became the focus of my attention. He had just finished drying a stack of dishes.

"You go on now and get out of here!" Mom demanded.

Her sudden outburst, driven by an unknown cause, exploded without warning. Dad's quick temper was not evident. Since Mom had not challenged him while he was in a sour mood, it did not make sense to me that she would confront him in a time of truce. I hadn't seen him do anything to provoke her. A puzzled expression clouded Dad's face. He was at the mercy of confusion, blind-sided and felled by Mom's sudden loss of clarity.

"You get out of here!" She stormed at him again. Dad stared, long and inquisitively at Mom, taking in her strange behavior. It was as if he could not tear his eyes away from her face.

In dazed silence, I watched him back away, flipping the towel from off his shoulder as he moved. Dad could not comprehend what was happening to her, nor to him. Mom appeared to be infuriated at Dad. I could see her anger rising.

"You go on now and don't you come back here!" She demanded. Fire flashed between them, as she ordered him out of the house and out of her life. Bitter words, spoken in anger, can never be retrieved. I could only wonder at what was going on inside Mom's head.

For what felt just shy of an eternity, Dad continued to search Mom's face for some sort of clue. He was lost in pandemonium, and seeking a means of escape that was short of leaving the house. All reasonable emotional exits remained blocked. Mom was not going to change her mind.

My feet were cemented in place. I was helpless to intervene. Time is mystifying. Leaving home should be a measured progression—as crossing over a brook from one steppingstone to another. Before the departure begins, you pack your belongings. Next, you say the farewells. And finally—a parting kiss, gentle hug, or at least a firm handshake is needed before the door closes. In dismay, I looked down at my feet, knowing that this is all wrong.

Dad left, but the screen door had scarcely banged shut before it swung open again. Mom raged at him once more. "I told you, I wanted you to get out of here!"

"I'm getting my bucket!" Dad snapped back. Routine activities suddenly feel out of place here in this kitchen battleground. It seemed so odd that Dad remembered to come back inside that hornet's nest to claim his dinner bucket. Our world was crumbling, and Dad's lunch was all he could salvage. Did he even know the finality of it? That nothing here would be ordinary any more?

For just a second, Dad and I made eye contact. And then he was gone, his footsteps fading away, echoing into emptiness.

Sometime later, it came on without any apparent reason. I was awakened by the muffled sounds of her crying into her pillow. The soft weeping suddenly turned into deep, body wracking sobs that shook the whole bed, leaving Mom's pillow soaking wet. My heart went out to her, and I felt a current of helplessness wash over me. The mattress quivered beneath us, and the sound of her anguish mingled with the squeaking metal springs in our shared bed.

The depth of Mom's sorrow made me reach out to her, and my hands were drenched in a river of her tears. I would have done anything to make it stop.

"Mom, what's wrong?" My words spilled out, interrupting her torrent. "Tell me what's the matter." I begged for an answer to her secret pain.

"Please, Mom, tell me what's wrong. It will be all right," I promised. "Maybe I can help you," I said, while trying to console her.

Mom lay curled up—with her back to me. Quieting herself, somewhat, she said, "Shirley Ann, you don't understand."

Her words struck me as so very sad. Though the bed shaking lessened, Mom's reply was crushing to my struggle to comfort her. Taking on Mom's sorrow in this moment, I was as moved by her brokenness as she.

Mom did not mention Dad or the turmoil connected with his departure. Something else was more troubling, more hopeless. What could be so abysmal? She shut me out, and there was nothing I could do.

Desperation drove me to grasp at the first thing that popped into my mind. Astrology literature became suspect number one. I turned a critical eye there because Mom was so absorbed in those particular magazines.

Evidently, Grandpa Alf was also troubled by Mom's fascination with the stars, calling her magazines, "That trash." I saw the worried glances he threw her way, knowing full well that in the face of this formidable opponent, her mental decline, he was rendered powerless.

Mom was not going to take fatherly guidance. Sometimes it proved taxing just to gain her attention. We had to overcome her inability to focus, before she would acknowledge us.

But Grandpa was not one to back down from a fight. In his younger days, I am told, he had been an amateur boxer.

"Norma," Grandpa said, "it ain't 'ery good for you to have your nose stuck in such rubbish as this."

Mom didn't bother to answer Grandpa, and he waded in to persuade her, warning: "It's a preyin' on yer mind." As usual, she ignored his counsel.

I wanted to blame the junk type reading material for adding to Mom's distress, exactly as my grandfather had. I recognized that he must have associated astrology books with some sort of mystical or addictive power. Grandpa's opinion influenced my thinking—more than it did Mom's.

As soon as the coast was clear, I hurriedly picked up one of the magazines in question, feeling quite guilty for it, all the while. Laying conscience aside, I needed to see for myself if the book's sinister reputation was superstition or fact. I simply did not understand how just reading about astrology, or tracking the positions of the stars and planets could harm a body, and yet Mom's condition was real enough. She was worsening, even slipping away from us.

Leafing through the ominous magazine, I searched for a cause to the illness that was enveloping my mother. What I read was a bunch of horoscope nonsense. The pages seemed harmless enough—nothing in there to steal my mind or make me cry. I tossed the suspicious magazine to the side and went on with my little girl life.

I could only wish for something typical. Everything was in turmoil when I learned that Dad had expressed concern and mentioned putting us in a children's home. That turned out to be idle talk, but the thought of it struck fear in my heart.

Carol and I were the young ones in jeopardy. I burned with anger that Dad would not want us for himself, and I thought that these two old people, our grandparents, were the only hindrance that stood between us and a fate worse than death.

CHAPTER 32

— ⚬ —

Brush With Eternity

WHEN MY FRIEND exposed the gun, I just knew it was loaded. Shannon plopped down on the couch next to me, holding out the gun for me to inspect. It was an awesome find in her estimation, but it looked cold and lethal in mine.

"Lookie what I got!" This boastful declaration seemed out of place for a young girl—we were both 13—because there was an assumption that only boys were fascinated with weapons.

Her finger was on the trigger, and I was frozen with fear of what was coming next.

"He wouldn't have a loaded gun in the house," Shannon said, but the warning of self-preservation roared like thunder in my ears. I scarcely had time to stretch out my arms in protest when the gun exploded.

The bullet grazed the rim of my eyeglasses, narrowly missing my temple. As in slow motion, I watched the gun fall from Shannon's hand and clatter against the floor.

It felt like the end of the world had come. My life was a short sequel. There was not much recorded yet, because I had just begun to live. Naively, I imagined God as a very wise man with a long, white beard.

"Oh my God! Oh my God!" Shannon cried. She wailed out the words nonstop.

I will never again question the value of a millisecond in time or a centimeter in space. My wish for a brighter tomorrow might have ended here—everything wiped out by accident, all in a bloody split second. My brains were not more than an inch away, at point blank range, from being splattered across the room.

How ironic that such a small and insignificant measure of time and space can decide life or death.

It was not just about me; the lives of the babies I had always dreamed of having hung in delicate balance. My life would surely miss the completeness they could offer it.

Yet I remained calm. How could this be? I had, of a certainty, just cheated death, and I felt crushed. It was over in a flash. I thought I was about to die, and the profound relief that it didn't happen overcame every other human emotion.

Later, I was devastated. But I would not allow myself to be mad at my friend, and I never told anyone. Only a wise God, the one with a long white beard, and my friend Shannon knew of my brush with eternity. I could not bear to think on it, so I put it out of my mind.

Once the shock of the moment passed, Shannon tried to cover her tracks. Survival mode kicked in, and the gun was returned to her stern uncle's nightstand. Shannon had done the unthinkable when she violated his trust, went into his bedroom and lifted his police revolver.

I recall that Shannon's temporary guardian was a grumpy sort of fellow—a constable and a rather impatient one. After the day's work and the evening meal, he generally settled back in his easy chair. It rather embarrassed Shannon that her uncle would strip down to his undershorts and then spend the rest of the evening watching television and guzzling beer.

Shannon found and pointed out the incriminating evidence. The stray bullet (which only by the grace of God was not meant for me) was lodged somewhere inside the wall. Placing a box fan, just so, in front of the hole, Shannon took a deep breath. It was as simple as that. She would never be found out, and neither of us spoke about it again.

A few days later, though, Shannon brought it up.

"Hey, Shirley, guess what?" she snickered. "Have I ever got something funny to tell you!"

My jovial friend covered her mouth, as she always did when she laughed to hide her badly chipped front tooth.

"I heard Auntie tell my uncle… " A wave of giggling erupted before Shannon could continue. "She told him, 'I just can't figure out what could have made that hole in my wall. I've looked at everything near it. Nothing matches it.'

I can say now, that if the close call had happened to some other luckless kid, I probably would have told somebody. When kids don't tell, it's because they are too traumatized. They can't speak out while wearing their own sensitive skins. Instead, they deny their feelings. The fear of repercussion and the pain of dredging up all the lowly details prevails. They cannot untie the knot.

That knot of fear was the reason I never told on Hunter when he pursued me to the point of stalking. A couple of times his advances came very close, but he never managed to lasso me. My guardian angel works overtime.

The crazy thing was this: Hunter would have wanted to marry me as readily as he wanted to attack. In my thirteenth year, I turned a deaf ear to every word he used to lure me. The world is so strange—a snare comes in many different forms.

CHAPTER 33

— ✿ —

Just Testing

WE WERE AN unlikely pairing of friends—Shannon and I—opposites all the way down the line. She was a darker complexioned, brown-eyed brunette. She possessed an uncanny, gutsy urge to try anything and everything.

I was fair, blond haired and blue-eyed. And I needn't get burned to know that fire is hot. It was similar circumstances that bound us together. We depended on one another for safe passage through the risky teen years.

I was the more restless one. Shannon could sit idle, watching soap operas for hours at a time. God saw fit to bless me with feet that never stopped running.

A taste for the bitter was something we did have in common. From the few, unclaimed fruit trees in the wilds behind Shannon's home, we gathered sour green apples. And then, there was that time when Shannon came around, toting a windfall sack of store-bought lemons, a saltshaker, and for afterwards—a pack of smokes.

Shannon clung to the tomboy phase a bit longer than I. While I was newly concerned with finding the one true love of my young life, she was fixated on taking down all male challengers in a bout of "Indian arm wrestling."

"I can beat any girl in town," she bragged, staring me down, "and most of the boys."

On one particular day, in order to impress me with her prowess, Shannon assumed a confrontational stance directly in my path, blocking the only exit to an amicable retreat. It was just in passing, that she offered her pumped-up forearm muscle for my inspection.

"Shirley," she urged, "just feel how hard my muscle is."

I wished I could think of a polite way to refuse. Weighing the need to be agreeable against maintaining a comfortable personal space, I reluctantly yielded to Shannon's persistence.

Pretending to admire her strength, my hands gingerly touched the much exaggerated and touted lump on Shannon's upper arm. She wallowed in the satisfaction of her moment in the sun.

Wrestling was her current interest. It was a pastime within a poor child's reach. Just off the back stoop of the shanty that Shannon's family of seven called home, a deep woods began.

"Come on," Shannon urged, as she motioned for me to follow her out into it. We proceeded on down a brushy trail until we reached a small clearing. All of this land was owned by a strip-mining company.

"This place right here," she pointed out a scrubby area with clumps of debris piled to one side, "is where I'm gonna build a wrestling ring." Her enthusiasm went unmatched by mine.

An expression of pride over her small success lit Shannon's face as she flourished the thus far fruit of her labors. "I just have to come up with some posts and a long rope," she said.

I surveyed Shannon's handiwork. Four mounds of black dirt marked the perimeter of her wrestling ring. Building supplies were conspicuously missing. She had managed to clear an area of underbrush and to dig some shallow holes. The next step would involve Shannon's confiscating an axe in order to hack away at a few of the mining companies' small trees, turning their trunks into posts.

When I suggested a problem with her building plans, she assured me, "Oh, they won't even care."

As nobody was handing out free ropes, and as Shannon was every bit as penniless as I was, it seemed unlikely that her endeavors would progress further.

Rather than discouraging Shannon's wrestling ambitions and taking the chance of awakening her competitive spirit (and finding it turned on me), I kept my fingers crossed and my opinions to myself. I didn't want to be dragged into a wrestling match with her, on this day—or any other.

Too late. It was nagging at her, and Shannon was not totally confident of besting me in combat, as she would like. I felt perfectly content to leave it so and would rather not have to prove myself in an unnecessary contest. Although we were close friends, I had nothing to say in the matter, once Shannon decided to take me on.

Striking a hold in an unexpected clash-of-wills moment, Shannon quickly tackled me. After she made the first move, she drew back. Then, she laughed as she downplayed the competition to "Just for the fun of it." To my growing uneasiness, she went on to suggest, "Let's see which one of us is the strongest."

Shannon ignored my feeble protest; she was determined to be sure she could whip me.

It dawned on me, that all this unwelcome rivalry—never mind the hard knocks to the ground that left me breathless—was meant to also be a psychological triumph for her ego. This stunt was really a testing that would hand Shannon a wanton advantage over me, and also, a physical confidence that I would just as soon she not have.

The idea that Shannon would, thereafter, have the bluff on me, gave fresh determination to my final efforts. In a lightning round that began on her terms, I fought to come out on top. In the end, I only held my own.

We scrapped a good one, grappling and churning on the hard ground, until my lungs begged me for mercy. My power-hungry opponent and I were red faced and breathless, and at long last our intense struggle was declared a draw. Shannon's question—who is the baddest?—remained unanswered.

Shannon laughed off the whole ordeal, but it was not that easily done away with for me. My insides were pumped up. Outwardly, I gasped for air and my arms were two useless, dangling nothings. Still, I forced myself to pretend otherwise—not willing to allow her the least bit of satisfaction. And I was darn good and mad at her for making me feel this way. Already primed, and now, with a second wind, I could have "whipped my weight in wildcats."

The toughest thing either of us wrestled with was smoking. Breaking my addiction was the most difficult thing I have ever done. Year after year, I was hooked, fighting frequent bouts of bronchitis. The cigarette called "Luckies" was anything but. It was even worse for Shannon. Sadly, in the final round, it took her down.

Years and miles put distance between us. We reconnected in the weeks before Shannon died. Our friendship withstood the only test that really mattered. Inside the ropes of time, it endured.

The last time I spoke with Shannon, we closed the gap of years that had separated us. She confided her heart problems, and I tried using encouragement, asking her to not give up without a fight. There was finality and acceptance in her voice when she responded, "It's too late. I'll not get any better now."

Shortly after, Shannon, now in her early 60s, ate a slice of her birthday cake, went to bed, and died peacefully in her sleep.

When I think of Shannon, I still imagine her as the same dark-eyed and courageous young girl who raced, side by side with me, through the mine field called youth.

CHAPTER 34

❧

Forever Friends

KATE AND I have a history of lost and found friendship. It was the summer of my eleventh year when we became acquainted through a chance meeting with her younger sister, Dana. All three of us hit it off immediately, and from that day forward we were almost inseparable.

This lasting friendship came about through a shoe exchange. I let the new girl at Bible school, Dana, borrow my prized Mary Janes for the morning, and she invited me to come home with her before we swapped back. She really was reluctant to return my black patent treasures. "We'll switch at my house," she said.

I met her entire family, and right away I felt at home. In a surprisingly short time, I think I would have parted with the classiest shoes ever to adorn my feet and gone skipping back home barefoot, if Dana had asked to keep them.

Just days later, on the walk home from my new friends' house, I was confronted by bullies. I found myself at the mercy of a boy named Grover and his older brother Harry. When they came sauntering up the road toward me, I knew by their swagger that I was in trouble.

The boys stood the ground in front of me—daring me to pass. I watched their chests puff out like a bullfrog's, as they blocked my retreat, taking advantage of my situation (fear and isolation). I was stuck, unable to move on or turn back. Grover, at Harry's command, went on the offensive, thrusting his leg behind mine and tripping me. Falling backward, my body hit the ground. I was so scared that I hardly felt the slam.

Never underestimate the power of a kick. Grover took a wild and lofty spin on my spontaneously uplifted feet, causing him to land on his head. It made a hollow conking sound. A look of shock covered Grover's face, as he scrambled to recover his coke bottle thick glasses. Harry continued to egg him on, shouting from the sidelines, "Git 'er Grover! Git 'er!" Still dazed from the blow to his head, Grover backed away. He brushed himself off and challenged his brother, "You git 'er yourself!" He quickly conceded his part in their mischief. Then I passed by the two of them, unharmed, and went on my merry way. So many close calls for one little girl.

I can still picture Kate and Dana—big as life. The three of us kept the sidewalks hot between our houses.

Everywhere within walking distance was our playground. On occasion, we hiked to another village scant miles away. The area around the Community Lake, formed by strip mining operations, was a favorite exploration site for us. We went swimming there, in our street clothes, and chased after lightning-fast lizards that zipped along the muddy banks.

Although we roamed across all the territory our wandering feet could cover, from daylight to dusk, there was a loose set of our own unspoken code of conduct that we kept in mind. There were lines we just would not blur. I carried the Wonder Woman ideals inside my head; Kate and Dana had a church-centered background in theirs.

The one diversion I best remember was a pastime the three of us made up. We called our creation the Movie Star Game.

It was actually more of a beauty contest, one that would begin with the selection of a judge. The remaining two girls sprawl out on the grass, readying themselves for their coming flight. Next, the appointed judge takes hold of one contestant's arm and leg. And the twirling begins.

I sailed through the air, flying in a wide circle. The wind rushed by as though I had wings. The world became a blur; it was quite the wild ride.

The object of our flight was to turn a fairly soft landing into something resembling a movie starlet pose—once the judge had lowered each of us to the ground and released our wrists and ankles. The outcome of our playacting required a certain trust in the ability of the dizzy swinger/judge to know when she had slowed to the point of making "the drop," without causing bodily harm.

The most theatrical pose at the finish of our flight was declared the winner. The prize was a hefty boost in self-esteem—movie star power—which was something of a rarity in all three of us poor kids. The judge had the final say in choosing a winner, but there was always a next time to fly and another chance to win beauty and fame. After minimal practice, we mastered the art of some very glamorous poses.

Though neither Kate nor I was very practical, her thoughts, more than mine, were influenced by the insincere promises ("I'll love you forever.") that young boyfriends are inclined to easily make and break.

Give and take in the sand box with the notorious Bobby, early in my life, had taught me to recognize malarkey when I heard it.

Wonder Woman was my idol until Kate introduced me to love story comic books. These tantalizing tales—were to die for. Nothing was ever quite the same after I had read something titled "True Romance."

Princess Diana, aka Wonder Woman, and her golden lasso of truth took second place in my new aspirations. I decided that some other young dreamer would have to fill those striking red boots, and to struggle at being her greatest fan. Defending the weak was a full-time occupation, and I had cast myself in a new fantasy role. Visions of great, romantic expectations whirled around inside my head.

The poetic nudging from immature reflection coincided with the arrival of passionate adventures that were tucked inside those comic books. The leap from imitating Wonder Woman's amazing exploits to finding myself captivated by pages spelling out the splendor of romance, all happened in a flash of discovery. Somewhere out there was the man of my dreams. And I laced-up my walking shoes.

231

Kate shared with me the limited knowledge of love making that had been passed along to her. We discovered years later that there were some glaring inaccuracies in our "birds and bees" discussion.

She introduced me to her childhood sweetheart, Carl, who had given Kate her memorable first kiss. "Now," she assured me, "we are just good friends."

It was Kate who brought Carl and me together. Love letters sailed back and forth between us. Our short romance consisted of walking together and holding hands—no kisses. Love words on paper, though, had a powerful effect. Reading each letter made my heart flutter. I sure was in love—with love.

When a girl passes on a former romantic interest to another girl, that speaks volumes about her, and it is a sign of true friendship. Kate gave the okay—and she meant it.

"Carl is too young for me," she said. "And anyway, he is not 'the one.'"

Everything changed for Kate when a handsome red-haired boy arrived from out of state. Marvin had come here to spend the summer with a relative who lived just across the road from Kate's family. She was 13 when she met Marvin. Romance blossomed on his granny's front-porch step. Their dates consisted of holding hands and attending evening church doings.

Through Kate's eyes, I saw young love at its fairest. Every thrilling, innocent detail in their closely chaperoned courtship she shared with me.

Then the dreaded day arose. Summer vacation came to an end, and that meant her new love must return to his home state of Michigan. When they parted, Marvin's teenage heart lay behind at Kate's feet. Distance is a force to be reckoned with, and the dreams they had built were crushed by it.

It's so difficult for the young to think beyond tomorrow, and love letters are not flesh and blood. Deprived of the closeness they had experienced all summer long, the bloom slowly wilted.

Kate's austere girlhood, in many ways, resembled mine. Both of us grew up in households with absent fathers, but because her mother stayed in the home, my lot seemed worse. Kate had some wearable hand-me-downs to choose from. When her father bought her a new dress for her eighth-grade graduation, I was as thrilled to see it as she was.

Kate never challenged me to a wrestling duel as Shannon had. There was no tomboy ways about her. And I never confronted death while with her. Instead, a deep trust developed between us. Kate and I shared secrets of the heart.

When she was in her thirties, Kate's sister, Dana, suffered a nervous breakdown, and she had to go away to a state hospital. Already a heavy smoker, her cravings for tobacco got the better of her.

When she got out, Dana confided to me, "I begged strangers there, who were just visitors, for cigarettes. I can't believe now that I did that."

Mentally, I journeyed back to our shoe-trading days. In a sense, the shoes that Dana and I had shared seemed a poor fit. I felt her humiliation, when she was reduced to begging random strangers for a smoke. The thought of it made my brief walk in her shoes miserable.

Putting my habit and myself in Dana's place, brought about a rude awakening. My first desire to quit smoking was formed by Dana's painful experience. The picture I saw in my mind—of me begging for smokes—caused me to panic. I had to quit. And eventually I did.

Dana died, as Shannon did, from heart problems while she was still a young woman. Hair that had started to gray in her 20s hinted at a future that was destined to be far too short.

CHAPTER 35

❦

Mopping Lioness

UNCLE AL SHOWED up in midday, his staggering drunk form darkening our kitchen doorway. He guided one clumsy hand over the other in the general direction of the screen door handle. From across the room, Mom scrutinized her brother as he stumbled across the threshold.

My gaze followed Uncle Al's wobbly legs. With each step forward, a trail of muddy shoeprints tracked up Mom's freshly scrubbed floor. The mop bucket was at her feet, and in her hands was the mop handle: a potential weapon.

She delayed her back and forth scrubbing motion, long enough to offer him friendly warning. "I'm mopping now, Brother."

He barged in, anyway, continuing to weave his way farther into the kitchen, step by wobbly, precarious step. Then, fumbling with the front of his trousers, he bellowed a startling announcement.

"I don't care if you are a moppin'. I'll take a piss right here on it!"

In full view of his shameful conduct, I froze in shocked disbelief. I was standing against the front room doorjamb. Before Uncle Al could perform the threatened obscenity or utter another word, Mom flew into action. I was amazed to discover, first hand, exactly where my Wonder Woman roots originated.

She was on him in a flash of wet mop head. The swiftness of her pounce shocked me. I felt the breeze fan right by me when Mom sprang like a lioness protecting her cub. All I could see was a blur of woman and mop.

"Whack-thud-crack! Crack!" The mop stick pounded its intended target.

With every swing of the mop handle, Mom berated him. "Don't you never, never do such-a-thing as that, in front of my little girl!" Mom, the lioness, lunged at Uncle Al, again, thumping him mercilessly. "Why, I'll beat you to death!" I'll knock your damn head off!"

Uncle Al resembled a slapstick clown, performing a riotous circus act. If it were not a serious matter, and if he hadn't been dying to get out of there, this spectacle would have been outrageously funny.

Zigzagging, while rushing to escape the wrath of his sister, Uncle Al overturned the mop bucket. Blow after blow rained down on his head and across his shoulders. I hoped the cracking sound I heard was not Uncle Al's skull.

Water flooded the floor, and he went skating on the wet linoleum. Legs and arms lurched and flailed wildly in all directions. He went down on all fours. Scrambling back to his feet, the beaten drunkard lunged desperately for the kitchen door.

The fear of Uncle Al exposing himself was crowded out by a new and even worse thought: I seriously considered that Mom could actually "do in" my uncle before he could get clear of the mop handle and skate to the safety of the back porch.

Uncle Al could not exit that kitchen fast enough to satisfy himself, nor me. He was lucky to get out of there alive. I was more than relieved when I heard the screen door bang shut after him.

The following day, Uncle Al reappeared. He looked around at us, somewhat sheepishly. I don't know what I expected out of those two, but there wasn't any telling sign of hard feelings between sister and brother. Uncle Al was sober, and he hadn't any obvious battle scars—other than a bandage across the bridge of his nose.

Uncle Al lived to an advanced age, despite the cost of lifelong alcoholism. It destroyed his marriage and ruined every close relationship that mattered to him.

CHAPTER 36

—— ✿ ——

Between Love and War

TUCKED AWAY IN thoughts from my youth and nearly forgotten is the memory of Aunt Lola's last visit with us at Grandma Mollie's house.

After dinner, Nancy and I were helping Lola wash dishes, when Lola and Nancy started reflecting on family relationships. Listening to their exchange of confidences gave me pause to reconsider the missed opportunities in the past—chances that would never come again.

"Why do you think," Nancy asked Lola, "Mom and Dad divorced? I mean, what really went wrong? And was there any one thing that caused the break-up?" Nancy could speak right up.

I listened intently, wanting to hear a logical response from Lola, whom I considered unbiased and who was more knowledgeable of their troubles than either Nancy or I.

"There really wasn't anything you could put your finger on," Lola said. "But separation during the war (World War II), when your daddy was away for so long, I think, was the beginning of the end. I was so sorry to hear of it. After Wib came back home, he and Norma couldn't get along."

Intentionally then, Lola turned to include me in her confidence. "The time apart took its toll, and I'm sure it contributed to their squabbles. Why, Carol was just a little thing when Wib came home to stay." Then, surprising to me, Lola went on to assure us, "I liked your daddy." I had not expected to hear that from our mother's side of the family.

Unanswered questions still troubled me. I wondered (wordlessly, because I wasn't born with Nancy's openness or her self-confidence)

236

why Dad enlisted. Was the military the only option available to him, during that time? One especially hurtful doubt lingered: Did he want to leave us? On down the line, I would be stunned by Dad's sharp reply to my supposes.

Lola's conclusion did not agree with some of my early childhood memories, leaving me questioning whether the war had actually sounded the death knell to our parents' marriage.

Having felt the atmosphere of resentment between them, in the way that only a perceptive youngster on the sideline can, I was led to a harder truth. In the eyes of one small daughter, their discord had more to do with Dad's impatient nature and Mom's mental health issues.

Years later, when I asked him why he enlisted in the Army, Dad glared at me as he hotly defended himself. Setting the record straight he snapped, "What kind of an asshole do you think I am?"

It never occurred to me that a father of six might be eligible for the draft. All this time, I had wrongly believed that it was Dad's choice to sign up, and that he wanted to leave us. Was there anything this girl child could get right?

CHAPTER 37

— ❧ —

Second Go Around

OUR MOTHER WAS an attractive woman. After she and Dad were divorced, it was not long before admirers pursued her. Mom's suitors seemed genuinely interested, inviting her to attend local events—such as the annual Fireman's Ball, street dances, and community picnics.

Somehow, these pairings never worked out. It may have been that Mom's beaus caught a hint of a grave mood disorder in her future, and they shied away because of it.

It was in the late 1940s when she met Max and the dating turned serious. He was different from the others, in that he was a "hanger-on."

Once they wed, it soon became evident that Max had brought his own set of issues into their relationship. Although he was a congenial fellow and a hard worker, there was also the jealousy factor and the downright stinginess that were a part of his nature.

Money disagreements were large in the failure of Max's first marriage. I recall his grumbling over his first wife's spending. He preferred to live as a pauper, demanding a bleak existence while holding tight to every penny. Life with Mom and her new selfish husband was not as my sisters and I had hoped. We were better off sharing in the poverty of our grandparents.

After Max took a job in the northern part of the state, working as a tenant farmhand, we moved away from Grandma and Grandpa and the home we knew. Dee, Sonny, and Mary, all had new lives elsewhere, so Nancy, Carol, and I were the only kids making the move.

We lived in a farmhouse there, and it was so remote that Max shouldn't have had to worry about Mom's fidelity. But he did.

At the end of Max's workday, it was not unusual to find him squatted down to examine the dusty lane leading to the house. He would be searching for any suspicious tire markings there, and if he found evidence of strange tracks in the dust, we would be grilled about them.

On one such occasion, he sought me out, demanding, "Who was here today?"

"Nobody came here," I answered. There was more hell to pay, as Max grew more hostile over some vague tire impressions left in the dusty road.

"Bull shit!" He bellowed. Throwing things was Max's initial response to my denial that we'd had any company earlier in the day. Finally, I did recall seeing the landowner drive down our lane to his barn, just that morning. When I reported it to Max, he didn't take back any of his outburst. The least a person should do, after making a cussing and stomping mistake, is to offer a "sorry."

It was not all bad; there were the many pleasant evenings when we played poker around the kitchen table. And after some time had passed without any evidence to the contrary, Max came to the conclusion that Mom was not going to run away with the next traveling salesman who happened by, which was highly unlikely in this forsaken place.

I would just have to make the best of it, but country living and long dusty roads to the nearest mailbox were slowly choking the life out of me.

Nancy and Carol made the leap from small town to country living with ease. Both of them formed new circles of friends without hesitation. It was not so for this homesick one. I felt left out in the cold among strangers and that my freedom to roam about had been stolen. For a town kid who was accustomed to a world that was wide open, as far as she could travel on foot, moving here was followed with a stab of loneliness. In this dull place, I was stranded, miles from civilization, with only soft-eyed cows to communicate my unhappiness to.

One lackluster day was followed with another, until I thought the monotony would last forever. Then when civilization seemed farthest away, along came "a bolt out of the blue." His name was David.

Grandma Mollie used to tell stories that had been handed down to her. Stories about how the "Gypsies" would come to town and steal children and hearts and anything they could lay their hands on. She warned me about strangers. She made me wary, but those fears did not prevail over loneliness.

I was 12, going on 13, when I had an unforgettable encounter with a young man named David.

David and I became acquainted at the movies when he asked if the seat next to mine was taken. After I indicated that it was unclaimed, he lowered his lanky form down beside me.

"Hi, I'm David," he said.

I guessed he was about 16 years old. At first I was too self-conscious to even follow the movie, but his easygoing manner soon eased my discomfort, and we became friends then and there. It was as though he already knew me.

The following day, during lunch break at school, David showed up. He had been waiting for me to appear. He was tall, standing head and shoulders above me. We talked, and he tilted his head to listen. He stared, searching my face and locking his dark, expressive eyes with mine. It was in this fashion that I found myself hand-in-hand with him on several lunchtime strolls as autumn progressed toward winter.

One day his voice was full of remorse. "If you really knew me, you wouldn't have anything to do with me," he said.

His solemn words stunned me, and I hastily denied them, protesting otherwise. He was my awesome rebel. "Nothing can be that bad," I said. "You know, we can just start from when we met."

There again was that bitter look of regret crossing his boyish features. "No," David insisted. Momentarily, he squeezed my hand, indicating that he was touched by my solace. "I've done things, things you couldn't imagine."

He fell silent for a moment. Then he said, "You're sweet, and I wish things could be different. But no ... if you knew all about me, you wouldn't like me anymore. You think you would, but you wouldn't."

David had lived on the road with his family his entire life, and even though Grandma Mollie had related the dangers posed by the nomadic people of her generation, her warnings went right out of my head when he was present. In the fleeting days when I saw David, he would simply materialize outside the school, and I accepted our friendship on his terms.

The mediocrity of my days was enlivened by his freedom. David was a pathway to a world apart from my current dowdy existence, and I felt unchained in the minutes that we strolled near the school.

One wintry afternoon, as we were walking, he provided a shield against the cold north wind. I was warmed by his protective closeness. As the gusts of wind pushed us along, he spoke of a dilemma.

"It's too late now," he said. "I could never leave the family. They will be moving on, soon. We've already stayed here longer than I expected."

Little by little, David planted a soulful vision in my mind, and I saw there a lonely young man who despaired of "laying down roots."

"I've never been in love," he wistfully acknowledged. "My first time was with an older woman. She took me under her wing and taught me everything."

That revelation was so puzzling that I didn't know what to do with it. David noticed my reaction, and he quickly added, "Oh no, it's not what you're thinking. I don't blame her for anything. She never seduced me. I wanted to be with her that way. I don't regret that part; I owe her. She was a kind woman, and she helped me out a lot. When I was younger and got in trouble, I ran to her and she hid me."

The principal's office was on the second floor of the building. It had a lengthy window that faced the school's entranceway, providing an unobstructed view down to the sidewalk below where David and I were ending our "sort of" date. David knew better than to come onto school property.

Inadvertently glancing around, a slight movement above caught my eye, and then I saw the principal looking down on us. I thought nothing of it, but when I got back to class I was summoned to that "scary place on high."

Each step up the stairway, stole another piece of my confidence. When I finally entered the office, the principal motioned to a chair across from him. Nervously, I sank down there, facing an uncertainty— just a desk width away. He ruffled a stack of papers, prolonging my discomfort. I didn't know what to expect next.

"I saw you, just a while ago, taking a walk with a young man," he said. "I think his name is David. And he was here yesterday, as well. You're a nice girl, and David is not someone that you should be spending time with."

A final thump on the desktop, leveling the edge of the bulky papers, meant business. He looked directly at me. "I know the family," he said. "They do not have a good reputation." Duly intimidated, I wanted nothing more than to escape from there.

The principal's scornful tone made my head swim. I had supposed that I would be "taken to task" over some minor infraction of the rules, such as leaving the grounds. I didn't expect this.

Regaining a semblance of calm, I carefully chose my words in David's defense. "He's been really nice to me," I offered.

My assertion of David's good character annoyed the principal, and he went from counselor to contender. In self-defense, his demeanor changed, and then he scowled at me.

"Look," he avowed, "I don't like doing this. It is my duty to warn you: David comes from a group that is not to be trusted. They are troublemakers."

242

I hesitated to say anything more. The principal rose to his feet and dismissed me. Moving to his viewing station at the long, long window, he turned his back to me. I walked out of there still foggy headed.

The weekend dragged by. On Monday, I was anxious to see David, but at our appointed time, the sidewalk was empty of him. David's family had left town after nightfall, taking him with them—along with everything they could lay hands on that wasn't nailed down.

Later in the day, the principal made eye contact with me when we happened to pass in the hallway. The impression I got of him was muted. Usually, I can read someone's face very well. He had every right to gloat, yet he didn't.

It was a disappointing finale. I never saw David again. As I ponder his fate, I think I'm better off not knowing the details that haunted David's life.

I'm not judgmental of the older woman in David's story—just puzzled by her. I always have a need to ask the "why" of things.

Would I have turned away if I had known David's past? I remember that he thought so: "You think you would (still like me) but you wouldn't."

CHAPTER 38

✂

Robbing the Cradle

THE ONLY HIGHLIGHT of the dreary sameness here was that Nancy gradually started to include me in her social ramblings. Although she was all of 14 to my 12, she let the years between us vanish.

In open country, Nancy could still draw friends—and she did. Shortly after we moved to an isolated piece of ground, Nancy began seeing a boy who lived a long drive away from our ramshackle farmhouse. But, as young admirers will, he was enamored enough with her to put a gazillion miles on his car to pursue her.

It just so happened that Nancy's suitor had a buddy that wanted to meet her younger sister. I could hardly believe my good fortune in receiving the sudden attention of an older boy. Growing up was taking far too long, and the prospect of having a boyfriend made me feel instantly older. That idea was thrilling, to say the least.

Everything was going well for the first couple of our double dates. Nancy and I were beginning to get comfortable with the boys, and the all-important first kiss was coming on strong. My beau was handsome, and at 16, old enough to shave. All of this was in his favor.

Snuggled into the back seat of his friend's car, after a trip to a soda shop in the nearest town, my date whispered something in my ear. He confessed to a surprising preference. "I love the taste of lipstick," he told me. Further, he asked a favor. "The next time I come to see you, will you put more of it on? For me?"

Well, this was something I had never heard before. The wonderment must have shown on my face, because he quickly added, "You can't wear too much for me. I love it—love it!" He insisted. "Put on as much as you can."

I studied him. He looked serious. I didn't know where this older guy had developed such a craving for lipstick. Nobody had ever expressed to me that the taste of it was the main objective of a kiss. Yet I did want it to be perfect.

Now, poverty precluded my owning a lipstick. Therefore, when I stood before our dresser mirror, applying paint, it was Nancy's tube of Pink Queen that was poised to accent my pale lips.

Layering a buildup, one application after another, I smoothed glossy color across my mouth. Up until now, I hadn't had much practice with globbing more on. It went sort of hit and miss after the first few smears. Getting beautiful lips is harder than it looks.

I continued to spread on an ample amount of Nancy's personal possession to the target area. After one quick inspection of my reflection in the large mirror, I felt well painted and ready for romance.

My tongue sampled shiny Pink Queen lips. The gooeyness didn't taste like anything.

There was this trivial second thought that I was having over the thickness of my plumped up lips. But then, I remembered that handsome older boy had whispered, "You can't overdo it. I love the taste of it—that much!"

Nancy had not spotted my new look until we were crawling inside of her boyfriend's car. Then suddenly, we locked eyes. "Oh, my gosh!" She unloaded on me. Nancy ranted on. "Shirley," she yelled, "what have you done to yourself? You look like a clown."

My face burned crimson. Heaping more fuel on the fire, Nancy declared, "Hey you! That's my only tube of lipstick. That stuff don't grow on trees, ya know."

I was crushed by her scolding, convinced that she made me look like a baby—and in front of my beau. The ground should open up and swallow me, I thought.

Handsome spoke out in my defense. "Don't yell at her," he told Nancy. "I asked her to do that."

Nancy's feathers were already ruffled by then. "Go in the house," she ordered, "and wipe at least half that goop off your face. You look awful!" She announced.

The outlook was dismal, as I trudged back to the house. Wounded pride hurt the most, even worse than the thought of my clown lips. My date was sure to think I was a big baby. It was all I could do to keep from crying and prove him right.

Later, if there ever was a kiss goodnight, I don't remember it. The romance with my lipstick-enchanted boyfriend was short lived.

Nancy's date told her why his buddy quit me. He said to her, "Shirley is too young. He needed to end it because he liked her a little too much."

My date's mother had objected to his seeing me, urging him against it because of our age difference. She reminded him that his little brother was my classmate. Everybody was against our romance. His friends ganged up on him, teasing and accusing him of robbing the cradle.

So, he was dumping me? And because I was a "baby?" That hurt. Nancy tried to let me down easy, explaining, "That boy really is too old for you."

They were right. There was an insurmountable age gap between us. And at this moment I can't picture his face or put a name to him. I guess the healing of my pride was complete.

This country ordeal did not last forever: it just seemed to. In truth, it was little more than a year. I was overjoyed on the day when I could finally shake the country dust from that longest of farmhouse lanes, off my feet. This big baby was more than ready to return to Grandma's house—my true home.

CHAPTER 39

Dark Days

ONCE WE SETTLED back in familiar territory, I breathed easier. It was not the same for Mom. Her mental breakdown followed in pursuit, affecting our whole family in one way or another.

Mom's personal anguish became clear to all. The tears she had once shed were dried and replaced with a pattern of compulsive habits and bizarre hallucinations. I could not determine which was the worst—Mom's sadness or her chaos.

In those days, mental health awareness was weak and treatment primitive. What looked like heartache to many was a deep-seated depression. The only remedy we could fall back on was a faith that tomorrow would be better. Call it positive thinking, if you will.

It bears repeating—I was her shy child, wherever Mom stepped, I was underfoot. Therefore, when she was leaving reality behind and slipping into another place inside herself, I could see it happening. In the same breath, I could never accept letting go of her. Holding on caused a steady tug-of-war. I so desperately needed her to get well. I needed to hear Mom singing and laughing as she once had, at appropriate things.

Time only served to immerse her deeper into depression. Mom's ability to concentrate slowly waned until I rarely saw her to even read. In some semblance of rationality, she managed to cook and keep house.

I could still talk with her, after a fashion, even though she was often detached from reality. Constantly, I would remind myself: Don't give up; tomorrow could be better. Tomorrow never was.

Out of doors was not any better. I had witnessed Mom being mired in a trance-like state. Under open skies, standing during long and awkward moments, she would become subject to her mood. She stared above at nothing at all. Whatever she saw was for her eyes only.

Her thoughts were often delusional, but Mom was never violent toward anyone. Just the opposite—she was more childlike than I was at 12. Slowly we were exchanging roles.

Her anger had been given to flare because of irrational thoughts. But it was directed at things and not at people—except for the time when she mopped up the floor with Uncle Al, which he well deserved.

Once in a heated dispute with a sizable mirror, she let loose, and it shattered. She also launched the iron like a missile and destroyed our radio.

Some of her thoughts were certainly outlandish. She moved on impulse, taking in imaginary sights and sounds. When I attempted to dissuade her irrational ideas, Mom would tell me almost anything to explain away her flawed logic. It wouldn't matter to her whether it made sense.

I never wanted to give up on the vulnerable loved ones who most needed me. To walk away from Mom while she was in turmoil and let her illusions run wild, I knew, was not helpful. A close relative saw things differently. He advised me, "Go along with their fantasy, and just agree with them. That's what you need to do."

Because I was so close to my mother, I couldn't think of her in terms of their or them, and I put aside his suggestion. However well-intentioned his counsel was meant, the idea of favoring mixed-up thinking, seemed as illogical as the reasoning of a troubled mind. The emotionally wounded already have enough jumbled signals coming into their brains without the added burden of another deceit, especially from someone they trust and depend on.

I could never have made temporary peace at so steep a cost to her. When the delusions struck Mom, I always stopped whatever I was doing and interrupted her rambling thought. She would respond to me then, and I could reach her. Mom trusted me. Whatever thought was holding her captive was not going to win easily. If I ignored the threat of mental illness taking over her, it would not just go away.

If need be, I resorted to touching Mom's arm or her shoulder, as I spoke. Calling out to her and saying her name gained me her attention every time.

Later the inattention to real life would return, I knew, but the distraction of my light touch would be enough to bring Mom back to herself and to make her acknowledge my presence, at least for the moment.

My early teens were trying. Sometimes I felt abandoned when I couldn't depend on either parent for advice, or to so much as share a confidence with them.

One memory awakens other. During Mom's second marriage, she was hospitalized for her emotional problems.

I knew that it was going to happen. She did not. I couldn't find it in my heart to go off to school, leaving her to face the inevitable all alone. I wanted to soften the impact of her duress as much as I could. Max went off to work, as usual—not that I could blame him for that. Staying home from junior high school that day was my decision.

I am old beyond my years. Whatever picture comes to mind of that awful morning cannot do it justice. The sheriff, his tall frame blocking the doorway, and the social worker ... Their somber expressions, are etched in my memory. This one was a very long day.

CHAPTER 40

— ❧ —

Love is Wasted on Kisses

AFTER AN EVENING date with my young man, I came home and my step-father stopped me in the living room.

"What's that on your skirt?" Max demanded. I didn't see anything. "No, on the back of it." He pointed as he fell in step behind me.

I turned to look at the back of my skirt. "I don't know," I said. Still not thinking much of it, yet puzzled over his show of rage, I added, "It's probably something I sat on. Maybe it's gum."

"Bull shit!" He exploded.

Suddenly, it dawned on me. Incredible as it seemed, he thought he saw evidence of sexual misconduct on my skirt. I wasn't guilty of anything more than a goodnight kiss, and Max's accusation made me furious.

After Max found he was mistaken, he backed off, and my resentment slowly faded. I hadn't an inkling that he had hidden desires he was dealing with, and that I should be wary.

Mine could be any young girls' story. Innocent ones who trust men in all circumstances should have second thoughts. Lapse of character does happen.

Looking back, I can't believe how naïve I was when it came to understanding the opposite sex. The only justification I can offer for being so trusting has something to do with spending my formative years in the care of gentle grandparents.

It would have been so easy to pull the wool over their eyes. Yet it was dreading a look of disappointment from these kind, old people that usually stopped me in my tracks and made the straight and narrow path the more appealing one.

After we moved back home from up north, we lived in the old place with Grandma for a while before Mom and Max found a small house at the edge of town, taking Carol and me with them. Nancy had gotten married soon after we returned, so it was just the four of us now. We lived dirt cheap.

Now, to tell it like it was, Max was not a man who would bathe regularly —if at all. I could hardly fathom how Mom reconciled with it. I do recall that she, being so attentive to cleanliness herself, was forever trying to lure him into a tub of bathwater. Max would have none of it.

In those days, Mom was sent again to a state mental hospital to get better. She was still away when I discovered how impossible it could be to see others in a true light.

Moods change, inhibitions break down, and high morals dissolve. None of us reacts in the same manner to things, day in and day out. The morning face is not exactly the night one.

Late in the night, I was awakened from a deep sleep by his lips covering mine. In a groggy state of misunderstanding, I bolted upright in my bed. A late night face confronted me. Startled and not fully awake, I responded with confusion. My thinking was foggy when I asked, "Max, what's wrong with you? Are you sick?" I was dumbstruck by the insanity of the moment.

He didn't answer. Staring at him, in chilling disbelief, I struggled to collect my senses. The crumpled form of my stepfather was poised on his knees at the edge of my bed. Sudden clarity hit, and I was racked by a feeling of betrayal—to find him there.

I can't say whether alcohol played a role in his judgment. To some degree in his favor—a lesser man caught up in the throes of passion, would not have had the will to choose differently, would not have turned away. Max stopped before anything else happened.

I had never heard, nor have not since, sounds to equal the torment-ed, guttural moans, as he literally pushed himself away from where he had crouched beside my bed. The man was truly shaken. His appear-ance was that of a wounded animal. He was not the person I knew and had passed the time of day with, playing a friendly game of cards. This was the last thing I would have expected from Max, and I felt sick when I realized that he must have been watching me while I slept.

Sometimes we don't know people as well as we think we do (night face). Some can fall to temptation.

My emotions ran all over the place. I was torn between pity and anger toward him. Why did I even care if he got hurt?

I was too young to predict what men might do when they become stirred. But the harm of it was—that the stolen moment never left my memory. Over and over, in my thoughts, the sloppiest kiss ever imag-inable was planted on my lips. It—was—disgusting.

I sat huddled on the bed, my back against the wall, until daylight. The wait for sunup took exhaustingly long.

It was only after I had sworn Grandma to secrecy that I felt com-fortable enough to tell. The notoriety would certainly have been more than I could bear. The scandal from the kiss would have hurt some and upset many.

In those days, fear of scandal outweighed all else—sometimes even topping the welfare of the most vulnerable. The reigning thought was "not on my doorstep."

In my mind, it is possible that my stepfather came to the doorway of my bedroom, not intending to trespass or steal a kiss but only to look in on me. And then, it went bad and desire brought him closer.

I would like to give Max the benefit of the doubt, (He never ap-proached me again.) supposing that it was strength of character, rather than fear of consequences, that set the standard for him in the turning away.

In second sight, it is distressing to note that I was so stricken over a single kiss. Given my reaction, what greater and longer lasting harm would have been done, if there had been more?

Until Mom came home from the hospital, I stayed at Grandma's house, which was just a ten minute walk away. I should add that Max's behavior, on that night, was uncharacteristic of him. Nothing of the sort ever occurred again. Neither of us brought it up thereafter. I forgave it, and we remained close family in the days that followed.

I struggled with this tumultuous chapter of my life—and the one that is to follow. I even leaned toward downplaying these pages and saving myself the grief of revisiting a bad phase in my youth. I especially wished to avoid making any more of it than a walk through ancient history. And then...I thought better of it.

If I could touch another's life and make a difference, then sharing my story will be worthwhile. Maybe another young person, facing similar trials, will read of these ordeals and gain from them.

CHAPTER 41

Ugly

THE WASTED KISS was not the only peril that I encountered in my early teens. Shortly after one calamity subsided, another transpired.

Evildoers, disguised in everyday form (ones that Grandma Mollie would have described as "ugly acting") decided to take a twisted path, and they conspired to drag me down it, along with them.

It was during the same time of Mom's worst distress, when it happened. Mom was now at home from what she termed "a little vacation" from the state hospital.

Early one evening Shannon and I set out walking along the train tracks toward the next town. We were heading to the theater there and we made the short, two-mile jaunt in good time. Traveling on foot to see a movie was something of an adventure. She and I seldom had the price of an admission ticket.

Night fell while Shannon and I sat inside the theater. After the movie ended, we began our trek home on the same route we had traveled to arrive. Although the highway ran parallel to the rails, we felt safer avoiding highway traffic.

About halfway home, we noticed a group of four boys lagging a short distance behind us. Picking up their pace and hurriedly gaining ground, they soon narrowed the gap between us. Still, nothing about them seemed threatening, even as their strides continued to widen. I didn't know we should be running away from them.

I had turned 13 and was still pretty gullible. When they whispered among themselves, Shannon and I were oblivious of their intent. My head was filled with notions of gallant knights and a code of honor that romanticized courtship. Anything other than their wanting company on the walk home, never crossed my mind. I did not know that violent young men feed off of each other's mob courage, in the face of their own cowardice.

They didn't prevent Shannon from running and leaving me there alone with them. I felt abandoned.

In a sudden turn, they went from a group of boys—to a gang of predators. One of the four of them cut away, avoiding the trouble that was brewing. As he stomped down the tracks, the last words he heard were taunting, "If you don't want any, get the hell out of here." And he went away. Panic struck as I was pulled, picked up, and carried across the highway into a nearby graveyard. I knew two of the attackers. One was Hunter. Another of the gang was Rob, who used to hang out with my brother, Sonny, before he left for the military and the battlefields of Korea.

I couldn't place the other boy. He was new in town. He said to the other two, "She's gonna fight."

"Let her," Hunter said. "That will make it that much better."

That night would come easier to relate if I were writing someone else's story. I can't go back to that time and place and unhear the bullies' voices. They talked over me, as though they didn't see me as a human being, at all. To the three of them, I was not much different from an object. An unfeeling blow up doll could have replaced me, in their minds.

Hunter and the boy I didn't know left Rob alone with me, while they went a short distance away. There, Hunter and he attempted to break the lock on the caretaker's tool shed to conceal themselves from a moonlit scene.

Meanwhile, in desperation, I focused on Rob's old boyhood connection to my brother. Trying to appeal to his sense of honor or a loyalty that was, sadly, not there in him, I began to reproach him.

"Some friend you are, Rob. You came to our house with my brother. Sonny is supposed to be your buddy."

While I wanted to cast shame on him, my words irritated Rob, and he sputtered, "Shut-up!"

After the two menacing figures paced the few yards back to where I was being held captive, Rob turned spiteful. Out of vengeance for my stinging comments to him, he shoved against my shoulder, knocking me down. One of the others (Their voices seemed to run together.) said to Rob, "Hey, don't hurt her!"

Rob lunged, as I lay on the ground.

I took on the fight posture that comes natural to me. With a will of their own, my legs bolted forward. The impact from my energized feet was a repeat of the kick that struck once before—back in Grover and Harry history.

After making contact with my charmed feet, Rob was carried skyward, and rewarded with a kick like a mule's. The "ugly" one landed justly—rattling his brains.

(If ever there was a wrong made right, in all my thirteen years, this moment was one. It is mine to cherish.)

Three bullies against one skinny girl meant help needed to be on the way. I could see a bad ending coming on.

Delay was my friend. Because I was not a pushover, that tactic bought me precious added minutes, and I stayed safe and fully clothed. The strength and the subtlety of survival is immeasurable. Words are also a means of defense.

Meanwhile, the friend that I felt so sure had deserted me to this pack of animals, was out flagging down a car on the highway, and they began to search to find me.

Caught in the sudden blinding glare of headlights, all three cowards scurried away, escaping by blending into the shadows of night—like the sneaky rodents they really were.

Their intent, although unsuccessful, was a bitter experience that affected my sense of trust.

A heroic figure arrived on the scene in a moment of saving grace— just like in the movies. I was rescued by a stranger and a pair of head-lights. I knew I wouldn't likely be that lucky twice. It made me more aware of my surroundings whenever I'm alone. The unknown feels risky, even today.

Max was outraged when he learned of the gang's attempt, and he immediately notified the sheriff. Mom could not take it all in. Her illness denies.

In a small community where everyone is acquainted with or is re-lated to all the others, it is very difficult to make waves. It is easier to place blame elsewhere when the perpetrators are members of their own families.

There were gossips who suggested that Shannon and I had some-how provoked the guys because we were walking the rails alone at night. Did society have a right to demand an escort for all girls, at all times? The sheriff, however, took our side.

"These two girls have as much right to walk there and to not be mo-lested for it, as anybody else," he said. And he arrested the three bullies.

Hunter was the leader of the pack. The few days that they lan-guished in jail for attempt, did very little to dissuade any one of them. Shannon gave me a warning.

"You better watch out," she said. "The new guy is bragging." She told me that she'd heard he'd boasted, "I did the time. Now, I'm gonna do the crime."

I couldn't contend with the stress of going to court. I didn't want further torment. But once out from behind bars, a different torment began. They taunted me whenever they saw me. In a small town—that was often. I tried to endure; I swallowed my fear and pride. I crossed the street whenever I thought I saw one of them approaching.

And then, for a second time, a man protected me. After overhearing their mocking calls, he stepped forward and warned all three bullies of consequences that would certainly befall if he ever witnessed "further torment to that young girl." The gallant gentleman shielded me from further harm, I could walk freely. This dear angel came to my defense, disguised as a tough talking mechanic.

I well remember the hurtful taunts hurled at me from Hunter's place of concealment. Yet adding his threats to my story and acknowledging them would, once more, give power to his words. I choose not to.

For a very long time, Rob continued to leer at me, but he kept his distance. His face wore a dark, smoldering hint of the obscenities floating around in his head. Without saying anything, his eyes revealed his thoughts.

Time passed and eventually this troubled fellow was sentenced to prison, convicted of a robbery.

Hunter was just Hunter—mean through and through. I had witnessed his bullying of others who were weaker than he was. In later years, he, also, served time for robbery.

The third boy was new in town, so I didn't have any knowledge of his family. I do remember that Hunter and Rob had older sisters. How was it possible to look into their sisters' eyes and feel alright with themselves?

The fourth youth (the boy who decided to bail), was Rob's younger brother. Anytime he exchanged glances with me, in a chance meeting during school hours, a twinge of conscience was there to remind him of his turning away.

There is a certain something about me—a vague sort of shyness that seems to attract and embolden weirdoes and bullies. If there is one or the other (with strange or aggressive intent) in a crowd, he will zero-in on me. Even though vulnerability is invisible to the naked eye, the opportunist seems to sense it.

I don't have a need for revenge against the young men who acted "ugly" to me. They brought on their own recompense. Certainly Hunter led a sad and loveless existence. But if this story had had a darker ending—as happens to countless other young people—I believe that I wouldn't be so quick to move on. Those less fortunate girls and boys, who have been brutalized and their futures marred, have a right to not let bygones be bygones. Why should they let the uglies of the world win?

CHAPTER 42

The Magic of the Snowflakes

BLESSINGS, JUST AROUND the corner, are sometimes slow in coming. Without weathering the storms of life that fate brings on, serenity could be unrecognizable even when we are showered with it.

An uneventful collection of days grinds by. After a while, the once bitter and angry young man—the father who did not cope well with fatherhood or the pain from a hasty divorce—would come back to his children.

Over the passage of time, how vulnerable this fellow had become. He was complicated in temperament, and I never fully understood him. Still, I am thankful to have been granted the "time and tide" to be there when a scrappy father of six, transformed into a sentimental family man. In his more mature years, my dad was made misty-eyed by the slightest show of affection.

Only God knows the workings of the heart. Dad suffered so many losses, in health as well as in family relationships. His personal life covering the length of my childhood is very much a mystery to me. If another woman ever filled the void that Mom left behind, I never knew of it.

Our parents' early separation improved neither their lives nor ours. We grew up in stark poverty, starved for money and love.

An ancient drinking man and a saintly old woman, governing from their judicial places and settled back in rocking chairs, led homeless, stair-step sized youngsters along the winding road to their coming of age.

Decades passed.

On the wintry morning when Dad came to us, he appeared gaunt. Years of poor health, including heart disease, were evident in his halting footsteps and in the slumping of his shoulders.

The short pace from Dad's car to our door had left him winded. "I just need to stay for a few days," he told me. Until then, I had not realized just how delicate his health had become. Dad was needing a helping hand until he could get back on his feet.

"Sure, Dad," I answered, welcoming him inside. I'm married now, but I knew Earl wouldn't mind. "We're glad to see you. Stay with us as long as you want to."

Many doors had closed on my father in his past. When this one shut, he was standing on the right side of it. Dad confided his helplessness to me.

"I'm feeling hungry, and I can't cook myself a meal," he said.

There my father stood, looking weary boned. He was a sick and lonely man, needing the love of family. A canvas valise containing a spare change of clothes dangled from a wide strap around his wrist.

It was not uncommon for Dad to make an overnight stay with us. He preferred to avoid the drive back home at night. Those evenings together gave Dad and me the chance to bond, time that we had missed when I was small. But this stay would be for longer.

Soon after he joined our household, Dad managed to throw off some of his misery. The look of defeat that etched his face when he arrived was gone. Though I knew he planned to return to the house that he and Uncle Bud shared, when he felt well enough, his decision to leave came about suddenly.

I wasn't prepared when, abruptly, Dad said, "I'd better get my old boat to rowin' and get my fanny on back to the ranch."

The ranch, in reality, was an empty red barn and a weather-beaten old farmhouse, without the comforts of indoor plumbing, all situated on a few acres of woods and croplands. These days, Uncle Bud and

Dad tramped through the timber and hunted squirrels, but they didn't plant the fields.

A note of bitterness, maybe it was regret, crept into his voice. Anyway, Dad seemed intent on not wanting to be a bother: a worry that he needn't have had. I still went about trying to get Dad to change his mind.

"I'm not sure you can take care of yourself yet," I said. "You may need some help."

"I'll be okay," he assured me. "I can fool around in the kitchen, again." Dad certainly was in his glory there, among the pots and pans. He had been a cook during his stint in the Army.

Voicing determination to set out for home, Dad said, "Your Uncle Bud will be concerned if I don't head on home by now." These two brothers had lived together for ages. Uncle Bud had never married.

Dad and I had the house to ourselves. It seemed quiet after the morning rush was over. Earl and our kids had gone their respective ways—he to work and the four of them off to school.

A second cup of coffee gave my hands something to do. I waited beside Dad, while he finished the egg and toast on his breakfast plate. Then scooting his chair away from the table, he moved to stand, solemnly, lost in thought and taking in the winter scene from our kitchen window. He watched a scattering of snowflakes drifting softly to the ground.

I was drawn to the window, and I stood there transfixed, next to my father. Sharing the magic of winter flurries, I drank deeply of the moment. There had never been a time when I felt closer to him.

The next thing I knew, Dad slipped his wallet from a back pocket. At once, I felt my shoulders stiffen. He pulled some bills out of his wallet, the same wallet that still carried a picture of my mother when she was young. The sight of him tending cash to me for his stay with us, made my heart sink.

"No," I said. "I don't want that." Whatever I did to comfort Dad throughout his bout of illness was because he needed me and because

I loved him. An exchange of money would ruin everything. It would take away my sense of belonging. "Put that right back in your pocket. I don't want it."

My emotions, by then, were wrecked, but my voice sounded even and natural to my hearing.

"Dad, you are always welcome to stay with us. If you need anything, anything at all, come here," I assured him, "and we will help you."

My open invitation brought him to tears. I purposely looked away, avoiding the sensitive response that my words had touched off. He blinked away the dampness.

My gaze fell on his hands. Dad's little finger on his left hand had an old injury that was quite noticeable. A reckless slide down from the barn loft, pitted flesh and blood against the friction of coarse rope, and Dad's little finger lost the contest. Later, while it was healing, stretching it out straight caused pain. Therefore, the rope-burned finger mended in place, damaged and tightly closed.

That was long ago. At this intended moment, I raised my eyes to look at Dad. His face held a trace of misty emotion. Our caring for him had touched him deeply.

The snow-covered landscape added urgency to Dad's travel plans. With the threat of more bad weather in the forecast, he quickly gathered up his things, thanked me for making him comfortable, and then he left for home.

I stood in the doorway, as Dad walked to his car. His back was turned to me, and I watched him go. My heart was overflowing with gratitude for our time together.

The drifting snowflakes fell softly, landing on the shoulders of his lanky frame. I saw my father in a new light, and I now found him so easy to love.

Dad was made lonely and frail, becoming disabled while he was still in his 40s. Mom's fate was even worse. She went from one empty relationship to another, never finding in her quest, a better man than our dad. In her mental confusion, she failed at her mission that she insisted was "to make a home."

Mom's futile dream of a comfortable fireside—home and hearth ideal—never materialized. Instead, what followed, on the heels of her heart's desire for endless change, was a long and terrible mental illness that engulfed her. In sickness and in health, Mom and Dad had not one another.

CHAPTER 43

—— ✧ ——

Searching For a Greater Good

IN DAD'S LAST years, I saw his life changing before my eyes. He became a better, more caring father and grandfather than many other men who had the advantage of watching their little ones growing up and of always being loved and understood by them. Dad was relatively young, only 58 when a heart attack struck.

Both of my parents came to depend on my family in their times of frailty. Dad's health failed before Mom's. Prior to his most serious health crisis, Dad was our frequent houseguest. I think his overnight stays helped him to feel less lonely.

We always had room for one more, and sleeping arrangements could be made at a moment's notice. The boys (Tracy and Lonnie) gave up their bedroom in favor of a party time. The two of them would spread out blankets for the night, happily sacking out in front of the living room television. In those days, TV programming was more family friendly.

Robin and Dawn would hurry to the kitchen, preparing to impress Grandpa with their culinary skills. Among the accidental spills and peals of laughter, treats were created. (I gave all four of our kids my blessing to run amuck in there.) They kept the hot buttered popcorn and brownies coming.

Shirley Owens

Cautionary bumps in the road were all behind Dad and me. We were close now, and I gladly let him lean on me. It was not always so good for us.

The resentment he harbored toward Mom spilled over and touched his children. Dad could not endure sharing the same physical space with our mother. Seeing her again stirred old hurts, so we never gathered as a family for major events, holidays or birthday celebrations.

As time went on, Dad seemed to mellow, and his religious heritage played an increasing role in his life. He was brought up in the Catholic faith, and his belief had never really faltered.

Slowly Dad's faith became an inspiration to me. It was the only unwavering constant in his otherwise stormy existence. I wanted that steadiness—something to cling to in the darkest hours. Once more, I was reminded that tomorrow could be better.

A reconciliation of my parents was a hope that I carried in my heart. It was not to be. I don't easily let go of a dream. But Mom's ongoing mental illness and her intact second marriage remained a barrier to this one ever coming true.

Mom had spent most of her life either running away from or toward things that did not exist. I could never distinguish which it was. Every time she was preparing to flee, it caused panic in the family. Daily lives would be disrupted by her sudden travel plans. Mom's days were filled with thoughts of a perfect life.

In adulthood, I knew my parents' imperfections as well as their goodness. I think it was their frailties that stood out most in my mind and even endeared them to me.

It's never too late. My dad, in many ways, more than made up for the neglectful relationship we had in my youth.

Dad passed away on June 6, 1976. Robin, Dawn, Tracy, and Lonnie have only positive memories of their grandfather. When Dad embraced them, it was the same as giving me that thoughtfulness. When Dad acknowledged them on holidays and on their birthdays, he celebrated

266

me. Nothing else can better heal or restore closeness with someone than to show kindness to their sons and daughters. Both of us got a second chance to get it right.

True happiness is found in using our God-given talents for good— sharing something of ourselves without regard for gain. There are many ways to say I love you to the ones who gave us life. The best one is to care for them when they grow old or become sick, physically or mentally. Whatever will be, will be.

Immediately after my stepfather died, Mom joined my family. I have never once regretted the decision to bring her home. Her happiness, at this point in her life, was foremost in my thoughts.

In every difficulty that transpired, my family came to the rescue. Earl and our four kids, willingly included Mom in their daily lives. Reflecting on their helpfulness, I do know how blessed I am to call them mine.

For some of us, our emotions are precariously suspended by a single delicate thread of clarity. My mother was one so vulnerable, and she grappled with illogical thoughts for all of her life.

The divide between those who can fully maintain control of their moods and those who lose the battle is narrower than many of us would expect. Who among us hasn't had a few questionable ideas? Compassion is the hoped-for response to the troubled soul who suffers. Most of us will be touched by mental illness of some sort, at some time in our lives. It could be ourselves or someone we know, and it could be serious or minor. For my mother, it was crippling.

One of the less harrowing incidents came about one morning, shortly before Lonnie, our youngest son, needed to board the school bus. He drew me aside and in hushed confidence said, "Mom, Grandma told me not to tell you, but I knew I had to. She asked me to go to the quick stop. She wants me to get her a quart of whiskey and a pack of cigarettes."

"That's quite the shopping list," I said. I was unprepared for this sudden obstacle before my morning coffee. What was puzzling was that Mom didn't drink, and she hadn't smoked in years. And Lonnie, of course, wasn't old enough to buy either.

Genuine concern filled his eyes. "I thought you should know before Grandma finds somebody who will do it for her," he said. "I told Grandma that I couldn't go get it because I have to hurry or I'll miss my bus."

Just days earlier Mom had acted on another impulse. After being subject to random thoughts, she calmly remarked to me, "Shirley Ann, I need you to call the sheriff and have him come here and arrest me."

I was confounded by Mom's request, and I was thankful once again that she never used the telephone. The headaches that this would have caused were too frightening to contemplate. I felt my heart sink. I knew her answer would be evasive, but I asked anyway. "Now, why would I want to do that?"

"Oh, I don't know, Shirley Ann," she said. "I just thought you might want to have me locked up."

A lump that wouldn't swallow away, formed inside my throat, and I answered. "No, Mom, I don't want that."

In that moment, I vowed to myself, as much as to her, that I would always protect her. Mom struggled with fantasy. Counting on the rightness of letting her just be herself, as much as safely possible, I reassured her.

"No, Mom. The sheriff will not be coming—not today, tomorrow, or any other day. I wouldn't ever do anything like that."

I wanted and needed her trust. Trust is big in my life. While Mom appeared unruffled by the whole conversation, it made me heartsick.

"Well, all right then," she agreed, suddenly content. "If you'll not, I guess I'll go on."

Her moment of irrational thought passed as quickly as it had come, and Mom's attention moved elsewhere. She walked slowly into the next room, where she settled into the rocking chair and a quiet peace of mind. I stood by speechless.

I came to realize that Mom's obsession to contact law enforcement was an effect of her illness and of a lingering memory. She was recreating a past trauma. One of her worst days was also one of mine. I was in the eighth grade when it happened. Both of us remembered that ominous knock at the door.

On that foreboding day when the sheriff arrived with that stone-faced social worker, Mom was taken away for treatment. This measure was taken because Max believed that Mom was considering travel plans that did not include him. Mom's thought to leave Max was probably a temporary desire. She had a nagging urge for change.

Eventually, after she joined my family and I observed some of her compulsions, I could better understand her. Mom didn't actually want to be locked up; she simply was at the mercy of an illusion.

The years (nearly fifteen) that Mom lived with Earl and me were possibly some of her best. Here, freedom (a most precious thing) was hers. Earl and our kids helped me to make it so. At our house, Mom enjoyed new clothes, a diamond ring, and weekly shopping trips. All of these things that she had wanted were denied in her second marriage.

My mother was, essentially, gentle natured. She depended on me, and we got along great together. Of course, there were days when Mom's thoughts would go awry, and there were other distressing moments. My family and I did need to make adjustments after she moved in.

Mom was a restless sleeper—in that respect she was very much her father's daughter—and she liked to cook. She couldn't be trusted to use the stove, without help.

One necessary precaution was to remove the burner control knobs from our gas range. Mom would cook while the rest of the family were sleeping, placing all of us in danger. A scorched dishtowel was evidence of an accidental blaze.

Reminding Mom of my greatest fear didn't dissuade her. I had first tried patience. "Mom," I pleaded, "You promised that you wouldn't use the stove, after I've gone to bed."

Her response was more nonsense. "The gypsies did it," she said. After that, the burner controls went, nightly, into my bedroom. Mom never once asked about them. You know, she really was a gentle soul, most especially to me.

Mom didn't try to use the stove, but she still wandered through the house at night. Before the sun rose, Mom had usually twice visited the living room rocker. Her sleep pattern didn't disturb the rest of the family all that much. The kids' bedrooms were upstairs, and steps were too burdensome for Mom to ascend. Actually, she was very quiet and considerate of us.

Medical screenings to track Mom's diabetes took advance planning. On the night prior to her doctor visit, I would tape shut the refrigerator door. Mom would not remember nor bother to fast past the midnight hour, as required for an accurate blood sugar count. Luckily, she would heed the tape. Somehow, there was a workable solution to nearly every problem that confronted me.

Despite her doctor's best efforts, Mom's mental health remained fragile. We put our best into making her feel at home. Earl and our four kids welcomed Mom, passing over her quaint ways and including her in everything. Their kindness to Mom was returned to us, many times over, in an unbreakable family bond.

I think that our family has benefited from our children growing up in a three-generation household. The friction you might have expected was nonexistent. Quite the opposite. We adopted the musketeer motto of one for all, and all for one.

Mom lived with Earl and me for the remainder of her life. Though she was pleasant natured, living with her presented us with challenges. My mother, Norma, through necessity, became a fifth child of mine. When she died on June 15, 1990, a piece of my heart went with her.

The children of Wib and Norma have missed so much. God in his great wisdom takes care to sift through the mess we make of ourselves, here on Earth. There must be a backup plan—faith and family for dummies—that He hasn't let us in on yet.

At this writing, it has been decades since my parents passed on. In my thoughts, I can see them now as clearly as before they left us. It is wholly impossible to endure such a loss without family beside me.

The stirring memory of my brother's profound grieving at our Dad's funeral service has left a lasting impression. It was then that Sonny turned to me and spoke of his feelings of helplessness. I heard him sigh, settling his nerves before he confided his own difficulties. Sharing that which, to my thinking, sounded like a premonition, he said, "I know it's Dad there, but I see me."

Sonny lived another four years before cancer took him, leaving his young children much too soon. Sadly, they didn't have a chance to know their father.

My sister, Mary, joined our brother. She was taken from us by heart disease. I think of her, often, and deeply regret our lost time.

Nancy became our next loss. Nobody else is just like her. Being the most social one of our siblings, she drew people to her everywhere she went. I do—so—wish life had been kinder to her. Nancy's children were her source of joy.

It is the hardest thing to say goodbye. Once the reassuring thought took form—a mental picture of Mary coming to Nancy's aid and leading her to the light—I found it easier to come to terms with both of their absences.

Dee, well into her 80s, is still quite the whirlwind. She helped me to soar. Every kid needs someone to look up to, imitate, and beyond that, bravely scrunch with into an ominous, dark place called Indian Cave. To me, my big sister was all that, and more.

Our youngest sibling, Carol, lives just a hop, skip, and a jump away. We make the holidays sparkle for each other. She is a true friend.

In the back of my mind, as I confront the mysteries along life's pathways, I sense that there remains an, as yet, unknown ending—a message of greater good to take away from the journeys of Wib and Norma. Hearts so easily broken in this world, God may, with purpose, restore in the next.

CHAPTER 44

—— ❧ ——

Heaven's Window

WHERE HAS THAT youthful, although misguided, sense of immortality vanished to? Not so long ago, I was a child who took risks, leaping off of roofs and running with the bulls. I was unbreakable.

Before an accumulation of days betrayed me, I was used to harsher living conditions, and the freezing blasts of winter couldn't faze me. My bare feet could dash in leaps and bounds against the threat of frostbite. It was a race against time, and to win it I completely disregarded the cold and snowy path leading down to the outhouse.

I steeled my willpower in anticipation of a sudden shock of cold traveling up from my shoeless feet. My breath hovered above me, in a frozen layer of vapor. If there is a good that comes out of a have-not upbringing, it is that adversity builds endurance for that which lies ahead.

They called young affection, puppy love. Above all else, the thing I most wanted (from as far back as I can remember) was for the magic, the laughter, and the romance—never to end. However, I have to admit that my finding the right one was nothing I had anything to do with.

Love coming into my life, had to have been an accident of fate—or the work of angels. During the turmoil of my thirteenth year, I surely didn't have a working brain in my head. At that unsettling stage, even had true love fallen in my lap, I would have unwittingly brushed it off.

I met Earl at a grade school sports event between our opposing hometown teams. He was 14 and I was 13. I was unexpectedly given the responsibility for the concessions, and I probably wouldn't have noticed if the place caught fire. What I did notice was a persistent, curly-haired boy, devouring candy bars (buying them one at a time) as an excuse to be near me.

After the game ended, my candy bar fanatic and I went our separate ways, still strangers and destined to wait until fate tapped our young shoulders again.

The next time we were thrown together, we were paired off with each other's best friend.

We floundered about as the too young will do, never sure of where we were going or how to be true.

After many moons had passed, the boy with the mop of dark, curly hair, teased: "You didn't think I was eating all that candy, did you? I wanted you from the first time I saw you."

Nothing could keep us apart—not even a cranky, old (although much loved) grandfather who tried to dissuade the boy. My sweetheart had walked four miles to see me, on that day, when my grandpa said to him: "Steamboat Bill, you better get yer boat to rowin'. Shirley ain't a goin' nowhere with you."

In the beginning of our friendship, I needed a wide boundary to feel comfortable. Earl, the 14-year-old boy that I would later marry, loved me from the start. It takes a slow hand to build my trust.

Earl worked at a local gas station, earning enough money to buy an engagement ring. I wore his ring for two years until we were old enough to marry (almost). We were finally wed on July 2, 1955, in Union City, Tennessee. I was still 16; Earl had turned 17 that past January.

A leap in time finds that trust alive and well. I am not as resilient as I was in my barefoot days. Presently, in my more settled and usually shod epoch, a chill attaches itself to my feet as soon as autumn returns. These days, I'm elated that when the cold winds blow, "out to the back" is located inside the house.

While the grace of time has left an imprint on my 5-foot-3-inch— and shrinking—stature, it has been mostly kind to me. While I acknowledge the silver in my hair, surprisingly, the childhood dreamer inside my head is still making herself at home there.

In defiance of the calendar pages, I never abandoned all the thrills of yesterday. My penchant to dream appears ageless, and the swift bare feet that once skimmed down an icy, outhouse path—dance on. Best of all, my lifelong dance partner is still game to keep step with me.

From school days filled with a long list of fantasy heroes and storybook romances, the flawless vision inside my head was of everything courtly, everything treasured—staying the same forever and ever. It is a beautiful dream.

Making time stand still requires commitment. After a few wear and tear years—birthing four babies and indulging in a wild craving for anything chocolate—saving the mental picture of my youth was becoming a lost cause. I found myself in a continuing struggle to compete with the prior week's weigh-in on that traitorous scale. My challenger is a relentless foe. To that rivalry, I faithfully dedicated my energy to turning back its numbers.

Romantic comedy takes over the next segment of my story. The man in my life and I have an uncommon bond. The ease of our relationship dates back to our friendship. Earl and I were so young when we found each other that we practically grew up together. In the course of the lifetime that we have known each other, I can count on one hand the number of times when we have fought.

One of my remembrances illustrates—more than anything else I have noted—the rare give-and-take of our unity.

On a late summer evening, nearing the end of a marathon jaunt— inspired by a recent chocolate melt down—I slowed my pace and pressed the key on my cell phone. My love greeted me in his usual manner. "Hi Babe," he answered. Earl's voice carries so well that it sounds as if we are talking face to face.

"Hey," I joked, holding the phone slightly away from my ear, "I'm just checking to see if you're on your toes."

Earl chuckled at the thought of toe walking, relating, "I'm on a chair." I picture my best friend relaxing in his easy chair—a rocker that is pulled up to the kitchen table. He was, no doubt, viewing his cowboy heroes on screen, pipe in his hand and the scent of tobacco surrounding him. The familiar pipe and zippered pouch containing Earl's favorite blend were never out of reach.

I think the cowboy attitude is a draw from Earl's boyhood. Some time ago, my thoughtful Western viewer caught me in the act of "making do" by using a kitchen chair in place of his stepladder. In the spirit of the moment, Earl took it upon himself to come to the rescue. I felt the reinforcement of two large hands encircling my waist. "Be careful," he warned. "You could fall and break a leg. Then, I might have to shoot ya."

Recently, an electronic pipe has become a substantial health benefit to him. I was used to locating Earl when we became separated during shopping, just by standing still and listening to hear his cough. Dawn ordered the vaping product for him. He much preferred watching cowboy movies over puzzling computer searches. She helped him to get the best possible deal on the lower, and eventually, zero-nicotine liquid. When the time seemed right, Earl quit the habit completely. Now when I want to find him, I have to call his cell.

Still on the phone with Earl—I on the hiking trail and he in his chair at home—I glanced westward at the glowing remnant of sunset. Watching its slow descent reminded me of how little time there is left for all things beautiful. Carried away in the moment, I suggested a date night.

"Can you rustle up a movie for tonight?" I asked the Western enthusiast. "I'm ready to quit out here."

I was circling the path on my final round at our local park.

"Be home," I estimated, "in about ten minutes" (which is my versatile measure of time that covers everything—no matter the length).

"You're my babe," he said, knowing how that term of endearment would ignite romance. The sound of that magical word is as moving as a gentle caress, and it never fails to summon a smile.

An expression of his true affection, thoughts too deep to share, intimate words composed for my hearing alone, flowed through the phone. Only once in a lifetime, a love like this comes along.

Emboldened by distance, and fanning the flames, I answered him in kind. "All I need is a little moonlight and romance. Call me babe, and I'll follow you anywhere."

My valiant one continued to court, boosting my self-worth. Then, purposely, he added... "Babe."

An exchange of sentiments is followed with a return to more obvious teasing from me.

"Hey," he protested, "that ain't fair."

"Love and war," I contended.

Then he laughed. "Okay, babe, you win."

"I'm pretty ugly right now," I said. "I promise I'll look better after I get back home."

Getting in the last word, Earl gave me his usual, goofy reply about looks. "Beauty is only skin deep, but ugly goes all the way to the bone."

"You take my breath away," I joked.

This uncommon man, who won my heart, has a generous spirit. He is willing to share space with the menagerie of stuffed bears that live in our bedroom.

Remembering the lyrics of another day's poem: truly, "The Heart Never Lies."

After over half a century together, the magic endures; laughter abounds, and the wonder of romance continues. And hearing my love say the magical words, "You're my babe," never grows old.

Somewhere above the parting clouds, in a place where miracles are born, Grandma Mollie is among the angels there.

Those bluest of eyes look down on kith and kin, ever observing their footsteps—just as she had when they were little tykes who played at her feet. Sometimes, I believe that she still puts words in my mouth.

A line of youngsters that stretched from as far as the eye could see, shared Alf and Mollie's crowded refuge that I, too, called home.

Reflecting on my childhood, brings the music of Grandma's laughter ringing in my ears. It is her way of reassuring me that Heaven is a joyful home, and that I shouldn't worry so much over every little passing thing. The Son of God has thrown open the door to all.

In his own gruff and grumpy manner, Grandpa Alf is a fine old gentleman. He has not overlooked Grandma's comfort before his own. I would venture that Grandpa obliges himself to leave the best seat for her—a place nearest to Heaven's window.

Paradise is kinder to Grandpa than were the days of underground mining and arthritic knees. All of the cares of this world are just a distant memory. The addictive "bottle of spirits" that so often claimed his paycheck—as well as his dignity—has lost its hold on him.

If only I could store the best memories inside my heart forever! Often the graces—or the pitfalls of everyday living—take precedence over documenting the past. Additionally, I have second thoughts, hesitating, flipping through the pages and fathoming the possibility that my book may be too open.

Recording my background—with a come-rain-or-come-shine resolve—has transformed my sentiments on what is most important in my life. In the beginning chapter, I did not expect my past to be recaptured so fully and in such detail. But here it is.

These pages have been with me for a very long time. I worry that they have a potential to come back on some tomorrow and haunt me. Committing meaningful thoughts to paper is exacting. There is a certain risk to be counted, and I don't take lightly my decision to share stories that have affected the course of my life.

Another year is waning as I pen the last page of my book. Focusing on ancient experiences bridges the gap of time, breathing new life into a dormant past. It is as though my cast-off days are having a rebirth. Grandma's stories, preordained to become intertwined with mine, are the heritage that came to me in the Shadow of the Rocking Chair.

Acknowledgment

I WISH A special thank you to Father Leo Hayes, author of *Evil in Mirror Lake*. His reading and encouragement were invaluable to the completion of this book.

Father's kind and helpful spirit inspires many.

Made in the USA
Lexington, KY
26 March 2017